Capitalism, Democracy, and Ecology

Capitalism, Democracy, and Ecology

Departing from Marx

Timothy W. Luke

University of Illinois Press

Urbana and Chicago

Manufactured in the United States of America
1 2 3 4 5 C P 6 5 4 3 2

♾ This book is printed on acid-free paper.

Library of Congress Cataloging-in-Publication Data
Luke, Timothy W.
Capitalism, democracy, and ecology : departing from Marx /
Timothy W. Luke.
p. cm.
Includes bibliographical references and index.
ISBN 10: 0-252-02422-2 (acid-free paper)/ISBN 13: 978-0-252-02422-1
ISBN 10: 0-252-06729-0 (pbk. : acid-free paper)/ISBN 13: 978-0-252-06729-7
1. Environmentalism. 2. Social ecology. 3. Capitalism—
Environmental aspects. 4. Marxian economics. I. Title.
GE195.L847 1999
363.7—ddc21 98-9100
CIP

For Kit

Contents

Preface

How does knowledge articulate power? What kind of power can be mediated through knowledge? Whose knowledge dominates whom? In what ways does ecology mediate the conduct of human conduct? In what ways can ecology embody implicit ideologies and express tacit technologies at work in the economy? How do class divisions and conflicts develop from unequal power and knowledge? These are fundamental questions for any advanced industrial economy or multicultural urban society, such as the United States, but attempts to answer them often bog down for the lack of a language to convey them.

This book addresses these questions after other attempts at answering them have stalled. It will explore power/knowledge from unconventional and even openly disfavored approaches. It also marks a series of departures from Marx, both because his practice of the ruthless criticism of all that exists has not been surpassed and because his nineteenth-century visions of advanced industrial life are now what must be surpassed if anyone is to change the world being made by the informational revolution. Initially I try to explicate the implicit ideologies as well as articulate the tacit technics embedded in the ecologies being made out of ordinary practices in our everyday life. Both ecologies and economies are now increasingly built environments whose continuing performativity guides the processes of informationalization toward new organizational goals, such as sustainable development, green governance, and industrial ecology. If what has been regarded as "nature" in the yet to be built environment is to survive development, then what is seen as "culture" in the built environment must be entirely rethought and rebuilt.

Because we often lack languages to capture such changes, this book twists old terms in new directions, hoping to snare some fresh meanings out of these shifts. Entering this tangle of concerns, I challenge categories of order and disorder, cause and effect, and purpose and structure that professional-technical experts have used to interpret modernity for nearly a century. Modernity is a mangle of practices, mostly associated with the globalized structures and activities of capitalist exchange, through which human beings create acts and artifacts to advance their sustained, purposeful, and organized instrumental control over natural and social environments. To accomplish this task, I will use two very problematic terms—the "new class" and "populism"—to discuss the class conflicts and contradictions of informational society, which are centered on who controls whom within the modes of interpretation, organization, production, and rationalization embedded at the core of informational ecologies and economies. These concepts will rankle many readers, but this also seems necessary to confront the peculiar qualities of the post–cold war era. The answer to Lenin's classic political question—"Who, whom?"—today is not entirely unlike it was in late nineteenth century industrial society, but then so too is it not exactly just like it ever was. So the figures of the new class and populist resistances provide some new provisional terms of analysis to tease out these similarities and differences.

To reframe my critical analysis of power/knowledge codes, which professional-technical experts use to define and drive contemporary economies and societies, I first return to Marx and then depart from him, recasting my critique of modern global modes of production and consumption in ecological terms. Along the way I cast doubt on many things: the historical meaning of the USSR, standard readings of Marx, the liberal productivist vision of advanced consumer economies, professional accounts of electoral democracy, the neglect of alternative technologies, elitist anxieties about local militias and mail bombers, and conventional dismissals of the populism driving ecological resistance groups. Most important, I question domesticated discourses of what is now accepted as modernity, pointing out how alternative mazeways in modernity always have existed alongside mainstream new class practices and suggesting why more ecological populist maps of other modernities could be followed to remake everything that exists. Such questioning now seems to be the only way that development can be made not "sustainable" but rather "survivable." In anticipation of probable criticisms, I admit this book will be seen as out of sync with the times, aggravating to many, and even unsettled in its use of both Marxian and non-Marxian critique. Nonetheless, such approaches are one of the only paths left for those who are uncomfortable with the settled disciplinary scholasticism of too many academic disciplines.

Pieces of my argument have been tried in several places over the past fifteen years as I have tested populist, ecological, or deconstructive readings of Marx against other interpretations in critical social theory. Writing this book took far longer than I originally had hoped, but its critical intent is now far more relevant to the inchoate new world order arising after the cold war inasmuch as the alternatives I explore here challenge the globalized informationalism of existing "liberal capitalist democracy" in the United States. Pitted against its disciplinary domestic stability and wild global instability is the promise of new ecological economies in populist municipalities, which become both more possible and more significant in the new world disorder billowing out of the ruins made by the revolutions of 1989–91.

Because I have been exploring various departures from Marx since 1980, sections of this book appeared earlier in much different forms, both longer and shorter. Pieces of the introduction are drawn from *Political Geography* 16 (1997) and *Quarterly Journal of Ideology* 7 (Fall 1983). Small pieces of chapter 1 first came out in *Telos* 46 (Winter 1980–81), *Current Perspectives in Social Theory* 13 (1993), and *Social Science Journal* 18 (Apr. 1981). Parts of chapter 2 come from *New Political Science* 7 (1981) and *Art Journal* 51 (Summer 1992). Passages from chapter 3 appeared in *Current Perspectives in Social Theory* 15 (1995), *New Political Science* 16 (1989), and a short essay in *Telos* 88 (Summer 1991). Parts of chapter 4 appeared in *Cultural Critique*, whereas sections of chapter 5 come from *The Annals of the Association of American Geographers* 84 (Sept. 1994), *Telos* 97 (Fall 1993), and *Telos* 100 (Summer 1994). Chapter 6 appeared in *Telos* 107 (1996). Chapter 7 continues arguments developed in *Social Science Journal* 24 (June 1987), and parts of chapter 8 come from *Telos* 103 (1995) and *New Political Science* 11 (Spring 1983).

During the time that I have explored these themes, many people gave me much assistance with their comments and criticisms. At the University of Illinois Press, some dedicated and very patient editors have encouraged me a great deal over the past few years, including Richard Wentworth, Larry Malley, and most important, Dick Martin. Dick Martin's understanding, good humor, and patience have been vitally important for me with this project. Likewise, Terry Sears and Bruce Bethell helped tremendously in its production. At one time or another, Ben Agger, Carl Boggs, Fred Dallmayr, Nicole Fermon, Ellsworth R. Fuhrman, Suzi Gablik, Glenn Harper, Robert D. Holsworth, John H. Kautsky, Christopher Lasch, Gearóid Ó Tuathail, Paul Piccone, Adolph Reed

Jr., Florindo Volpacchio, and Stephen K. White all provided their insights on this manuscript. Kim Hedge, Terry Kingrea, and Maxine Riley in the Department of Political Science at Virginia Polytechnic Institute and State University also contributed invaluable word-processing assistance throughout this manuscript's long evolution. I have been able to improve it thanks to their very dedicated and professional efforts.

Capitalism, Democracy, and Ecology

Introduction: Power/Knowledge in Coevolving Ecologies and Economies

Over the past century, a new order of things has evolved from the power/knowledge systems embedded in every operational layer of advanced industrial society. The effects of this order are found where the workings of large organizations such as major research universities, professional-technical associations, corporate enterprises, and bureaucratic states conjoin in the daily management of the global economy and nation-states. As big science and applied technology have been mobilized by corporate managers to rationalize industrial production over the past few decades, an entirely new bloc of professional, specialist, technical experts has emerged to organize and administer these new means of production. This group is often labeled, for the lack of any better term, the "new class."[1] This term is quite contested, and it is also in many ways inadequate and perhaps even anachronistic. Nonetheless, it is in widespread use, and it serves a good provisional purpose here. These symbolic analysts, professional experts, technical planners, administrative specialists, and design consultants have been empowered through their knowledge in both the private and public sectors to command and control the ecologies and economies first of advanced industrial societies and now of advanced informational societies.[2]

The "informational revolution" turns on defining, developing, and then deploying specialized systems of expertise whose power/knowledge codes constitute a new collective regimen to arrange resource scarcities, organize institutional rent seeking, and manage social reward systems. Informationalization rests on new technologies to produce, circulate, consume, and accumulate information as a value-added good and service. Still, it is not so much technology that matters but rather "the human skill and social organization which lie behind it . . . [;] it is the professional experts who have constructed the system, which in turn has created them."[3] The labor performed through the new classes' many diverse and divided disciplines of expertise in turn generates most of the productive power driving contemporary economies and societies. The valorization agendas of capital remain in play, of course, and much of what the new class does is pitched at protecting and preserving the profitability of highly organized and increasingly transnational networks of capital. In some ways the accumulation problem today is not unlike that addressed by Marx. In many other ways it is entirely dissimilar. At the same time, the action of such expert elites inside formal organizations remakes old class contradictions by presuming the inaction of lay populations outside these complex organizations. This elite presumption of mass acquiescence to new class authority has never entirely held true, however, for many oppositional forces have always tested the power of new class elites from above, below, and within. Rule by shifting, variegated blocs of expert elites, then, brings along with it resistance from ever-changing, semiorganized populist oppositions.

The power/knowledge organizing such economies of signs and space in transnationalized informational society does not operate on its own as abstract necessity. The fast capitalist markets underpinning global informationalization coevolve with its practices inside complex networks of technical expertise defined and dominated by new professional elites. As Christopher Lasch observes, such elites include "not only corporate managers but all those professions that produce and manipulate information," and with their commitment to making, mastering, or monitoring informational assets—"the lifeblood of the global market"—they are "far more cosmopolitan, or at least more restless and migratory, than their predecessors."[4] In ways that most environmentalists do not appreciate, this new class already "thinks globally and acts locally," for this slogan ironically captures not only an ecological ideal but also the basic realities of transnational commerce within and between informationalizing societies.

Harold Perkin ties the economic and cultural processes of informationalization back to the institutionalized hegemony of the professional expert, arguing that such new class agents transform society from top to bottom by mobilizing their power through expertise. The new class rules because

> it raises living standards not just for the few but for every member of society. It puts most of its man- and woman-power into services rather than agriculture and manufacturing. It substitutes professional hierarchy for class as the primary matrix of the social structure. It recruits to those hierarchies by means of meritocracy, entailing an increase in social mobility from below. It extends this to women, thus ensuring their (admittedly limited) emancipation. It entails the massive growth of government, including the universal benefits of the welfare state, which enlarges

> and moralizes the concept of citizenship. It expands the provision of higher education in order to create human capital. It concentrates production of both goods and services in large business corporations whether private or state-owned, in a new structure of corporate neo-feudalism. And, paradoxically perhaps, it threatens to erode the nation state by internationalizing corporate neo-feudalism and creating a global economy.[5]

Perkin concludes that all contemporary informationalizing economies and societies are now dominated "by those who control the scarce resource of expertise in its manifold forms."[6] These professional-technical experts (taken collectively, the new class) derive power, prestige, and privilege in state bureaus and corporate firms from "their possession of specialized knowledge, based on education, competitive merit, and experience on the job—in a word, on their human capital."[7]

The Coevolution of the New Class and Populists

It is not the best label for them, but these elites are, as Lasch asserts, a new class. Unlike the new class of party *apparatchiki* staffing the elaborate *nomenklatura* of the now defunct communist people's democracies, this diverse bloc of professional and technical elites is not the entire ruling class. Yet the new class shares with the old *nomenklatura* of state socialism their nearly monopolistic hold over most sources of information and many positions of power in key cultural, economic, educational, political, social, and technological institutions. The new class is composed of people who are, as Robert Reich defines them, "symbolic analysts."[8] As Lasch argues, they often are also essentially deterritorialized souls "who live in a world of abstract concepts and symbols, ranging from stock market quotations to the visual images produced by Hollywood and Madison Avenue, and who specialize in the interpretation and deployment of symbolic information."[9] For Lasch, it is quite significant that Reich turns to Hollywood to represent the rule of symbolic analysts in the United States' globalized informational economy.

> Washington becomes a parody of Tinseltown; executives take to the airwaves, creating overnight the semblance of political movements; movie stars become political pundits, even presidents; reality and the simulation of reality become more and more difficult to distinguish. Ross Perot launches his presidential campaign from the "Larry King Show." Hollywood stars take a prominent part in the Clinton campaign and flock to Clinton's inaugural, investing it with the glamour of a Hollywood opening. TV anchors and interviews become celebrities, celebrities in the world of entertainment take on the role of social critics. The boxer Mike Tyson is-

> sues a three-page open letter from the Indiana prison where he is serving a six-year term for rape, condemning the president's "crucifixion" of assistant attorney general for civil rights nominee Lani Guinier. The star struck Rhodes Scholar Robert Reich, prophet of the new world of "abstraction, system thinking, experimentation, and collaboration," joins the Clinton administration in the incongruous capacity of secretary of labor, administrator, in other words, of the one category of employment ("routine production") that has no future at all (according to his own account) in a society composed of "symbolic analysts" and "in-person servers."[10]

The silent majorities of "routine producers" and "in-person servers," however, are now becoming restive over losing control of their future in the "revolt of the elites" being mounted by these mobile minorities of systems-thinking symbolic analysts.

Because the idea of the intellectual is still deeply embedded in older registers of critique and resistance, it is difficult to regard many in the new class as intellectuals.[11] The new classes' application of formal cognitive skills in symbolic analysis rarely rises above quibbling over methodological assumptions or sniping at another's disciplinary advances.[12] Even so, an element of refinement typically has been associated with new class labor. As any corporate psychodemography of ZIP code communities indicates, new class individuals tend to be sophisticated encoders and decoders of commercial differentiations: BMWs, *Scientific American,* PBS, eurodesign, M.A.s, and Evian flow heavily through their shared mythos of meaning and identity. Indeed, many new class elitists imagine that their consumption of these more upmarket commodities proves their elite status, because the people they dominate drive only Chevies, read *The National Enquirer,* watch *WCW Nitro* matches, shop at Sears, have G.E.D.s, and drink Budweiser. To mistake such preprogrammed acquisitiveness as signs of either avant-garde radicalism or proletarian quietism, however, is more dream than reality.[13] Such signs of living well are instead little more than the tawdry referents of new class revenge against the alienating apparatus of global production, whose ecologies of operation marginally empower these elites as new class technocratic experts even as they dispower any of their friends and family who might remain somewhat more "ordinary" workers and consumers.

As the authors of power/knowledge codes, whose normalizing influences shape the acts and artifacts of everyone in contemporary informationalized societies, members of the new class may share a few tastes, but they do not share a common ideology or work at the same occupation. Instead, these individuals constitute "a new class only in the sense that their livelihoods rest not so much on the ownership of property as on the manipulation of information and professional expertise. Their investment in education and information, as opposed to property, distinguishes them from the rich bourgeoisie," but these differences must not minimize "their continuing fascination with the capitalist market and their frenzied search for profits."[14] As architects of empowerment zones, networks of influence, or fundraising food chains, such new class experts coalesce in their own lifestyle niches in ways that have little resemblance to local communities of any traditional sort. And although many pretend to profess deep faith in ecology, the new class remains "populated by transients . . . [who] lack the continuity that derives from a sense of place and from standards of conduct self-consciously cultivated and handed down from generation to generation."[15]

There are as many orders of professional-technical experts as there are bodies of specialized expertise to ground their authority, and knowledge-based work ranges from pursuits rooted in very arcane medical and legal knowledge to tasks tied to much less complex financial and managerial information. However, the key players clearly are "the professional managers of the great corporations and their counterparts in government, the state bureaucrats. They stand at the apex of the new society, controlling its economy and administering its policies and, increasingly, distributing the income and arranging its social relations."[16] These differences are vital. Since it is the labor of these executives and engineers that sustains the informational revolution, the activities of the new class must be reconsidered to judge how broadly and deeply their work also is reshaping the Earth's many environments.

The articulation of intellectual skill, professional labor, and institutionalized power in any economy is a complex puzzle, and this book only begins to pull together a few of its pieces. More important, it reconsiders some of the strategic possibilities for staging populist resistance against the new class. Indeed, the formation of "power/knowledge-endowed" new class forces simultaneously implies widespread "power/knowledge dispossession" among most nonelites without ready access to such restricted formal cognitive skills.[17] Although widespread opposition to the new class continues today, these resistances arguably first began during the 1880s and 1890s in the United States, when the original populist movements protested the authoritarian expropriation of their members' autonomous economic "competence" and localistic democratic "community," which were vested in relations of individual independent producership, close local exchange, and real personal property. Their expropriation was undertaken by a loose but potent alliance of corporate capital, professional expertise and national bureaucracy.[18] Truly democratic habits, the populists argued, require certain personal practices, such as responsibility, self-reliance, and initiative, which are best acquired "in the exercise of a trade or the management of a small holding of property. A 'competence,' as they called it, referred both to property itself and to the intelligence and enterprise required by its management."[19] The new, highly organized capitalism of the Second Industrial Revolution, as many have observed, brought into the public marketplace large formations of oligopolistic private firms that could not work at peak efficiency unless and until they destroyed such local sources of competence and community by building broad domestic dependencies on their goods and services.[20]

Localist, communal, entrepreneurial, populist forms of everyday life, then, were marginalized in the Gilded Age by finance capital and big technoscience as nationalized, corporate, monopolistic, elitist systems of lifestyling remade the economies and ecologies of most North Americans' everyday lifeworld. The free exercise of individual trades or freeholding of real property also declined as social knowledge about economic production was professionalized or technicized via formal schooling and as real property increasingly came to be held by banks, corporations, or the state, leaving more and more people dependent on tenuous salary and wage incomes. With comparatively high incomes and social statuses, new class elitists exercised greater executive authority, but vast lay populations, who had less real property and income, became more and more "incompetent" as a dependence on huge, highly organized corporate machines came to dominate their now "individualized" material existence. While Progressive intellectuals attempted to dress up these dependencies as "the new freedom," "industrial democracy," or "the promise of American life," the populist movement rightly resisted such nationalizing initiatives of dispossession and dependency as rationalization without representation.[21]

Like the notion of a new class, populism clearly carries a lot of excess baggage as a political concept. Nevertheless, it is still useful, because it taps into those alternative mazeways in modernity that new class experts, government bureaucrats, and agents of big business have worked to close from consideration for decades. Populism embodies a vital tradition of democratic thought, albeit a very conflicted one, that opposed the social contracts of industrial democracy, consumer society, and service state drawn up by the new class and big business from the Gilded Age through the New Deal era amid the consolidation of the Second Industrial Revolution. "Populism," as Lasch understood it, "was never an exclusively agrarian ideology. It envisioned a national society not just of farmers but of artisans and tradesmen as well. Nor was it implacably opposed to urbanization."[22] Today, in the aftermath of the cold war, it is clear that new notions are needed to sustain, if not resuscitate, American democracy amid the collapse of the welfare state, the crises of consumer capitalism, and the contradictions of industrial democracy. Populism could provide some of these much needed answers, because populists have held that "democracy works best when men and women do things for themselves, with the help of their friends and neighbors, instead of depending on the state. Not that democracy should be equated with rugged individualism. Self-reliance does not mean self-sufficiency. Self-governing communities, not individuals, are the basic units of democratic society."[23]

As the violence of the 1990s confirms, the basic premises of populism are attacked ardently in current political debates. Some dismiss all populists as the disgruntled followers of xenophobic America First!ers such as Pat Buchanan or H. Ross Perot, while others stigmatize populism by associating it with tragic incidents of paramilitary fanaticism such as those at Ruby Ridge, Idaho, or Waco, Texas, and violent episodes of terrorism such as the Oklahoma City bombing or the Unabomber affair. Contemporary populism is bigger than mass media accounts of these events suggest, however, and differs from their descriptions markedly. Nonetheless, these facets constitute a sure sign of a new antigovernment populistic upsurge that merits consideration not simply as a threat to the existing regime but as an indicator of its failures. Consequently, I will explore other, less violent readings of populism—interpretations that highlight its possibilities as an alternative set of practices to answer government and market failures by organizing an ecological, democratic, and self-reliant way of life in modern communities out of the anti-environmental, managerialist, and dependency-generating lifestyles concocted by new class designers, advertisers, and executives over the past century. The environmental justice movement, site defense organizations, bioregional fronts, and NIMBY ("not in my backyard") coalitions at the local level all can be seen in part as vital expressions of such populist impulses whose organizational logics and political values need to be articulated in a more theoretical fashion. As Mark Dowie notes, these "fourth wave" environmental groups are "multiracial, multiethnic, multiclass, and multicultural," and as a result, they have many of the same traits that characterized "the American Revolution—dogged determination, radical inquiry, a rebellion against economic hegemony, and a quest for civil authority at the grassroots."[24] Such environmental justice movements are efforts to rescue the United States from the miseries of division and discord in which a nation of the rich tussles with a nation of the poor, a people with access and education fights with a people without access or education, and a community of less polluted and poisoned lands struggles with a community of more polluted and poisoned lands.

Rereading Contemporary Populism

There are other, more anomic answers being advanced from below to cope with Lasch's "crisis of competence," and such responses in the 1990s have taken violent, militant forms. Nonetheless, not all this violent turmoil should be blamed on populism. Likewise, not all forms of populism should be associated automatically with white-hot rhetoric about hate crime, gun fetishism, or religious zealotry. Whether they are discussing the Branch Davidians at Waco; Randy Weaver at Ruby Ridge; Timothy McVeigh and Terry Nichols at Oklahoma City; Ted Kaczynski at Lincoln, Montana; Richard McLaren at Fort Davis, Texas; or the Freemen at Jordan, Montana, many academicians and most of the mass media cast these violent episodes—in which at most a handful of psychotics allegedly manifest their supposed psychopathologies in shootouts, bombings, or other antisocial hate crimes—as examples of "populist" resistance. This interpretation is much too easy, however, and it misses more deeply seated resentments boiling out of the heartlands of the United States and many other nation-states at the close of the cold war.

The militia movement, or as its followers prefer, "the patriot movement," fears the immensity of the U.S. state. Many analyses of the contemporary state claim that no institution can exercise sovereign authority without systematically using armed violence or constantly increasing its police forces. In the United States, for example, institutions at all levels of government have increased in size, number, and complexity since 1945, and total government spending has doubled every decade since 1960.[25] The bombing of the Alfred P. Murrah Federal Building in Oklahoma City on April 19, 1995, could have been an act of mindless sociopathology, but it also might be a study in how two average Americans who fashioned themselves as "patriots" believed they could "fight the power." After Waco such individuals hoped someone could "strike back" against what they regarded as a new Behemoth, growing in size, complexity, and power before their eyes. In other words, a "people's terror" might be needed to counter "state terror." But should this angry assumption by small factions in the militia movement be taken as everything that defines populism today?

Most contemporary populists advance a far more situated reading of the state; and as the environmental justice movements or NIMBY-minded site defense groups show, they often do contrast its professed liberal agendas with its actual illiberal bureaucratic practices. Even if the state is our enemy, as Andrew Kirby concludes, populists have many more choices than the simple "fight or flight" response expressed in McVeigh's and Kaczynski's misdeeds.[26]

Moreover, the opponents of populism are not limited to those individuals working in the bureaucratic organs of the state; as a result, populists need more complex coping strategies to deflect or defuse state power when and where it is possible so that those state agencies do not become as overwhelmingly powerful and pervasive as McVeigh or Kaczynski have dreamed. We should acknowledge the rage that many militant individuals and violent groups express against the state at all levels of its operation, and we must take their anger seriously at face value. These movements are not the work of democratic populists. Nonetheless, we also must be cautious about condemning contemporary populists by using all the old stigmas that elitist voices of state power have used against the people, because the embedded elitism of the liberal values in U.S. governmental institutions and the intrinsic populism of collective sovereignty in the nation's communities cannot be fully reconciled.

The Contradictions of "Liberal Democracy"

Most defenses of progressive liberalism in its essentially New Deal statist forms gloss over serious contradictions in U.S. politics, namely, the conflict between liberalism and democracy and the distrust that "the best and the brightest" among the new class usually feel regarding "the heartland" of contemporary U.S. society. Many new class experts support liberal statism with its strong track record of guaranteeing individual values through bureaucratic intervention. Using state power to force the people to be free operates in accord with a belief that "people are inherently equal, that they have a right to pursue their individuality in an open society and that the state must use its power and authority to secure their rights and help the needier among them."[27] New class experts push these managerial values because such practices benefit them and their interests. Social privilege and intellectual solipsism go hand in hand for most new class agents. They see the social gains of affirmative action or abortion rights as permanent fixtures in the liberal state's bureaucratic apparatus; fortunately for them and the United States, more new class managerialists are always needed to define and supply such state services. They tend to see any populist opposition to these values from the heartland not as the actions of a sovereign people but rather as the misdeeds of religious fanatics, tax avoiders, abortion clinic bombers, gun nuts, or domestic terrorists. For them, such apocalyptic fringe elements are the sine qua non of populism.

This new class analysis misses how much liberalism contradicts and confounds democracy in the United States. Liberal statism may appear to guarantee individual values, but these precepts might be the values only of individual liberal statists who believe they are empowered to keep "the people" equal by impelling them to pursue individuality in an open society, to secure various abstract enactments of individual rights, and to assist the needier elements of society. Such agendas of enlightened managerialism from above and without will frequently conflict with those of more self-reliant people struggling to rule themselves in a fully functioning democracy that fulfills decisions made by, for, and of "the people," not by liberal statists. Many populists, then, ask a troubling question: who actually sets the rules of governance, and for whom?

Elitist statism arguably is contemporary liberalism's first contradiction. A proliferating panoply of entitlements and rights, once meant to protect individuals from states, has perhaps come to constrain real democratic choice, reducing communal self-governance to the individual ratification of expert decisions taken elsewhere. State and corporate managerialists transmogrify popular democracy into an elitist technocracy legitimated by formal bureaucratic practices intent on protecting only their moralizing abstractions, such as their vision for equal rights and full entitlements. Whereas real people in many actual communities might choose through open and free democratic means *not* to accept affirmative action, *not* to endorse abortion rights, *not* to pay for antipoverty program entitlements, or *not* to impose restrictive gun control laws, liberal statists can intervene in their lives contrademocratically to force such statist policies down their throats as the freedoms they must accept.

As Ulrich Beck observes, governments now try to reduce risk—to themselves and their constituents—by reprocessing the dangers of democratic governance into the more predictable certainties of expert rulings.[28] Politics becomes "subpolitics," insulating real political choices from the democratic hurly-burly of popular elections or partisan wrangling while empowering small networks of experts to rule on the basis of their professional-technical disciplinary codes in networks of professionalized interest articulation and aggregation where more networks of other experts make, enforce, and interpret the rules separate and apart from more open electoral and parliamentary processes. The exercise of expertise creates a "subpolis" whose subpolitics often vitiate the democratic politics of the national polity. Hence the main political conflict zones today are no longer necessarily those between labor and capital, left and right, persons of color and WASPs, or women and men; rather, they are cut along new contours of control between those who know and those who do not, those who can and do participate in elitist managerial decision taking and those who cannot, or those who intervene in the personal spheres of others and those who cannot. For many, "the land of the free and home of the brave" is becoming estranged from its own historical discourses of republican democracy by dint of such liberal statist practices, making it just one more land of the unfree or roost for the cowardly as managerial experts seek to dominate or exploit lay persons, local communities, and legal systems.

Liberalism also carries a second contradiction tied to its deeply rooted market fixations. This also endangers democracy inasmuch as neoliberal doctrines of market expansion, free choice, and bureaucratic deregulation are counterposed to what were once democratically enacted policies—affirmed by the people at the ballot box—to constrain markets (wage guarantee laws, workers' rights legislation, social welfare provisions) and endorse regulation (occupational safety codes, food inspection procedures, environmental protection legislation). The informational revolution comes after the end of classical state-based imperialism with "the domination of the global economy by a few hundred TNCs [transnational corporations] based to an overwhelming extent in the same ex-imperialist countries. The professional managers who control them have the means to benefit the world or to exploit it to their own benefit."[29] At this juncture the opening of U.S. society to global market competition or foreign business investment appears in the form of a race not to "the top" of the world's economic hierarchies but instead to "the bottom." For many neoliberal market advocates, the United States should no longer benchmark itself against the welfare states of Western Europe. Instead, it is urged to emulate Chile, Hong Kong, Mexico, Singapore, or Brazil. Although the "successful fifth" of Reich's symbolic analysts may benefit from such policies, the "unsuccessful four-fifths" of nonsymbolic toilers suffer even more downward mobility. What should be the allegedly clean magic of the marketplace appears to work too many dirty tricks against contemporary society. The frustration with such governance is also being expressed in the voting booth. Unfortunately, the protest vote is often captured by nationalist, authoritarian, or racist politicians. As shown by the successes of individuals ranging from H. Ross Perot or Pat Buchanan in the United States to Jean-Marie Le Pen or Jörg Haider in Europe and Pauline Hanson or Winston Peters in Australasia, the 1990s have moved many anxious people to vote for dangerous politicians in protest against the programs of neoliberal rationalization, globalization, and informationalization being promoted by the new class. Globalization could perhaps be resisted, and many in the United States might vote to follow antiglobalization paths in the republic's public policies. Instead, they see experts accelerating the processes of globalization, selling out their country to the new world order and turning the United States into NAFTAland.[30]

Popular Sovereignty and the New World Order

Reconfiguring any nation's heartland to suit managerialist designs often creates populist resistance against such programs of transnational reconfiguration. Global flows of capital, national codes of expert meddling, and local structures of coercion all combine within practices of cold calculation into a formal order of bureaucratic legality in which everything is foreign, strange, and threatening. If what was "a homeland" for Americans has now become alien for too many people because Japanese executives, Washington bureaucrats, Hollywood scriptwriters, Harvard professors, or ATF agents are all rudely intruding uninvited into their lives in apparently authoritarian ways, then, some militants reason, why should this new world order not ignite violent counterstrikes? After all, no one elected any of these seemingly malevolent agents of change in free democratic elections.

As many observers assert, the United States is a violent country, and it has been so since the time of its English, French, and Spanish foundings in the seventeenth and eighteenth centuries. As the Black Panthers asserted in the 1960s, "violence is [as] American as apple pie." From its violent revolutionary origins in the 1770s, this nation has frequently seen "the people" use militia movements against the state and its officials from below and within.[31] Such violence might be endemic to the processes of nation building and state formation as such. Centralizing authorities and nationalizers must in turn diminish or destroy any and all competing blocs of local and regional authority as they reimagine their built nation in terms of one privileged governing canon of linguistic, religious, racial, ethnic, and gender myths—namely, their own against all others. Nonetheless, the popular violence of the present era does seem to be distinctive, and how we interpret its many distinctions will be significant. New pressures from within and without seem to be cracking the old canonical centers of imagining a larger nationalistic community within territorialized nation-states.[32] Now amid the remaining fragments, odd bits of popularized political knowledge in retronarratives, countercanonical readings, and subjugated myths—ranging from Koresh's prophetic rereadings of the Bible, to the Republic of Texas militia's repudiation of the admission of Texas to the Union, to the Montana Freemen's *lumpenproletarian* reinterpretations of common law—are rising up through the insurrection of subjugated movements. Moreover, unlike most liberal statists or technocratic managers, the people behind these new apocalyptic reimaginings of political community seem unafraid to admit that power ultimately does come from the barrel of a gun.

We must ask, along with many populists, whether institutionally situated new class readings of the state are visualizations that simply reconstruct their managerial vision of the state from their elitist readings of the current populist situation. Instead of giving us a well-contextualized reading of state power, they may simply reposition troubling news reports about governmental practices, such as those recounting how environmental legislation may privilege the protection of bird or fish species over humans' logging jobs, how ranchers and game officials clash over repopulating natural habitat with wolves, or how apocalyptic religious movements seem to attract "warrior males" who are no longer welcome in the nation's postmodern military. Waco, then, can be understood as a tragic loss of innocent lives incurred when duly appointed authorities sought to bring unruly fanatics to justice. However, it also can be read as an incident of exocolonial violence (tanks, SWAT commandos, helicopter harassment) directed at endocolonial targets (true believers, Texas towns, born-again children) that broke the social contract between the federal state and its citizens and then induced McVeigh, Nichols, and company to counterattack against such endocolonizing agencies allegedly working out of ATF, IRS, DEA, and INS offices in Oklahoma City.[33]

Over two hundred militia or patriot groups operating in thirty-nine states now openly oppose what they imagine is an "occupation government," engage in acts of civil disobedience, and encourage tax avoidance, militia activity, or domestic terrorism. All these developments are occurring in the United States, but how they influence our readings of contemporary populism is less clear. Most of them are fairly marginal, quite small in overall numbers, heavily concentrated in isolated Mountain West states, and mostly lacking any broad-based popular following. Is this populism resurrected, or anarchism again, or simply signs of a sinking lower middle class turning to petty crime as its outmodedness in a globalizing informational economy becomes obvious even to itself?

There are, of course, alternative interpretations of this turmoil. Rather than see the state as growing in size and authority, perhaps we should see it as shrinking and losing control through corporate-supported campaigns of national government downsizing, public agency underfunding, and public personnel cuts. The rise in violent crime, a mafia economy, and the allure of gangster culture could reflect spontaneous communal efforts to order everyday life in the downsized, underemployed, rust-belted economies of the post-1973 era. Ineffectual police, uncaring bureaucrats, and formalistic proceduralism in court or bureaucracies do not control criminals, so individuals and communities arm themselves. Runaway shops, mindless regulations, and overpriced labor do not support jobs with a living wage, so contraband economies in drugs, liquor, weapons, gambling, or illegal workers pay the bills. Multiculturalist ideologies, liberal elitist privileges, and white-collar prejudice do not create a truly civil society, so bunker mentalities tied to race, religion, or residence create a militant spirit of closed community that conveys identity and solidarity. Perhaps the state is becoming not an aggressive occupation government but an absent force, an empty shell, or a decolonized presence that most of the time and in many places possesses little hegemonic weight. To compensate for this unbearable "liteness" of its authoritative being, the state episodically may reappear in DEA raids, IRS shakedowns, ATF investigations, FBI SWAT teams, or INS inspections. Such dramatic state action might suggest a vast potential force with great state power, yet if these open spaces were so hegemonically subdued, such force levels obviously would be unnecessary. Because these spaces are so wild, government employees instead must move ham-handedly in heavy formations.[34]

Operational readings of the state by the new class now suggest how contested and contestable its basic jurisdiction—or its essential position as a center of legal diction, a mode of speaking lawfully or a form of law-making speech—is becoming. The vertical displacement of power upward from periphery to core, lower to higher organizations, and local to national institutions has always been an ongoing effort to maintain jurisdiction over entire populations and whole territories that has sought to center state power in a single country, territory, or domain. Acquiring jurisdiction equals seizing the power to speak and act lawfully as the duly recognized sovereign authority over certain terrains and groups, an authority recognized both by those inside the spaces in question and by those outside them.

Autonomous spaces (i.e., self-legislating, self-limiting, self-ruling places, such as nation-states) are sites at which autonymous (i.e., self-naming, self-ruling, and self-defining) elites name the games that define and delimit their rules, making them rulers. Those who now regard the state as their enemy dispute its rights to jurisdiction; they are challenging its law-speaking qualities, questioning its self-legislating authority, and attacking its self-naming capabilities. Many small militant movements today would have another kind of law (God's law, market logic, ethnoracialism) speak against statist jurisdiction while naming other selves (religious, racial, revolutionary) and other games (race purity, faith in God, regional culture, solidarity with family, property rights) to serve as the foundation of a new coexistence beyond, beneath, or behind the state. When the state is our enemy, these small circles of freemen and -women apparently believe its dominion over their homeland leaps from broken homes, dysfunctional families, and home-wrecking bureaucracies. Governmentality thus elicits its own contragovernmentalities as "contradictive" resistances question "juris-dictive" fixities with alternative visions of ways to more rightly dispose of things in relation to new kinds of people in the service of other ends and a different sense of conveniences.[35]

If populists are to resist the implicit liberal statism of traditional civic interpretations and dispute the purportedly benign nature of new class authorities, despite academic assurances to the contrary, their efforts may lead at the end of the day to their owning weapons or discharging firearms. As some militants suggest, it is possible to condone violence without supporting the politics of hate. Before the advent of modern war machines, classical visions of republican citizenship required the individual and communal ownership of weapons and condoned violence as part and parcel of citizenship. One can begin with Thucydides' account of warrior citizens in Pericles' funeral oration during the Peloponnesian War, then go to Machiavelli's republican musings in Renaissance Italy, and continue with Rousseau's sense of the social contract in the Enlightenment. At the end of the day, being armed has always been regarded as a basic duty or primary obligation of self-rule in republics. To be a warrior has been a collective dream of republican civic obligation as well as a lone project, a familial obligation, a community expectation, and a regional duty. Where these precepts are accepted widely in popular practice, the state often is not the people's enemy, because its magistrates tend to be few and weak. Armed citizens, warrior constituents, and duty-fulfilling freeholders constitute its "state power." Today's militia movements, then, might be only faint echoes or last gasps of such old myths of collective empowerment, which overdeveloped state formations, operating at times as unchecked and unbalanced war machines, have driven out into the badlands of Montana, Texas, and Idaho.

The militias of today are testing, once again, many of the age-old contradictions between authority and autonomy, the sovereign state and sovereign individuals, putatively legitimate jurisdictions and allegedly illegitimate contradictions. Today's Koreshes, McVeighs, Nicholses, McLarens, and Kaczynskis, however, as well as many other less violently aggrieved individuals, are also pushing far beyond democratic populism.[36] They no longer regard the U.S. state as "their state." Terroristic violence is directed by the bombers or militias against an alien state, secular humanists, or big technoscience as putatively righteous counterstrikes against a "them" opposed to "us," an "other" no longer like "me," "the strange" threatening "the familiar." New class experts may dispute such popular apocalyptic accounts of the state's estrangement and oppose the resulting violent acts, but why have so many people come to fear that the state is no longer theirs? Plainly one need not respond to their plight with bloody shootouts, bank fraud, mass suicides, or mail bombs. Violent responses constrict "us" and "ours" so narrowly that any sense of political community on a larger scale is lost. To reclaim a sense of shared community, contemporary populists must return to vital questions: who is "us," and what or who is "them"? In answering these questions, contemporary populists should determine openly and democratically which individuals residing where and at what particular places might (re)constitute sovereign authority in ways that could empower and enrich all those who could be counted as "us" without unduly disregarding or seriously harming all those who remain "them."

New Class Conflict: Populists and Experts

The monotone modernity associated with classic Weberian-Parsonian narratives of modernization, which combine highly unstable elements of complex organization, atomized individuality, strategic reasoning, extensive urbanization, scientific management, high mobility, or cultural secularization in one-way progressive currents of ever-increasing technoscientific rationalization, is not a historical inevitability, even though professional canons of social science have often constructed this story of modernity as humanity's "true and only heaven." Populism reminds us that there are many paths in modernity. Populists point to other, more polychromatic possibilities lying latent within this organizational monoculture, either as suppressed alternatives or as subjugated knowledges, possibilities for creating different modernities that would rely more on personal empowerment, not corporate empowerment; local community, not national solidarity; individual producership, not personal consumership; and popular self-reliance, not bureaucratic entitlement. More important, because their environmental arrangements would be based on shared common goals captured in small-scale economic operations and grounded in everyone's backyard, these localistic alternatives, as imperfect as they are, could prove to be less ecologically harmful than those overdeveloped transnational ecologies of global businesses and the major international powers that no one wants in his or her backyard.

The structures and functions of modern industrial life as we find them are not "natural." The "naturalization" of their artificiality is instead another disciplinary expression of class interests, corporate agendas, and control systems that has been kept in operation for decades to contain the subjugated power and insurrectional knowledge of popular communities, which have often been ardently opposed to the managerial command exercised by new class actors.[37]

Of course, the new class should not be seen as a uniform, well-organized, or self-conscious force that always acts cohesively or consciously in its own interest; it is as divided and diverse as all other social classes. The same market forces that have colonized the environment also generate fragmentation, competition, overspecialization, and unsophistication among the various members of the new class. More traditional humanistic and even quasi-critical values occasionally become embedded in the business plans of corporate firms or the standard operating procedures of state agencies. One perhaps should not jump, as do Alvin Gouldner or Jürgen Habermas, to rosy final conclusions about the inevitability of humanistic critical values or ideal speech situations in undistorted moral communication emerging full-blown from the everyday procedures of new class workers' professional-technical labor. Nevertheless, there are, as Scott Lash and John Urry maintain, quite a few self-reflexive possibilities built into many new class structures of administration.[38]

The fragmentation caused by "powerful knowing" creates a highly dispersed, if not contradictory, competitiveness among many new class occupations and disciplines, making commonly shared sets of interests difficult to arrange. At the same time, the diffuseness of intellectual labor in traditional university or college settings, as shown by the rise of many new corporate or municipal research campuses dedicated to highly applied scientific missions, weakens old humanistic norms of critical thought and practice by injecting highly subjective commercial considerations into what was once more objective scholarship, transmuting its many intrinsic rewards into the superficial simplicities of "knowledge production," "patent generation," or "fundable research." The elective affinities in professional-technical expertise between value creation in the market, power formation for the state, and careerist advancement in the profession, which Jean-François Lyotard identifies as logics of performativity, are where one sees many new class groups forging agendas and values that are antithetical to preserving either nature or culture as they have been defined naturally and culturally.[39] The ecological impulse to preserve the autochthonous ecologies of "first nature" is in part rendered obsolete as the new class technocrats fabricate an ever more comprehensive "second nature" out of artificially built environments in which their codes of power/knowledge define the naturalized histories, events, and forces in "situated knowledges" or "cyborg" power systems that are appropriate for managing these new artificial hyperecologies.[40]

To respond to these dilemmas, I attempt in this book to push beyond the important insights outlined by Christopher Lasch in his book *The Revolt of the Elites and the Betrayal of Democracy.* I will look at the roots of the organizational revolutions staged by new class experts, which Lasch saw as a local revolt of national elites against the mass populations they simultaneously serve and disserve. As new class experts secede into the realms of symbolic analytical work, they disempower others as well as redefine the normative horizon for all collective decision making. With this book, then, I also hope to address, as Lasch did, more important questions lying beyond debates over "the culture war" or "the end of history." Those who are concerned about the quality of democratic ways of life today must consider "the crisis of competence; the spread of apathy and a suffocating cynicism; [and] the moral paralysis of those who value 'openness' above all."[41]

To find for all of us some new sense of competence, engagement, and hope that might loosen the grip of those who proclaim the value of openness even as they have forbidden its practice to the public, my analysis looks to ecological sites of struggle. The one moment of certain reflexive practice freely permitted to most people is ecological, because we are all still allowed to worry about our own backyards. Moreover, many now do center their collective thoughts about others and individual emotions of care for nature on their immediate environmental conditions. This analysis seizes this reflexive opportunity and presses it toward much more fundamental conclusions. If ecology is a disciplined examination of the totality of forces and factors shaping organisms and their environment,[42] then why not push beyond the conventional biophysical borders defined by professional-technical experts to bind these ecological totalities together and then examine how the governmental agencies, economic processes, and cultural conditions constructed by the new class have been reshaping the organisms and environments of human ecology in the United States' advanced industrial society over the past century?

The difficulties of resisting the new class crop up as soon as one questions the good life of material abundance as it has been styled under the command, control, and communication of corporate consumerism. It is quite hard to reinvoke an ethic of personal responsibility, because so much individual independence has been given up, as Wendell Berry asserts, for "the cheap seductions and shoddy merchandise of so-called 'affluence.' We have delegated all our vital functions and responsibilities to salesmen and agents and bureaus and experts of all sorts. We cannot feed or clothe ourselves, or entertain ourselves, or communicate with each other, or be charitable or neighborly or giving, or even respect ourselves, without recourse to a merchant or a corporation or a public service organization or an agency of government or a style-setter or an expert."[43] Hence, the people, as clients, customers, and consumers, enter "this state of total consumerism—which is to say a state of helpless dependence on things and services and ideas and motives that we have forgotten how to provide ourselves—all meaningful contact between ourselves and the earth is broken."[44]

This book constitutes an ecological critique of the informational revolution, albeit an incomplete and imperfect one. Such a criticism is necessary, for the informational revolution has also been in many ways a control revolution, a managerial revolution, a design revolution, or an organizational revolution organized by new class experts and aimed at disembedding human communities from their mostly localized organic ecologies in natural bioregions to reposition them within more globalized inorganic hyperecologies designed by others in artificial technoregions.[45] The fashions in which it has worked, the bases from which it can be resisted, and ends at which alternatives could be aimed are in turn the focus of the following chapters.

One can protest that everyone is complicit in reproducing informational society, and that claim would not be entirely wrong. But this complicity is forced on most individuals by the monological quality of advanced industrial ecologies, which has colonized more and more dimensions of the everyday lifeworld for over a century. Certainly everyone is implicated in reproducing this ecological-economic totality. Its totalizing logic always operates so that its high standards of living become within its ecology and economy a living of high standards. More substantial forms of freedom, however, cannot be found by turning mall visits into a subversive act or taking countercultural parody as revolutionary resistance. As even the Unabomber sees, the organization-dependent technics managed by the new class survive by co-opting such empty alternatives endlessly into its always expansive visions of modernity as new progressive innovations. Effective populist resistances must push through these illusory changes into sites and structures where alternative modernities with entirely different relations of independent producership, communal competence, and individual power/knowledge can invent new ecologies more in harmony with nature.

The Outlines of Marxian and Populist Critique

People who favor radical ecological change can gain much from returning to Marxian critical theory. In reaffirming the close ties many local cultures have to the land, this nation's deep ecologists, nature activists, and social ecologists are tapping into powerful ecological currents in the United States that are as familiar and populistic as critical social theory has been esoteric and elitist.[46] Despite its intellectual contradictions, as chapter 1 claims, Marxian critical theory still carries the moral rage and analytical sweep needed to redefine the struggle over the remaining free spaces in today's globalized capitalist marketplaces, while it ethically inoculates the communities occupying those spaces against further intrusions.[47] Despite occasional missteps and fundamental mistakes, political alternatives inspired by engagé ecofeminism, environmental justice groups, radical social ecology, and even deep ecology could release the energies needed to build qualitatively new, ecologically rational forms of communal production and personal autonomy within those free spaces. While musing about the failures of today's "spectatorial left," Richard Rorty is all too eager to close the books on this sort of politics.[48] As someone more open to a "participatory left," I want to see an America where wealth, opportunity, and income are equitably distributed. The pessimism of the cultural left today does not warrant retreating from this goal, and there are many worthy visions of reconstruction, reform, and revitalization now available in the environmental movement that would be useful for realizing change. In fact, Rorty's spectatorial left has not entirely replaced a participatory left, nor has the pragmatic participatory project of improving the United States lost any of its merit.

By incorporating the critique of instrumental reason that critical theorists have leveled against both modern capitalism and socialism, some streams of radical ecology articulate important new thinking about the emancipation of nature.[49] Their ecological values defend a number of basic precepts as ultimate ends that must be intellectually and organizationally counterposed to the corporate technocracy's continuing reliance on the subjective-instrumental reason of efficient means in the marketplace. Ecological discourses, as an evolving set of ultimate moral ends, delimit new moral goals in a contextual, substantive rationality attuned to the continuing reproduction of nature as their alternative to strategic formal rationality posed in terms of the production of commodities, which chapters 2 and 3 discuss in more detail.

By providing new insights into the association of nature and culture, which can be continually reconnected to the perpetually shifting flows of the personal and social lifeworld, ecologically informed theories might tap into more survivable values to anchor human technoscientific activities. Chapters 7 and 8 explore how social, political, economic, and cultural rereadings of ecology by local populist movements could serve as a core discourse for discussing "the true nature of things and the correct pattern of living"[50] in more comprehensive ecological terms. Ecological judgments, not cost-benefit analyses; natural reasonability, not administrative rationality; and transcendent ecological ends, not immediate managerial calculations—these could emerge as a reflexive basis for developing moral values and guiding technical activities.

An ecological populism guided by many streams of contemporary critical theory could in turn shield this new type of community from instrumentalizing influences that would bend its operations to the economistic needs of corporate environmentalism. As chapters 5 and 6 maintain, the current order of instrumentally rational cost-benefit analysis, which has legitimated environmental degradation with languages of risk in small, incremental steps taken in tradeoffs between calculable quarterly business returns and incalculable long-run ecological costs imposed by large corporations or national governments, sets the bottom line of "environmental protection agency" for bureaucratic greens and ecobusinesses devoted to sustainable development. Such environmental protection policies bear about as much relation to the ends of local ecology as the now familiar "social security" policies bear to the transcendent ends of socialism, namely, little true relation at all. The administrative rationality of corporate and state technocrats denies the existence or validity of other ultimate ends held by local communities or individuals (such as protecting forests or owls for their own sake) by interposing its own more limited profit-oriented goals to be fulfilled by the efficient ends-means rationality of corporate calculation (such as destroying owl habitat by producing lumber to provide a few local jobs and short-run company profits).

As chapters 6 and 7 assert, populist ecological reasoning might resist as antithetical to the larger balances between human and nonhuman beings the unanticipated costs that society at large incurs in serving such corporate goals, as transnational corporations build new hyperecological macroenvironments based on social hierarchy, technological complexity, political centralization, scientific domination, and cultural reification. By opposing these destructive tendencies with new values, as chapter 8 indicates, ecological populists might also renew nonhierarchical social relations, technical simplicity, small-scale economies, political decentralization, civic science, and cultural vitality within the free spaces of present-day society. Unlike the new class, whose programs promote greater corporate managerialism, many radical ecological populists and critical social theorists favor mobilizing immediate producers and consumers to reconsider such crucial decisions about human beings' relation to nature rather than surrendering this prerogative to new class state and corporate technocrats.

The new class always seeks, as Wendell Berry claims, to "think big," but individual populists are oriented toward "thinking little." A new discipline of thought and in behavior shared by many is what will solve the environmental crisis. Populism is not about people voting for right-wing demagogues to make the trains run on time; it is instead about people taking responsibility for their own actions by making fundamental changes in the ways they are living. Most people still have control over many aspects of their individual existence, and these sites are where populism must operate. Even though the new class continues to study problems and organize solutions inside of large governmental and corporate institutions in its "think big" mode,

> nothing is being done. But the citizen who is willing to Think Little, and, accepting the discipline of that, to go ahead on his own, is already solving the problem. A man who is trying to live as a neighbor to his neighbors will have a lively and practical understanding of the work of peace and brotherhood, and let there be no mistake about it—he is doing that work. A couple who make a good marriage, and raise healthy, morally competent children, are serving the world's future more directly and surely than any political leader, though they never utter a public word. A good farmer who is dealing with the problem of soil erosion on an acre of ground has a sounder grasp of that problem and cares more about it and is probably doing more to solve it than any bureaucrat who is talking about it in general. A man who is willing to undertake the discipline and the difficulty of mending his own ways is worth more to the conservation movement than a hundred who are insisting merely that the government and the industries mend their ways.[51]

Populism, then, is a new kind of more conscious action, rooted in built and unbuilt environments, that reclaims responsibility and agency from experts and specialists as a strategy for opposing the polyarchical society and megatechnical economy discussed more in the chapters ahead.

This reconstruction and contestation of ecology as a new critical sensibility could revitalize political debates over the key issues of who decides, who pays, and who benefits in the complex economic and technological relations of people with nature. A renewal of nature, ecologically constituted and mediated as free sites for self-created being, promises to reorder the relations of the individual to the collective, of personality to society, and of these dual social relations to nature. This ecological sensibility, then, must reinvest individuals with the decision-making power to order their material relations to the environment in smaller-scale, nonhierarchical, ecologically sound technical relations between independent producers in local and regional commonwealths. States and businesses will not act responsibly in every instance. Therefore, ecological populism must reaffirm the responsibility of all individuals for preserving their ecological inheritance and passing it on to future generations. To confirm the virtues of self and social discipline in living within the renewable cycles of natural reproduction, this ecological sensibility should point to the most promising paths out of the megatechnical consumerism of corporate capitalism. Rather than encourage passivity, dependence, and purposelessness, which social theorists have criticized the corporate technocracy for fostering and perpetuating, the theory and praxis of ecological populism should presume greater social activity, personal autonomy, and reasonable balance to preserve nature. With these goals the labor of competent, conscious communities could be guided to ecologically reconstitute their social, economic, and political mediations with each other by interacting reasonably with nature.[52]

Furthermore, the successful establishment of new social relations organized along these ecological lines might radically alter the social constructions of nature in relation to society, making nature again into a subject, not an object; an agency, not an instrumentality; and a more than equal partner, not a dominated subaltern force. Many living and inorganic constituents of nature could be entitled to rights and privileges as worthy of defense as many human rights and social privileges. At the same time, no rationalizations of nature's continued destruction could be countenanced in exchange for the false promise of more jobs, greater prosperity, added growth, or closer technological control. Guarantees of ecological security should in turn ramify into greater freedom, dignity, and reasonability for the human beings whose own autonomy suffers in nature's abusive indenturing to corporate enterprises' instrumental rationality.

For centuries the industrial approach toward nature has emphasized a relation of instrumentally driven *mining*, the brutal appropriation of resources with little concern for the ways in which the never-ending growth of consumption overloads and exhausts stocks of natural resources, degrading the environment for all beings who occupy it. Shifting from these relations of "mining," which prevail in most contemporary technologies of mineral utilization, corporate agriculture, water usage, timber exploitation, commercial fishing, and atmospheric pollution, to a relationship of contextually anchored *minding* is a pressing need. Such caring collaboration between nature and culture, which could survive an equitable exchange between social resource utilization and natural resource renewal, might better balance the currently unbalanced cycles of growth and decay, present consumption and future production, and technical efficiency and ecological reasonability. A popular local culture for "minding" nature should assume human coevolution with nonhuman life in the environment.[53] As each of the following chapters asserts, these practices of nature minding also should evince several principles: the necessity of planning for permanence rather than obsolescence; the worth of maintaining natural and social diversity over the ill-fated imposition of a monological uniformity on nature; the importance of sustaining renewal, reusability, and reasonability as central principles of nature-culture linkages; and the need to balance past environmental destruction against present communal use and future ecological renewal in one common set of accounts. In developing these principles, new discursive representations of ecology should guide local communities hoping to make the transition from economies subjected exclusively to narrow corporate profit to ecologies rooted more closely in a broader democratic communalism.

Notes

1. The peculiarities of "new class" terminology are a function of sociological borrowings from formerly state socialist societies in which members of the *nomenklatura*, which was often a new table of ranks that the communist party-state assigned to its key personnel, were put "in authority" by virtue of their party membership, state office, or professional-technical labor. This statist intelligentsia in turn became almost entirely coextensive with anyone who was any kind of "an authority" in society. For more discussion, see Milovan Djilas, *The New Class: An Analysis of the Communist System* (New York: Praeger, 1957); or George Konrad and Ivan Szelényi, *The Intellectuals on the Road to Class Power* (New York: Harcourt Brace Jovanovich, 1979). These analyses also see new class blocs of elitist experts at work in most liberal capitalist democracies today; however, their pluralistic hierarchies are more confused, inconsistent, and open than those of state socialist one-party dictatorships. In liberal capitalist democracies, higher education and formal training of individuals confer the roles and statuses of becoming some kind of "an authority" within a disciplinary context, a professional organization, or occupational assignment. These individuals in turn gather into competing elite groups that divide ceaselessly over control of power/knowledge creation, interpretation, or operationalization. The winners of such struggles, if only partially or temporarily, then are placed "in authority." For more articulation of these circumstances in an informationalizing global economy, see Robert B. Reich, *The Work of Nations: Preparing Ourselves for Twenty-first Century Capitalism* (New York: Knopf, 1991).

2. The nature of the informational revolution is addressed in my *Screens of Power: Ideology, Domination, and Resistance in Informational Society* (Urbana: University of Illinois Press, 1989). Also see Fredric Jameson, *Postmodernism, or the Cultural Logic of Late Capitalism* (Durham, N.C.: Duke University Press, 1991); Ernest Mandel, *Late Capitalism* (London: Verso, 1978); Lewis Mumford, *Technics and Civilization* (New York: Harcourt, Brace, 1934); and Jaques Ellul, *The Technological Society* (New York: Vintage, 1964).

3. Harold Perkin, *The Third Revolution: Professional Elites in the Modern World* (London: Routledge, 1996). At one level, Bertrand Schneider of the Club of Rome is correct in asserting that "today's threat has no face . . . [;] we ourselves are the enemy." On another level, however, this conclusion is much too easy. It fails to ask how and

why we are organized by professional and technical elites so irrationally and inequitably. It does not question who this "we ourselves" might be, especially who should be rightly included, or has been wrongly excluded, in any attempt to understand where the threat lies as "the 20:80" society develops all over the world. See Hans-Peter Martin and Harald Schumann, *The Global Trap: Globalization and the Assault on Democracy and Prosperity* (London: Zed, 1997), 34.

4. Christopher Lasch, *The Revolt of the Elites and the Betrayal of Democracy* (New York: Norton, 1995), 5.

5. Perkin, *Third Revolution,* 8.

6. Ibid., 1.

7. Ibid.

8. Reich, *Work of Nations,* 171–84.

9. Lasch, *Revolt of the Elites,* 35.

10. Ibid., 38.

11. Raymond Aron, *The Opium of the Intellectuals* (New York: Norton, 1957); and Robert J. Brym, *Intellectuals and Politics* (London: Allen and Unwin, 1980) cover this ground effectively.

12. See Zygmunt Bauman, *Legislators and Interpreters: On Modernity, Post-Modernity, and Intellectuals* (Ithaca, N.Y.: Cornell University Press, 1987). Of course, there are socially conscious members of the new class, and many of them are moved by a genuine concern for the less privileged. Nonetheless, the majority of the new class is the same bloc of professional-technical workers that Reich sees seceding from the rest of society into gated communities, guarded office towers, and gilded resorts. In these changes, "the 20:80 society" feared by Martin and Schumann begins to acquire considerable heft and scope. See Reich, *The Work of Nations,* 282–300; and Martin and Schumann, *The Global Trap,* 1–11.

13. For more discussion of these interesting cultural variations, see Pierre Bourdieu, *Distinction: A Social Critique of the Judgement of Taste* (Cambridge, Mass.: Harvard University Press, 1984), 397–465. This analysis runs straight against the grain of many other treatments of the new class and populism. Like Lasch, I see the new class as far more numerous, complicated, and contradictory than do many New Right observers, who in the crassest misreading of Djilas simply dismiss any public sector employee as a new class operative. Also like Lasch, I see the people who become populists, communitarians, or localists as much more complex, multidimensional, and conflicted than do some New Left commentators, who in the grossest overinterpretation of Marx easily classify any local activist as a conservative popular reactionary. For a more orthodox left-wing reading of contemporary conflicts between the new class and local populist movements, see Boris Frankel, "Confronting Neoliberal Regimes: The Post-Marxist Embrace of Populism and Realpolitik," *New Left Review* 226 (Nov.–Dec. 1997): 57–92.

14. Lasch, *Revolt of the Elites,* 34.

15. Ibid., 40.

16. Perkin, *The Third Revolution,* 6.

17. See Michel Foucault, *Power/Knowledge: Selected Interviews and Other Writings, 1972–1977*, ed. Colin Gordon (New York: Pantheon, 1980), 109–93. Wendell Berry correctly observes, "The result of the short-term vision of these experts is a whole series of difficulties that together amount to a rapidly building ecological and social disaster, which there is little disposition at present to regret, much less to correct"; see Wendell Berry, *A Continuous Harmony: Essays Cultural and Agricultural* (San Diego: Harcourt Brace, 1972), 96.

18. See Christopher Lasch, *The True and Only Heaven: Progress and Its Critics* (New York: Norton, 1991).

19. Lasch, *Revolt of the Elites*, 7.

20. For consideration of these themes, see Noble, *America by Design;* Stuart Ewen, *All Consuming Images: The Politics of Style in Contemporary Culture* (New York: Basic, 1988); and William Leach, *Land of Desire: Merchants, Power, and the Rise of the New American Culture* (New York: Pantheon, 1993).

21. For further analysis, see Carleton Beals, *The Great Revolt and Its Leaders: The History of Popular American Uprisings in the 1890s* (London: Abelard-Schuman, 1968).

22. Lasch, *Revolt of the Elites*, 8.

23. Ibid., 7–8.

24. Mark Dowie, *Losing Ground: American Environmentalism at the Close of the Century* (Cambridge, Mass.: MIT Press, 1995), 207. For more discussion of such groups, see Robert D. Bullard, *Dumping in Dixie: Race, Class, and Environmental Quality* (Boulder, Colo.: Westview, 1990); Kirkpatrick Sale, *Dwellers in the Land: The Bioregional Vision* (Philadelphia: New Society, 1991); Roger Gottlieb, *Forcing the Spring: The Transformation of the American Environmental Movement* (Washington, D.C.: Island, 1993); and Bunyan Byrant, ed. *Environmental Justice: Issues, Policies, and Solutions* (Washington, D.C.: Island, 1995).

25. See Andrew Kirby, "Is the State Our Enemy?" *Political Geography* 16 (Jan. 1997): 1–5.

26. Ibid., 7–11.

27. R. Rosenblatt, "The Triumph of Liberalism," *New York Times Magazine*, January 14, 1996, p. 34.

28. See Ulrich Beck, *The Risk Society* (London: Sage, 1992), 183–236.

29. Perkin, *The Third Revolution*, 186.

30. These forces are being felt by many Americans, and other political interests beyond the closed circles of the militia movement have sought to address them as well. Presidential contender Pat Buchanan in the 1996 campaign even appeared to co-opt the themes of the patriot movement in his stump speeches when he claimed: "The men who stood at Lexington and at Concord Bridge, at Bunker Hill and Saratoga, they gave all they had, that the land they loved might be a free, independent, sovereign nation. Yet, today, our birthright of sovereignty, purchased with the blood of patriots, is being traded away for foreign money, handed over to faceless foreign bureaucrats at places like the IMF, the World Bank, the World Trade Organization and the U.N." See

Patrick Buchanan, "Republican Candidate for President," *Vital Speeches* 61, no. 15 (1995): 461–63.

31. See Hugh Davis Graham and Ted Robert Gurr, *The History of Violence in America: Historical and Comparative Perspectives,* rev. ed. (New York: Bantam, 1970); and Catherine McNicol Stock, *Rural Radicals: From Bacon's Rebellion to the Oklahoma City Bombing* (Ithaca, N.Y.: Cornell University Press, 1996).

32. See Timothy W. Luke, "Discourses of Disintegration, Texts of Transformation: Re-Reading Realism in the New World Order," *Alternatives* 18 (1993): 229–58.

33. See Paul Virilio and Sylvere Lotringer, *Pure War* (New York: Semiotext(e), 1983).

34. See Paul Virilio, *Popular Defense and Ecological Struggles* (New York: Semiotext(e), 1990).

35. Timothy W. Luke, "Governmentality and Contragovernmentality: Rethinking Sovereignty and Territoriality after the Cold War," *Political Geography* 15 (July-Sept. 1996): 491–507.

36. For similar observations, see Robert D. McFadden, "The Tortured Genius of Theodore Kaczynski: From a Child of Promise to the Unabomb Suspect," *New York Times,* May 26, 1996, pp. 1, 22–25.

37. These points are raised in my *Screens of Power,* 207–58.

38. See Alvin W. Gouldner, *The Future of Intellectuals and the Rise of the New Class* (New York: Seabury, 1979); and Jürgen Habermas, *Theory of Communicative Action,* vols. 1 and 2 (Boston: Beacon, 1984, 1987). The self-reflexive potentials of symbolic analysts are explored thoroughly by Scott Lash and John Urry in *Economies of Signs and Space* (London: Sage, 1994).

39. Jean-François Lyotard, *The Postmodern Condition* (Minneapolis: University of Minnesota Press, 1984).

40. See Donna Haraway, *Simians, Cyborgs, and Women: The Reinvention of Nature* (New York: Routledge, 1991).

41. Lasch, *The Revolt of the Elites,* 91.

42. For the original conception of "ecology," or "Oecologie," see Ernst Haeckel, *Generelle Morphologie der Organismen* (Berlin: Reimer, 1866). A critical discussion of Haeckel's innovation of ecology can be found in Donald Worster, *Nature's Economy: The Roots of Ecology* (Garden City, N.Y.: Anchor Doubleday, 1979), 191–220.

43. Berry, *A Continuous Harmony,* 76. Manuel Castells also surveys these changes in *The Information Age: Economy, Society and Culture,* 3 vols. (Oxford: Blackwell, 1996–98). Although this preliminary survey is a bit bloated, Castells also recognizes that localistic, populist movements for new vision of environmental justice are one of the most promising forms of popular resistance against the workings of informational economies and societies. See Castells, *The Information Age,* vol. 2, *The Power of Identity,* 128–33.

44. Berry, *A Continuous Harmony,* 77.

45. See James R. Beniger, *The Control Revolution: Technological and Economic Origins of the Information Society* (Cambridge, Mass.: Harvard University Press, 1986);

James Burnham, *The Managerial Revolution* (Bloomington: Indiana University Press, 1960); David Noble, *America by Design: Science and Technology and the Rise of Corporate Capitalism* (New York: Knopf, 1977); and Robert Vance Presthus, *The Organizational Society* (New York: Knopf, 1962).

46. For additional consideration of other ecocritiques, see Cheryll Glotfelty and Harold Fromm, *The Ecocriticism Reader: Landmarks in Literary Ecology* (Athens: University of Georgia Press, 1996). Also see Robert Gottlieb, *Forcing the Spring: The Transformation of the American Environmental Movement* (Washington, D.C.: Island, 1993); and Kenneth M. Stokes, *Man and the Biosphere: Toward a Coevolutionary Political Economy* (Armonk, N.Y.: M. E. Sharpe, 1994).

47. See Ben Agger, *Fast Capitalism* (Urbana: University of Illinois Press, 1989); Stanley Aronowitz, *The Crisis in Historical Materialism: Class, Politics, and Culture in Marxist Theory* (New York: Praeger, 1981); and Trent Schroyer, *The Critique of Domination: The Origins and Development of Critical Theory* (Boston: Beacon, 1975).

48. Richard Rorty, *Achieving Our Country: Leftist Thought in Twentieth-Century America* (Cambridge, Mass.: Harvard University Press, 1998), 36.

49. Some examples of these efforts to rehistoricize ecological concerns in economics, politics, and society can be found in Murray Bookchin, *Post-Scarcity Anarchism* (Berkeley: Ramparts, 1971); Alexander Cockburn and James Ridgeway, eds., *Political Ecology* (New York: Quadrangle, 1979); Barry Commoner, *The Poverty of Power* (New York: Bantam, 1976); David Dickson, *Alternative Technology and the Politics of Technical Change* (Glasgow: Fontana, 1974); Richard C. Dorf and Yvonne L. Hunter, *Appropriate Visions: Technology, the Environment, and the Individual* (San Francisco: Boyd and Fraser, 1978); Hazel Henderson, *Creating Alternative Futures: The End of Economics* (New York: Berkley Windhover, 1978); Amory Lovins, *Soft Energy Paths* (Cambridge, Mass.: Ballinger, 1977); and E. F. Schumacher, *Small Is Beautiful: Economics As If People Mattered* (New York: Harper and Row, 1973).

50. Max Horkheimer, *Eclipse of Reason* (New York: Seabury, 1974), 14.

51. Berry, *A Continuous Harmony*, 80–81.

52. For additional discussion, see Andrew Szasz, *EcoPopulism: Toxic Waste and the Movement for Environmental Justice* (Minneapolis: University of Minnesota Press, 1997). Another useful approach to the "constructedness" of nature can be found in Klaus Eder, *The Social Construction of Nature: A Sociology of Ecological Enlightenment* (London: Sage, 1996).

53. See Carolyn Merchant, *Earthcare: Women and the Environment* (New York: Routledge, 1995), 209–24.

1 Departures from Marx: Rethinking Ecologies and Economies

This book begins with the belief that almost everything should be otherwise. Most important, people and things, which now are mixed and matched in black boxes known as "the environment" and "the economy" allegedly by invisible hands in the marketplace, could become associated in other, far more ecologically sensible and economically equitable ways. Therefore, this book attempts to render such hidden hands more visible so that at least some closed and darkened boxes can be opened and brightened. Once unpacked and illuminated, various ensembles of power/knowledge that intermix human beings with nonhuman beings and things, both natural and artificial, might be refashioned through new theories and practices in a manner that is more economically just and environmentally sound.

Because things could be otherwise and are mostly as they are because of pervasive state power, subtle techniques of marketing, and rigid technoscientific authority, we must depart, once again, from Marx. Jacques Derrida is dead right in *Specters of Marx: The State of the Debt, the Work of Mourning, and the New International:* "It will always be a fault not to read and reread and discuss Marx."[1] This directive, however, is not an invitation to revisit those dark mausoleums of Marxism scattered profusely around the planet at the close of the cold war. Visitors to those tombs will not gain any good guidance, for such dogma machines were built to address a long-ago departed working class. Replaying old marches and melodies about the direction of their proletarian revolution on the eve of the twenty-first century will not do any good. Any real bid to depart from Marx, as Derrida suggests, instead must recognize that there can be no future "without Marx, with the memory and the inheritance of Marx: in any case of a certain Marx, of his genius, of at least one of his spirits. For this will be our hypothesis or rather our bias: *there is more than one of them, there must be more than one of them.*"[2] Francis Fukuyama could be correct in closing his ledgers on one Marx at his "end of history" in our new world order,[3] yet he would be mistaken to suggest that there is, and has been, only one Marx, namely, the Stalinist stick figure from the twentieth century's now widely discredited soviet unions, dialectical materialisms, or people's democracies. The new world order, as Derrida suspects, still carries too many crises and contradictions to be history's endpoint. Moreover, their resolution requires us to return to and then depart from another actually existing Marx: the ruthless critic of capitalism.

At the close of a century in which Marx's multiplicity is all too painfully obvious in the dusty doctrinal dialogues between the Party and the People in so many misbegotten people's democracies, Derrida's hypothesis has merit. My favor for another Marx, the one whose spirit evinces the ruthless criticism of all that exists, also automatically assumes that this Marx cannot be found amid the smashup of state socialism. The crash of global communism, whether one dates it from 1921, 1924, 1939, 1945, 1956, 1968, 1979, or 1991, fully and finally releases the ruthless critic of capitalist commodification from his imprisonment in the gulags of socialist industrialization. One "state of the debt" to Marxism—of which Derrida speaks—is our need to acknowledge Marxism's role in the tragic misadventures of Leninism-Stalinism-Maoism, but another equally valid project for any "new international" rising behind and beyond these necessary acts of mourning must be rediscovered in Marx's approach to transformative critique.

Returning to this Marx reunites us with a thinker who dared, as Derrida suggests, be foundationally antifoundational: "Who has ever called for the *transformation* to come of his own theses? Not only in view of some progressive enrichment of knowledge, which would change nothing in the order of a system, but so as to take into account there, another account, the effects of rupture and restructuration? And so as to incorporate in advance, beyond any possible programming, the unpredictability of new knowledge, new techniques, and new political givens."[4] By recovering this powerful perspective, new departures from Marx can outline fresh criticisms of knowledge, technique, and power as they operate now. Most important, this Marx might help us to construct another vision of the rapid informationalization of global capitalism while taking into account the widespread ecological effects of its ruptures and restructurations.

Crisis and change plainly are two of the most overworked notions in modern social analysis. On a world scale, however, the history of the last seven decades—in both the advanced industrial societies of "the West" and less advanced, semi-industrialized regions of "the Rest" outside the West—is riven by constant crisis and continual change. During the cold war, the centered, stable lifeworld of industrial societies in discretely territorialized nation-states slowly shattered as the decentering networks of a new informational economy formed globally from within transnational capital's destabilized flows and fragments. With the implosion of the old industrial lifeworld, however, few social analysts have acknowledged the nearly total collapse of many once tried-and-true conceptual categories that were grounded in these now sublated industrial forms of life, relations of power, and codes of culture.[5] We must begin to dig out from underneath these collapsed categories while working to outline a strategy for finding new meanings amid the rubble of old rhetorics in the new world order.

Returning to Marx

At this global turning point, it is imperative to "return to Marx," even though his Victorian conceptual frameworks remain thoroughly industrial in many ways. Most exponents of Marx's critique of industrialism—which was expounded as nationally propounded economies tied to modern industrial production gained political hegemony over regionally entrenched economies grounded on agriculture—still believe that Marx's "productivist" conceptual system, assisted by few innovative theoretical tweaks, can reveal how informationalism will ultimately replace industrialism.[6] In sharp contrast, the following chapters assert that this sort of orthodox Marxist analysis is doomed to failure.

As Derrida argues, fresh critical studies begin by believing that "one may still find inspiration in the Marxist 'spirit' to criticize the presumed autonomy of the juridical and to denounce endlessly the *de facto* take-over of international authorities by powerful Nation-States, by concentrations of techno-scientific capital, symbolic capital, and financial capital, of State capital and private capital."[7] The inspiration derived from such Marxist spirits is essential, because the dynamics of informationalization, which are at the root of contemporary technoscientific, military, and economic development, now maintain "an effective inequality as monstrous as that which prevails today, to a greater extent than ever in the history of humanity."[8] In fact, any celebration about "the end of history" simply masks the history of many human and nonhuman lives coming to violent, wasteful ends. Far too many things at the close of the twentieth century are unsettled, unraveling, and unsustainable. Derrida maintains that we find ourselves

> at a time when some have the audacity to neo-evangelize in the name of the ideal of a liberal democracy that has finally realized itself as the ideal of human history: never have violence, inequality, exclusion, famine, and thus economic oppression affected as many human beings in the history of the earth and of humanity. Instead of singing the advent of the ideal of liberal democracy and the capitalist market in the euphoria of the end of history, instead of celebrating the "end of ideologies" and the end of the great emancipatory discourses, let us never neglect this obvious macroscopic fact, made up of innumerable singular sites of suffering: no degree of progress allows one to ignore that never before, in absolute figures, never have so many men, women, and children been subjugated, starved, or exterminated on the earth. (And provisionally, but with regret, we must leave aside here the nevertheless indissociable question of what is becoming of so-called "animal" life, the life and existence of "animals" in this history. This question has always been a serious one, but it will become massively unavoidable.)[9]

A new approach to ecological critique, then, can be taken from Derrida's representations of deconstruction as radicalized Marxist critique. That is, "deconstruction has never had any sense or interest, in my view at least, except as a radicalization, which is to say also *in the tradition* of a certain Marxism, in a certain *spirit of Marxism.* There has been, then, this attempted radicalization of Marxism called deconstruction."[10]

Most important, this radicalization of Marx disconnects Marxian critique from the staid partisan orthodoxies to which it has been welded for over a century. Deconstruction in this new register of critique must refashion its activities as a strategic style of reading, resting on the contragovernmental questioning of fixed practices or the supertactical loosening of determinate interpretations. Remaking deconstruction as another disciplinary formation guaranteed to deliver surefire results will only bolt Marxist critique back onto the failed routines of scientific socialism and diamat discourse.

Attempts to decipher new outlines of a contextual futurology for informational production from traces left by textual archaeologies in orthodox Marxism simply misconstrue new classes as old classes, miscode new power relations as ongoing traditional modes of power, or misinterpret the new culture as one more permutation of an old culture.[11] The currently most promising path of returning to Marx involves making entirely new departures from Marx, guided only by his critical commitment to deciphering the hieroglyphics of the commodity form. Within the still inchoate upheavals of informationalism, however, we must examine how corporate capital elaborates its productive powers on a transnational scale while in the process destroying much of what was traditionally regarded as the realm of nature and the domain of society. Nonetheless, in developing informational modes of production, which are designed, built, and managed by a new global bloc of professional-technical experts, local and global capital are reconstructing their roles under new economic and political conditions of reproduction as the ultimate guarantors of humanity's "sustainable development" and "environmental security."

While the contemporary proletariat is being displaced by new installations of robotic apparatus, divided up into competing national labor reserves within a transnational capital market, and diluted into indistinct categories of increasingly underskilled work, transnational businesses can expand, amplify, and elaborate their markets as the world's most important revolutionary economic and political force. For the first time in the ontogeny of capital, informational modes of production can commodify everything on a planned, rational, mass scale. Not only can the raw resources of the Earth, the manufactured things of social production, and the social services of human interaction be submitted to capital's logic of reproduction, but even words, codes, memories, sounds, images, and symbols can be designed as value-adding fungible products intended for rapid transit through mass markets as instruments of production, accumulation, reproduction, and circulation. Even life itself, whether in the form of designer genes, engineered tomatoes, bionic joints, synthetic skin, or patented mice, is turned into a commodity. A critique of the commodity in these informational forms can be undertaken only by decoding the phantom objectivity of such reifying dynamics. It also must question the ideological horizons projected by development, modernity, or liberal democracy under transnational corporate capitalism as it engulfed the culture, politics, and society of the post-1945 world.[12]

Information technology is not per se the cause of the informational revolution. Such interpretations merely desocialize social change and deculturalize cultural shifts by abstracting technics out of everyday lived experience only to return them as an autonomous external force that relentlessly reshapes values, institutions, and beliefs to fit its technical imperatives.[13] Instead the technification of information embodies divisive social changes and conflicted cultural shifts that are reshaping heteronomous social forces through contingent political processes articulated through the restructuring of capital, states, and technics. The planet's ecology, in turn, is the most crucial domain that must be reappraised. We must ask a key question: who and whom? Whose information for whom; whose revolutionization by whom? The advent of network society forces us to interrogate all the informationalizers much more closely. How is the informational revolution playing out as a struggle for control, profit, and organizational authority, and in what ways are the winners and losers promoting the further domination of nature?

A simple return to Marx will result only in more misrepresentations. For over a century many of the most systematic, thoroughgoing critiques of advanced capitalist industrial society have been grounded in Marxian political economy.[14] Nonetheless, because Marx's thoughts also were used to legitimize the Bolshevik Revolution in Russia, and because the Soviet Union collapsed in 1990–91, some experts now consign Marx's work to the ash heap of history.[15] On the one hand, the peculiar nineteenth-century European context of Marx's theoretical writings as well as the less than successful revolutionary strategies endorsed in his many political writings make it wise to leave his work behind. Many contemporary forms of capital, labor, value, and power render Marx's tactical interpretations of their interplay in today's terms anachronistic, for the referents of what he called the bourgeoisie and proletariat, city and countryside, and state and society have all assumed very different forms in the twentieth century. On the other hand, Marx outlines a decisive reading of commodification, technology, and class that can still deliver painfully accurate insights into the capitalist mode of production. So any critique of contemporary informationalism must depart from Marx's work.

Ideological Ironies: Marx and the USSR

To return to Marx, one also must account for the Soviet Union and all the other "actually existing socialisms" of the twentieth century. State socialism's greatest success, ironically, seems to have been its provision of a weak systemic negativity that forced classical capitalism continually to reinvent itself in more progressive forms in order to persuade the working classes to support its increasingly more modern ways of life. Socialist alternatives, as barbaric as they were, indirectly served to humanize, democratize, or personalize capitalism, making it far more productive and destructive at the same time. The rise of informational capitalism all over the West, not the fall of industrial socialism in the East, makes it necessary to depart from Marx in this ecological critique of informationalism.[16] And departing from Marx now implies completely leaving behind most of those practices tested as state socialism in the former Soviet Union. This break must be drawn explicitly, because Marx has been directly blamed—at least in most Western analyses about Soviet communist practice—for the tragic course of the October 1917 Russian revolution during the twentieth century.

Recently, however, the Western sciences used to explain cold war conflict between East and West over the past five decades have crumbled, like the USSR, into chaos and confusion. Now that the nations and states of what *were* "the Soviet Union," "the Second World," "the Warsaw Pact," and "the Communist Bloc" have experienced violent or "velvet" revolutions in their economies, governments, and societies, one often cannot account easily for what happened in 1989, 1990, or 1991. In what perhaps still are "the United States," "the First World," "the NATO Alliance," and "the Capitalist Bloc," however, many interpretations of what has happened east of the old Iron Curtain, which now are ironically labeled "post-Soviet studies," remain thoroughly grounded in a strongly centered cold war subjectivity. They still seek to judge, sentence, and condemn state socialism for its Marxist origins and Leninist practices.[17]

Most aspects of the theoretical discourse and disciplinary practice of Marxism-Leninism deserve our condemnation. Any uncritical celebration of contemporary capitalism in the wake of its apparent triumph over this communism of the old centrally planned economies, however, is unwarranted. The advent of "capitalism" and "democracy" in most regions of the former Soviet Union has not made life much better; instead, it has often proven much worse for most members of society. Concerning the breakup of the USSR, one hears that this pivotal event "disproves" the insights of Marx, "invalidates" the possibility of realizing greater material equality in a socialist society, or "affirms" the rightness of capitalism over the errors of communism. Yet there is little evidence supporting these specific claims. What discursive terms such as *socialism, equality, capitalism, democracy,* or *communism* might mean now is problematic.

Although the Communist Party of the Soviet Union and the USSR itself are gone, much remains the same under the postcommunist regimes that replaced them. In many republics of the former Soviet Union, ex-communists dominate the national legislatures and executives. Yeltsin's brutal moves in Chechnya differed little from Brezhnev's in Afghanistan. Just as the transition to socialism failed in the USSR during the 1920s, so too is the transition to capitalism failing during the 1990s in most parts of the former Soviet Union. Capitalism in Russia is mostly synonymous with gangsterism, and commodification is mutilating many of the precious few recesses of human dignity remaining in the former Soviet republics. Self-congratulations in the West are much too hasty and overdrawn. First, the general understanding of Marxism today is clouded by cold war conceptions of Marx's project. Second, the attribution of the USSR's successes or failures to Marx's political economy is far too simplistic. Third, the affirmation of capitalism's apparent successes totally ignores its endemic flaws, which are surfacing virulently across the former Soviet Union even as capitalism's advocates gloat over the demise of a communist order that never seriously approximated the practice of its own purportedly Marxist ideals.[18]

With regard to the claim that the cold war culminated in victory for the West and defeat for the East, this too is problematic without a clear sense of how infrequently this trial by combat involved much real trial or actual combat. Whether the "victory of capitalism" disproves the merits of Marx's theoretical project is even less clear. In fact, since 1945–47 most informed individuals in what was the "capitalist West" who were or are seriously concerned with politics and society in the hitherto "socialist East" have traveled mainly in the extended discursive orbits of anti-Marxist disciplinary networks grounded in closed cultures rooted within the worlds of the academia or state intelligence agencies. The historical record is far more mixed. Marx did not provide a method for revolution making in Russia; at best, he afforded a myth for revolutionaries there to motivate themselves and others to modernize Russia. As a comparative "latecomer" to industrialization, tsarist and Soviet Russia did not retrace the same steps to industrial modernization initially set down by European or U.S. industrialization strategies. As the USSR industrialized, it experienced a strange mixture of outcomes in its economic development that are both the "same as" and "different from" those in the West. Marx's role in these historical dramas, however, is ambiguous.

At best, Western discourses about the Soviet Union circulated in the restricted disciplinary networks of "comparative politics" or "international relations." At worse, they intentionally spoke in the even more damaged disciplinary dialects of "Kremlinology" or "Sovietology." This point is important because, as Michel Foucault suggests, "No body of knowledge can be formed without a system of communications, records, accumulation and displacement which is in itself a form of power and which is linked, in its existence and functioning, to the other forms of power. Conversely, no power can be exercised without the extraction, appropriation, distribution or retention of knowledge. On this level, there is not knowledge on the one side and society on the other, or science and the state, but only the fundamental forms of knowledge/power."[19] Any knowledge about the nature of Soviet systems since 1917, therefore, has often also been liberal democratic capitalist evidence of power acting against them. In particular, the condemnation of Marx, Marxian approaches to political economy, and Marxist political movements has remained a fundamental first principle in all Western knowledge codes accumulated in the struggle against state socialism. Inasmuch as the conceptual expressions of Western Sovietology gained acceptance in professional debates of government policies as an ordering of power/knowledge, they also became cognitive acts of containment, normative blows against the totalitarian, or instrumental acts of self-affirmation in the socialist other's negation.

The West's organized scientific studies of communism, Marxism, and socialism were not objective: they were instead anticommunist, anti-Marxist, and antisocialist from the outset. To know Marxism better was to seek a fuller philosophical prevention against its political effects or larger operational limits over its cultural influences. Not surprisingly, many of the theoretical constructs used to "understand" Soviet communism are not addressed directly to Marxism in Russia. Although a few leftist fellow-travelers sought to visit a workable future, the Bolsheviks were almost ignored after the Russian civil war of 1918–21 except by freebooting capitalist firms that wished to sell them modern industrial goods in the brief heyday of pragmatic modernization during the 1920s. More serious analysis of the Kremlin gained ground only during the 1930s as Stalin's dictatorship rose in Moscow at the same time as Hitler's formed in Berlin. Many categories and concepts were dragged into Kremlinological discourses without much modification, the analysts moving back and forth from studies of fascism in Nazi Germany or Mussolini's Italy as part of a frantic quest to root out the origins of "totalitarian society," even after the Axis powers fell in 1945.[20] Kremlinology/Sovietology, as an allegedly objective mode of engaging in scientific knowing, has been soaked to the bone in the ideological agendas of anticommunism and the geopolitical programs of containing Soviet power. Similarly, the disciplines of comparative government and international relations continued for decades to spin out fantastic taxonomies to show how state socialism remained a mostly retrograde, immoral, or dysfunctional form of rule even as its antagonism toward democratic capitalism anchored the stability of the bipolar international state system.

As the entire cold war global order now slips further and further into yesterday, any survey of the standing systems of Sovietological power/knowledge becomes more like Foucault's reading of an old Chinese encyclopedia's categorizations of the animal kingdom that Jorge Luis Borges mentions. That is, in the spirit of empirical analysis, "it is written that 'animals are divided into: (a) belonging to the Emperor, (b) embalmed, (c) tame, (d) sucking pigs, (e) sirens, (f) fabulous, (g) stray dogs, (h) included in the present classification, (i) frenzied, (j) innumerable, (k) drawn with a very fine camelhair brush, (l) *et cetera,* (m) having just broken the water pitcher, (n) that from a long way off look like flies."[21] Sovietology's conventional classifications of bureaucratic centralist regimes, as they were manufactured to explain everything from the Soviet Union to Albania to Poland to the People's Republic of China, were cast in equally arcane codes for methodologically rigorous data collection as (a) those belonging to Marx, (b) inhumanely evil, (c) centrally planned economies, (d) totalitarian, (e) authoritarian, (f) neo-Stalinist, (g) bureaucratic centralist, (h) worshipping Lenin, (i) state capitalism, (j) new class dictatorships, (k) dynamic/expansionist, (l) bureaucratically deformed proletarian rule, (m) red fascism, (n) those that from a long way off look like meaningful people's democracies. In far too many ways, these different taxonomic variants of political analysis from "comparative communism" are no less bizarre than Borges's old Chinese schema for defining animal species. Now that the cold war is over, it is clear that the knowledge they provided about Marxism's operation in the USSR was rarely any more certain or conclusive than the knowledge that Borges's Chinese encyclopedia might provide to zoologists studying animals today.[22]

The astounding wonder of Sovietological studies was the remarkably serious acceptance of their categories and exponents during the cold war. Actions taken first by Gorbachev and his allies in the USSR and next by Yeltsin and his associates in the former Soviet Union have shattered the stabilized referents of such power/knowledge codes. Landmarks that were formed with the extraction, accumulation, and circulation of this cold war power/knowledge in the West must shatter in our laughter. Like Foucault reading Borges, "*our* thought" now also must change, "the thought that bears the stamp of our age and our geography—breaking up all the ordered surfaces and all the planes with which we are accustomed to tame the wild profusion of existing things, and continuing long afterwards to disturb and threaten with collapse our age-old distinction between the Same and the Other."[23] Capitalism, democracy, and freedom have been defined for so long by their opposition to communism, authoritarianism, and repression that now, with the end of the Eastern other, the real meaning of the Western self also encounters doubts.

Marx and Critical Criticism

To extract Marx from this impasse, we need to rethink the radicalism embedded in his ruthless criticism of the commodity form. To make this move, we need also to reclaim the notion of "collectivization" from its Stalinist uses in twentieth-century Marxism-Leninism. Bruno Latour uses "the word 'collective' to describe the association of humans and nonhumans"[24] in everything that knits together the networks of people and things making up what is regarded as modernity.

These hybridized assemblies of subjects and objects, humans and nonhumans, agents and structures, or actors and artifacts compose Latour's key associations, which like Marx's hybridized vision of commodities "are *simulta-*

neously real, like nature, narrated like discourse, and collective, like society."[25] Marx's historical materialism positions the nonhuman things of humanly constructed social existence as the determinate force in society responsible for shaping the consciousness of humans. When Marx asserts in the preface to *A Contribution to the Critique of Political Economy* that "it is not the consciousness of men that determines their being, but, on the contrary, their social being that determines their consciousness," he also struggles to open the black boxes of the environment and the economy.[26]

In describing "the modern constitution" that underpins the contemporary mode of capitalist production, organization, and information, Latour sees what has been taken to be modernization as resting on a doubled ontological distinction:

> Modernity is often defined in terms of humanism, either as a way of saluting the birth of 'man,' or as a way of announcing his death. But this habit itself is modern, because it remains asymmetrical. It overlooks the simultaneous birth of "nonhumanity"—things, or objects, or beasts—and the equally strange beginning of a crossed-out God, relegated to the sidelines. Modernity arises first from the conjoined creation of those three entities, and then from the masking of the conjoined birth and separate treatments of the three communities while, underneath, hybrids continue to multiply as an effect of this separate treatment.[27]

These multiple links, intersecting influences, and continuous negotiations between the human and nonhuman, as well as the temporality of humanity and the transcendence of divinity, are what preoccupy Marx in much of his writing. Coming back at him through Latour's reading of modernity, most of Marx can be seen as an extended critique of Latour's sense of collectivization, inasmuch as he uses the notion of the commodity to describe the association of humans and nonhumans. Since Marx's examination of the commodity form under capitalism looks at ways in which human labor is mixed with nonhuman things to create value, much of his analysis is a careful study of who dominates whom in the processes of such collectivization, with commodification leading to the endless "co-modification" of human and nonhuman beings in both nature and culture. These ties now define coevolution.

Marx's vision of communism also promised human beings another, better means of associating people and things in highly socialized collectives beyond the distorting dictates of market-mediated commodification. In making the transition to communism, Marx argued, all the most destructive effects of bringing people together with things through the cash nexus could be simultaneously overcome, eliminated, and then banned by communist communities, which would no longer suffer the exploitation from class conflicts expressed by coercive governments, for they would realize emancipation out of their joint liberatory administration of things. This utopian vision of communist living was in turn predicated on creating an entirely new ecology (i.e., remaking all the relationships between human society and its environment) beyond the dictates of market pricing, competitive labor, private property, and commodity production. In the final analysis, Marxism predicted that materialistic historical forces were knitting together new, more rational, equal, liberating, and emancipatory means of associating human beings and their things in fresh social collectives whose tenor and tone would be communist rather than capitalist.

For many reasons, all forms of socialism practiced from 1917 to the present failed to reweave people and things into these emancipatory associations of humans, property, institutions, and technology from the economic, political, and social threads that were spun out of their revolutions.[28] Marxism-Leninism departed from Marx, rushing headlong into all the ill-considered quasi-statist, semifeudal, cryptocapitalist, or paramodern practices that have deformed twentieth-century state socialism since the October Revolution. Sovietology made a science of sorts out of studying these aberrant attempts at actualizing Marx's project, but it really provided very few insights into how Marx's postrevolutionary communist collectives of people and things actually were to operate. Yet it is precisely Marx's utopian reimagination of all associations that tie people together with the things they create that must anchor a thorough reappraisal of the economies, ecologies, and ethics of modernized living after the implosion of communism in the twentieth century.

The founding of state socialism in the former Soviet Union did not detonate a string of global explosions that might have made such changes possible. Meanwhile, Marx's internationalizing myths were quickly turned to the chauvinistic purposes of national economic and technological modernization in the former tsarist empire. The Communist Party of the Soviet Union struggled to do little more than first compete with, and then equal, existing forms of bourgeois capitalism in its statist strategy of national industrialization.[29] In doing so, the Soviets accepted ecological irrationalities as wide ranging and deep as those in the West, but they pushed harder and faster in their economic planning system to create even more extensive levels of environmental destruction.[30] This misbegotten Marxist-Leninist heritage is not what we should take from Marx; instead, we must depart from other, more emancipatory paths to modernity kept in stasis as unrealized potentials within the fixed and frozen mazeways of existing capitalist modernity. Not necessary, but possible; not foreordained, but feasible; not inevitable, but practical—these other conditions of collectivization, or the possibilities for rebuilding the associations of people and things, can be actualized. However, another constellation of political decisions, social structures, and cultural values must congeal to assemble them as workable alternatives to the established means of market-mediated collectivization. What can be done now is far different from what Lenin imagined must be done nearly a century ago.

The Critique of Commodification

To gain insights for the present from Marx, one must look far beyond the many misadventures of the dialectic in Eastern Europe and the Soviet Union to Marx's original critique of political economy, which focuses on the ravages of commodification. Most significantly Marx focused on the economic and social interactions that distort each human being's relationships with nature, other humans in society, and his or her own inner psychic life. Marx saw the commodity form becoming the universal basis of all social relations, and his entire political project is based on overcoming its destructive effects. During his lifetime, however, the commodity form did not completely dominate the outer social or inner psychic life of most people. Although the initial intimations of planned corporate capitalism could be detected along the commanding heights of the U.S., English, or German economies, many precapitalist cultural, economic, and social relations still survived outside most modern factories in big industrial cities, allowing nature to be viewed by many as an autonomous and indestructible force.

For Marx, commodification occluded the exploitation of both humanity and nature in the ordinary market relations constructed between humans and nonhumans in the everyday relationship of things. When caught in the webs of monetized exchange, the origins and existence of all socially produced artifacts become mystified. Commodities have "absolutely no connexion with their physical properties and with the material relations arising therefrom."[31] Instead, "a definite social relation between men . . . assumes, in their eyes, the fantastic form of a relation between things. In order, therefore to find an analogy, we must have recourse to the mist-enveloped regions of the religious world. In that world the productions of the human brain appear as independent beings endowed with life, and entering into relation both with one another and the human race. So it is in the world of commodities with the products of men's hands."[32]

Marx represents commodities as volatile, mysterious entities through which real human relationships between men and women, as well as humanity and nature, are "co-modified" in objectified, mystified social relations. In commodities, "the social character of men's labor appears to them as an objective character stamped upon the product of that labor: because the relation of the producers to the sum total of their own labor is presented to them as a social relation, existing not between themselves, but between the products of their labor."[33] Fetishizing the products of labor as concrete things tracing the tangible tracks of abstract exchange value occludes the fragile webs of social understanding, cultural creation, and collective action in the strategic calculations of instrumental rationalization. Through exchange value, humans modify things and in turn things modify humans in a circuit of commodifying relations.

In keeping with *Capital,* Georg Lukács recaptures the essence of commodification's co-modifications under more modern conditions of production: "A relation between people takes on the character of a thing and thus acquires a 'phantom objectivity,' an autonomy that seems so strictly rational and all-embracing as to conceal every trace of its fundamental nature: the relation between people."[34] Gradually this reified phantom objectivity of commodity creation, exchange, and accumulation unfolds all its many different dimensions until it becomes the universal basis of all social relations under capitalist exchange. "Only then does the commodity," as Lukács asserts, "become crucial for the subjugation of men's consciousness to the forms in which this reification finds expression and for their attempts to comprehend the process or to rebel against its disastrous effects and liberate themselves from servitude to the 'second nature' so created."[35] Things have changed a great deal since Marx's death over a century ago. Commodity exchange clearly has come to dominate the outer and inner life of the global economy and each natural society. As a result, in the 1990s, "There is no problem that does not ultimately lead back to that question and there is no solution that could not be found in the riddle of commodity-*structure.*"[36]

In contrast to the looser, entrepreneurial forms of capital discussed by Marx, contemporary corporate capitalism is much more organized, efficient, and scientifically grounded, and it has mobilized many different disciplinary discourses to organize exchange around the managerially planned enterprise.[37] As chapter 2 will suggest, the service-oriented economies of the most developed societies now predicate their future growth on the further commodification of culture, personality, and social relations to realize new increments of growth. Informational capitalism strives to erase the once meaningful distinctions between the logic of work and leisure, the realm of reason and desire, or the boundaries of nature and society. As Max Horkheimer and Theodor Adorno would argue, corporate plans aim at "no more than the achievement of standardization and mass production, sacrificing whatever involved a distinction between the logic of the work and that of the social system. This is the result not of a law of movement in technology as such but of its function in today's economy."[38]

New modes of postindustrial behavior and belief are emerging from the complex interactions of global media markets, product cycles, and capital flows, which in turn frame the outlines of a new informational culture, economy, and society. The phantom objectivity of this newly shaped "second nature," however, has yet to be fully explored, particularly with regard to its ecological impact on the "first nature" of Earth's biosphere.[39] Marx's own discussions of ecology, the environment, or nature are not extensive.[40] At different turns Marx articulates a respectful engagement with nature, seconding Rousseau's romantic reading of nature as an emergent subjectivity needed to ground or even direct human action. In other stretches Marx affirms the modern bourgeois capitalist project of dominating nature technologically and economically. Without this total pacification of necessity, the material wherewithal of total abundance essential for the realization of full communism cannot be realized. Others have tried to read Marx for more messages of redemptive ecological guidance, but on the whole, it cannot be found there.[41] Like most people of his age, Marx was captured by the Victorian era's uncritical celebration of technological development as being equivalent to the conquest of nature. Still, Marx can yield some useful leads for building a case against the informational revolution. His contradictory reading of technology and his critical appreciation of technics in the capitalist mode of production provide the most promising places to begin.

Technologies and Markets as Collectives

According to Marx, human beings relate to themselves, one another, and nature through the social organization of their labor. Making objects, controlling powers, and generating productive systems—both in nature and outside nature—defines humanity: "In the treatment of the objective world, therefore, man proves himself to be genuinely a *species-being.* This production is his active species-life. Through it nature appears as *his* work and his actuality."[42] Although such activity alienates nature from humanity as well as each human from him- or herself, "it makes *species-life* the means of individual life. . . . It is life begetting life."[43] The conditions of associating humans and nonhumans in ancient, Asiatic, feudal, or capitalist relations of collectivization can thus be used to understand how power, knowledge, and conflict co-modified people and their things in any given society.

One needs to take Marx at his word. If technical activity is what defines humanity, and if social individuality creates the means of individual and social life, then nature itself changes within the mode of association connecting human and nonhuman beings. Indeed, the ecology of the Earth becomes increasingly an anthropogenic construct:

> As plants, animals, minerals, air, light, etc., in theory form a part of human consciousness, partly as objects of natural science, partly as objects of art . . . so they also form in practice a part of human life and human activity. Man lives physically only by these products of nature; they may appear in the form of food, heat, clothing, housing, etc. The universality of man appears in practice in the universality which makes the whole of nature his *inorganic* body: (1) as a direct means of life, and (2) as the matter, object, and instrument of his life activity. Nature is the *inorganic* body of man, that is, nature insofar as it is not the human body. Man *lives* by nature. This means that nature is his *body* with which he must remain in perpetual process in order not to die.[44]

To the degree that nature is our "inorganic body" with which we must remain perpetually engaged, ecology should study the direct bases of human life, which are the matter, objects, and instrument of all human life activity. These conceptual foci also should renew our interest in all forms of organized technics by which human societies transform nature into humanity's inorganic body in the form of food, heat, clothing, housing, and so on. The conventional antinomies of nature/culture, environment/society, human/nonhuman, and subject/object all implode in Marx's rendition of these links as one active organic/inorganic project. Instead, they express Latour's sense of the collectives binding together people and things. Technical formations permit humans to constitute systems for all life to help beget their lives in the elaborate urban-industrial ecologies of an increasingly anthropogenic nature; in the process, however, all life now naturally unfolds in terms of these artificially emergent practices. Whether it is early humans burning savannahs to organize the hunt or contemporary commuters altering the atmosphere with pollution, nature/society can be understood as ecology/humanity coevolving through their consciously co-modifying collective associations in technology, society, and economy.

To depart from Marx does not demand elaborate Marxological justifications of everything that must be done, but it does require modifications to Marx's frameworks. Much of the power in Marx's critique derived from his identification of allegedly inherent tendencies in nineteenth-century capitalism and the class struggles they engendered, which revealed how revolution could occur as well as why the proletariat was destined to play the leading role in all coming revolutionary upheavals. Because of their ownership and control of the means of production, the bourgeoisie built self-serving arrangements in the relations of production to relentlessly extract surplus value from the proletariat. The workers' unending immiseration coupled with the ultrarationalization of the productive forces would set the stage for a general crisis. To a large extent, then, the means and relations of production could be steered under capitalism to favor the bourgeoisie because of their simultaneous control over the organization of production on the shop floor, in the marketplace, at the bank, or back in the laboratory. Being a capitalist as an owner, as Marx affirmed, also required the capitalist to act as a commander, which created the conditions of bourgeois private collectivization out of these direct configurations of ownership and control during the First Industrial Revolution.

Rereading the Mode of Organization

Many relations of organization, information, and control have changed profoundly since Marx died in 1883. On the one hand, the organizational transformations of the Second Industrial Revolution increasingly decomposed ownership and management into different groups of actors, degraded labor and skill, divorced equity holding and business administration, or divided technological innovation and technique application. On the other hand, they also disturbed consumer demand and producer supply, distorted public goods and private interests, and diffused capitalistic exploitation and proletarian immiseration through massive state interventions in both the economy and society. Similarly, the informational directions of the Third Industrial Revolution, which are now reshaping the time, space, and speed equations of contemporary production and consumption, must be considered if Marx's insights are to be adapted for any serious critique of the current conditions of capitalism.

As the organization and control of the productive forces have become far more complex problems, who owns them or who works for whoever owns them become somewhat less important. Indeed, the modes of organization, information, or control assume much greater significance. Likewise, the new elite class of organizers, informationalizers, or controllers, who may or may not share equity stakes in the productive forces even though they are now the decisive economic, political, and social elites, now deserve far more attention than do Marx's classical bourgeoisie.[45] At the same time, the many new social movements of antiorganizers, noninformationalizers, or contracontrollers, which emerge inside and outside the workplace as anti-elitist populist movements, also must be reexamined with much greater resolve.[46] In departing from Marx, the capital/labor contradiction still stands, yet it also is quite clear that many facets of the struggle between capital and labor now manifest themselves in flare-ups around the means of organization as local populists question distant elites, consumers challenge producers, radical environmentalists assail corporate engineers, scientists criticize managers, or end users oppose product managers.[47]

The risk-driven organization of highly technological production in the informational revolution has empowered an indefinite but quite decisive ensemble of experts to manage, design, plan, and extend the scope of commodification on a global scale.[48] As Ulrich Beck asserts, the chaotic complexities of organizing for profit making in the increasingly disorganized marketplace of transnational capitalism are generating costs and benefits whose risks require continuous assessment and management, but "the problems emerging here cannot be mastered by increased production, redistribution or expansion of social protection—as in the nineteenth century—but instead require either a focused and massive 'policy of counter-interpretation' or a fundamental rethinking and reprogramming of the prevailing paradigm of modernization."[49] Here, then, is where another Marx—one tied to ruthless criticism—must reshape our counterinterpretations of the present. The nub of conflict shifts with ecological resistances in informationalizing societies. New class experts systematically produce risks and rewards through their economically rational execution of organizational imperatives in the capitalist marketplace, whose ecologically irrational implications and costs must be aggressively counterinterpreted and counteracted by new resistance movements of radicalized people from all walks of life. These populists become intent on rethinking and reprogramming the prevailing patterns of capitalist modernization, which seem to assume nature's destruction.

It is possible, then, to conjure a critique from the effects of the information revolution. Deciding which forgotten choices, repressed possibilities, or hidden options should be teased out of the advanced technics underpinning the new world order is an entirely different question, however, particularly if one is to radicalize existing approaches to cultural criticism and political resistance. One might choose, as Derrida does, to revitalize an international ethicized law by casting it as "the *worldwide* economic and social field, beyond the sovereignty of States and the phantom-States."[50] At the same time, one might opt to revive an intranational localized community, embedded in specific natural ecologies and particular cultural places, to resist the appropriation of power/

knowledge "by concentrations of technoscientific capital, symbolic capital, and financial capital, of State capital and private capital."[51]

An ecologically grounded populism can and does develop inherently from the contradictions of technoscientific capital. Such contradictions are intrinsic to the organization of production by new class elites against nonelites, producers against consumers, managers against labor, owners against users, or engineers against technicians. Inequalities in power, knowledge, status, or income spark tremendous conflicts, and these conflicts are fought out along the fronts of power/knowledge disparities as well as in the trenches of status/income inequities. The unthought inaction of organizational structures pits elites against popular agents, opposes lay consuming audiences against expert producing spokespersons, and confronts unprogrammed clients with overprogrammed service workers. Departing from Marx, then, requires that attention to the old contradictions of capital versus labor, owner versus worker, and bourgeoisie versus proletariat be refocused through optics trained now on the means and relations of organization to expose new structural conflicts between expertise and inexpertise, servers and clients, or the organizer and the organized within the collectives built by informationalizing societies.

Although it is presumptuous to assert that some potential unity exists amid such disunity, perhaps there is, as Derrida asserts, a basis for some "new international." Linkages, alliances, or communities could now be emerging in the crises and contradictions caused by informationalization.

> It is an untimely link, without status, without title, and without name, barely public even if it is not clandestine, without contract, "out of joint," without coordination, without party, without country, without national community (International before, across, and beyond any national determination), without co-citizenship, without common belonging to a class. The name of new International is given here to what calls to the friendship of an alliance without institution among those who, even if they no longer believe or never believed in the socialist-Marxist International, in the dictatorship of the proletariat, in the messiano-eschatological role of the universal union of the proletarians of all lands, continue to be inspired by at least one of the spirits of Marx or of Marxism (they now know that there is *more than one*) and in order to ally themselves, in a new, concrete, and real way, even if this alliance no longer takes the form of a party or of a workers' international, but rather of a kind of counter-conjuration, in the (theoretical and practical) critique of the state of international law, the concepts of State and nation, and so forth; in order to renew this critique and especially to radicalize it.[52]

Those who would depart from Marx, then, include everyone who can adapt Marxian approaches to understand and change the world as it reshapes itself today. The prevailing paradigms of informationalizing modernization can be rethought and reprogrammed, but that will not happen unless and until the endangering dimensions of the new organizational modes of production, consumption, accumulation, and circulation face the insurrections of subjugated knowledges (counterinterpretations, rethinking, reprogramming) from many zones below, without, or beyond their control against the hegemony of their disciplinary power prevailing in fixed paradigms of modernization exerted from many zones above, within, or at the center of large human populations.

Under a capitalist mode of production, these collectivized products of nature-human associations appear almost exclusively in the commodity form. The totality of all human relationships with the environment "presents itself as 'an immense accumulation of commodities'"[53] in which the environment is constructed from these commodified clots of alienated, externalized labor. As commodities and as private property, nature as humanity's inorganic body reappears co-modified in the alien quasi-subjective power of capital, the state, and markets. Consequently, capital formations, governmental authority, and everyday exchange now become environmental forces, mediating the condition of all human beings' collectivization of their alienated human being, natural ecology, and social product. As Marx suggests, alienated labor is the crucible of co-modification as commodification transforms "the *species-existence of man,* and also nature as his mental species-capacity, into an existence *alien* to him, into the *means* of his *individual existence.* It alienates his spiritual nature, his *human essence,* from his own body and likewise from nature outside him."[54] Labor makes the world for humanity, but this processed world simply creates a coevolutionary order in which corporate capital, state power, and consumer culture jointly create nature, or now "ecologies" and "environments," as part of their own work and as their material actualization in rational economies.

Marx's political economy can help us construct an ecological critique of the informational revolution, because it again identifies the key material forces at play in any given social order. In his materialist conceptions of history, Marx accentuates the centrality of labor and technology for co-modifying nature as the substance and symbol of humanity's inorganic body for every society, polity, and economy in the ever-changing collectives of people and things. Such a sense of collectivization is expressed in *Capital* when Marx asserts, "Technology discloses man's mode of dealing with nature, the process of production by which he sustains his life, and thereby lays bare the mode of formation of his social relations, and of the mental conceptions that flow from them."[55] This observation should guide any contemporary ecological critique, and it provides my point of departure from Marx.

By rereading organizations and technologies in a critical, deconstructive fashion, we can observe how contemporary economies and societies produce their organic and inorganic bodies—out of and in nature—as they associate their human members, nonhuman beings, and things through labor and exchange. Whether the labor in this exchange sustains or undermines life in general provides essential knowledge needed for any successful ecological resistance. By having us look again at technical forces and dynamics, Marx helps us understand how social relations, cultural assumptions, moral values, and political programs generate human ecologies out of the co-modifications of humanity and nature through commodification. The current ecological crisis is one result of informational society's destructive abuse of nature as exchange systematically deforms humanity's inorganic and organic bodies. Those who benefit most directly from control over the collectivizing conditions of commodification adopt anti-environmental practices of production to bolster their powers, profits, and privileges while deploying the co-modifications of commodity consumption to occlude how they choose among and benefit from their decisions.[56] Chapter 2 will explore these issues in greater detail by turning to the most dynamic political economy of the post–World War II era—liberal democratic capitalism—to investigate how an entire hyperecology of consumption emerged from the industrial ecologies of production driving its polyarchical politics and megatechnic economics.

The New Class

The ideological agitprop celebrating new class power/knowledge constantly courses across corporate screens of power in our informationalizing society, prophesying and legitimizing the limitless abundance that high-technology industry and scientific research allegedly will make possible. Unfortunately, these promises of universal abundance, and implicitly of a more egalitarian distribution of its many benefits, have proven to be false. Within the United States the material inequalities between the top 20 percent of society and the lower deciles have widened, not narrowed, since 1967, and the growth in such inequality has only accelerated over the past ten years. Systems of complex technics, which the Unabomber identifies as "organization-dependent technology" (see chapter 6), have provided remarkable affluence to small elite groups of symbolic analysts working in the United States and a few global cities abroad, but these technics have not spread enough wealth to bring everyone on the planet up to even moderately comfortable standards of living. Within the national borders of advanced core economies across the world, as Reich observes, the successful simply secede from the rest, living in enclaves of affluence amid stagnation and poverty. Earth's already severely strained ecosystems can not carry this existing load.[57] There are limits of ecological sustainability, and exceeding or violating them really will make a difference in what tomorrow brings, particularly if new class corporate technicians continue to assume that since in the long run today's well-off average Americans will all be dead, they may as well consume in the short run as if there is no tomorrow.

The new class, if it can be assigned any definitive institutionalized position, basically is the professional-technical intelligentsia, or the affluent members of the symbolic-analytic knowledge class, which applies its expertise in workplaces at both state bureaucracies and corporate enterprises.[58] The new class is hard to pin down, difficult to define distinctly, and split internally on its politics and interests, just like the bourgeoisie and proletariat were when Marx defined his idealized types of bourgeois empowerment and proletarian powerlessness. The ranks of the new class encompass both the adversary culture and the technical elites, the liberal reformers and conservative technocrats, the bureaucratic apparatchik and the cybernetic entrepreneur. They can be owners and operators of capital as well as nonowning workers for it. The new class sends checks to Greenpeace and the Republican Party, Amnesty International and the National Rifle Association, Operation Rescue and the National Organization for Women. Moreover, as chapters 4 and 5 illustrate, new class experts can espouse technocratic geo-economy or therapeutic ecodiscipline equally in their politics.

Outside of their specific areas of expertise, new class experts have much less claim to authority, and some share values and views with nonelite individuals. Still, their command over knowledge and information continues to set them apart. Consequently, new class experts share a common position amid the organization of production inasmuch as their professional commitment to knowledge-driven projects of historical progress, technological development, and economic growth engage them in elaborate arrangements to use their expertise in ways that continually disempower and devalue the insights and interests of nonelite workers and citizens. With the growing informationalization of contemporary economies and societies, the knowledge workers of the new class acquire a peculiarly powerful role in the value-adding processes of economic production, the trend-defining cycles of social consumption, the meaning-giving ripples of cultural reproduction, the wealth-amassing circuits of commercial circulation, and the agenda-setting apparatuses of political administration.

Nature often is treated by many wings of the new class as an alien entity that must be subjected to expert domination from above and without by Washington's bureaucratic fiat or Wall Street's financial manipulations. As a vast storehouse of what are identified as "natural resources," the dead matter of nature is subjected to new class administrative designs and scientific expertise to provide all the modern goods and developed services of advanced industrial society. Such operations also strangely mystify the brutality and irresponsibility of new class power by associating it with the incredible bounty of material goods, cultural benefits, and social services that formal knowledge can produce, even though it comes from unsustainable rates of environmental exploitation in the short run to benefit only a few. Once nature is reduced to an alien entity, an abstract individualism—disconnected from the organic diversity and richness of close-lived coexistence with nature—easily arises from modern consumer societies, which are vast machinic formations organized to produce and consume the matériel ripped from its supposedly dead alien body, as chapter 3 addresses in greater detail.

The ideological assumptions behind many new class practices, as well as political interests served by existing new class structures of power and knowledge, must be carefully reexamined. Against a backdrop of whatever concrete possibilities exist for staging popular resistance to the polyarchical order of liberal capitalist democracy, today's systems of political economy constantly generate power for professional-technical experts working in state agencies and private firms. The politics of this polyarchical order continually pit different fractions of the new class against one another for more privilege or higher position, and these struggles in the marketplace and state usually cut in many directions over most issues. Therefore, the prospects for populist democratic communities organizing successfully against new class power—with such projects being exercised largely as lay resistances to the specialized expertise, privileged decision-making power, and exclusionary discourses of the professional-technical intelligentsia—need to be more fully charged by the spirit of the other Marx.

At this juncture some of the best grounds for staging oppositional direct action are afforded by nonelite communities' ecological resistance to the informational modes of production created by new class power/knowledge formations. In a world where corporate capital can pretend it brings all good things to life, one must ask how the built and yet to be built environments are shaped to sustain such good things, what ecologies generate which forms of life for whom, and where good things do and do not get brought into being when corporate science and technology get down to business. Here is where a "new international" can coalesce its alliances, linkages, and communities. The historical negativity of the proletariat has been virtually neutralized by transnational modes of production, which increasingly replace the human working class in the organic composites of capital with informatic, cybernetic, and robotic instruments of production—now known ironically as "steel-collar" or "silicon-collar" labor forces. The remaining inputs of necessary human labor are in turn becoming either "professionalized" (as technical-managerial "white-," "pink-," or "gray-collar" work for "mental workers") or "marginalized" (as unskilled, low-wage "blue-collar" work for temporary, migratory "manual workers"). From this perspective, transnational enterprises have been either idiosyncratically degrading or systematically destroying their proletarian opponents quite successfully over the past fifty years. As the following chapters begin to suggest, a deconstructive reading of Marx feeding into currents of ecological populism might contest the conditions of producership as well as ownership in a new struggle for more humane ways of life for all human beings without destroying all other nonhuman beings. Such ruthless criticism must aim toward reimagining informational production along more ecological, decentralized, municipal modes of socially reasonable community production.

This book, then, asks whether the most comprehensive critique of instrumentally rational corporate capital may now be populistic rather than proletarian and whether the most radical negation of today's transnational modes of production could be ecological rather than economic.[59] Reasonable limits of resource renewability and ecosphere reproduction, which the discourses of a critical social ecology can define, are violated systematically on a daily basis by transnational businesses in the global marketplace. Transnational businesses, of course, are not completely monolithic, omnipotent, or malevolent. Significant sectoral, national, and international divisions still hobble their strategies and effectiveness. Some firms do much good, and other companies do great evil in their everyday business. Nonetheless, it does appear that transnational corporate capitalism, as it continues to develop on a global scale, serves fewer constructive social purposes than are required for all to attain truly humane forms of being.[60] As the modern welfare state and transnational firm have become committed to the ever more rational production of goods and services, they also spit out greater and greater waste and pollution. And these long-term costs pile up as death, destruction, and decay in many more niches in the biotic chains sustaining human, animal, and plant life all over the planet.

The Soviet experience *as such* sheds little light on Marxism in practice, but the actual workings of the USSR and the its Communist Party ironically may provide some intriguing parallels for this history of the present. The workings of many transnational business firms now strangely mimic many features of Moscow's dominion over the former Soviet Union. The party *nomenklatura,* as a bloc of new class apparatchiks, imposed its abstract designs for their unrealizable scientific utopia on all the goods and services of their socialism, which quickly turned into the evils and disservices of a bureaucratic centralism.[61] Populistic revolts from below inspired in part by limited *perestroika* from above during the 1980s and 1990s eventually toppled this regime, despite the expert judgments of most Western Kremlinological experts, who foresaw only enduring permanent power for the Soviet regime. In the world's more affluent regions, such as North America, Western Europe, and Australasia, the public goods of nature are being increasingly despoiled by a transnational capitalist economy under the guidance of new class experts for the benefit of a relatively small handful of more prosperous individual consumers at the expense of all life that once lived, lives now, or might live in the future. The prevailing model of modern mass consumption, as it has been packaged by new class professional-technical experts in charge of managing both corporate capital and the welfare state, thrives on destroying natural habitat as it fabricates the artificial milieux of a commodity consumption monoculture in the midmarket suburbs and upmarket downtowns of a few megacities around the world. Perhaps this regime too could be toppled by populist resistances from below. Even though its new class managers and administrators have been madly experimenting with a top-down *perestroika* of their own through corporate "downsizing" and governmental "rightsizing" initiatives in the 1990s, this regime also rests on its own unrealizable scientific utopia rooted in a metaphysics of microeconomics. If enough people give up on its false promises, then, like the state socialism of the USSR, consumer capitalism could collapse from within on its own.[62]

Despite the serious ecological and economic crises that have emerged from the reengineering of traditional human communities and their natural environments that transnational business have performed over the past fifty years, most new class experts maintain that these crises stem from *too little* rather than *too much* reliance on the purposive rationality of corporate science and technology.[63] In seeking to attain complete managerial control of both economic production and social reproduction, some corporate enterprises and technical experts want to expand their control over nature by scrapping almost all strong environmental regulations in the name of "downsizing big government," by turning to "wise use" and "open markets."[64] Working with self-defined mandates to "reinvent government," new class technocrats in the United States are pushing public policies toward opening the last unspoiled regions of the planet to unchecked, disorganized, and inefficient economic exploitation. As the few surviving reaches of wilderness in Alaska, the last stands of old growth timber in the Northwest, and the final handful of undammed rivers in the Rocky Mountains face the disciplinary designs of corporate planning, precious natural resources continue to be consumed wantonly by an overdeveloped consumer economy that perpetuates a dual domination of nature and humanity, as former secretary of state James Baker claimed during the Gulf War, always in the name of "jobs, jobs, jobs." Many voices in some new internationals are raised to resist these moves—ecofeminism, deep ecology, bioregionalism, sustainable development, conservationism, and wilderness protection.[65] Nonetheless, their antidevelopmental preservationist tendencies are essentially marginalized in current policy debates, because human beings continue to need natural resources to live. How these resources are gathered, who controls their use, what technologies will be needed, and where benefits might flow, however, are serious political questions about collectivization that tend to be slighted both by ecological preservationists and new class experts.[66] The following chapters explore how new alliances between radical social ecology, contemporary critical theory, and ecological populist initiatives at a local or regional level might offer practical alternatives and political perspectives to answer these questions—once again, by departing from Marx.

Notes

1. Jacques Derrida, *Specters of Marx: The State of the Debt, the Work of Mourning, and the New International* (New York: Routledge, 1994), 13. Like Derrida, I could not disagree more with Richard Rorty's premature dismissal of Marx from contemporary political discourse. Conflating the Marxism of actually existing socialism with Marx, Rorty concludes, "It would be a good thing if the next generation of American leftists found as little resonance in the names of Karl Marx and Vladimir Ilyich Lenin as in those of Herbert Spencer and Benito Mussolini." Even though I agree that the American public should be asked "to consider how the country of Lincoln and Whitman might be achieved," this ideal would be realized much sooner by knowing those things that are still useful in Marx's critical criticism and everything that is dangerous in Lenin's vanguardism. See Richard Rorty, *Achieving Our Country: Leftist Thought in Twentieth-Century America* (Cambridge, Mass.: Harvard University Press, 1998), 51, 92.

2. Ibid.

3. See Francis Fukuyama, *The Last Man and the End of History* (New York: Basic, 1992), 55–81.

4. Derrida, *Specters of Marx,* 13.

5. For discussion of these forms of life in a more Marxological voice, see Timothy W. Luke, *Social Theory and Modernity: Critique, Dissent, and Revolution* (Newbury Park, Calif.: Sage, 1990). Moreover, we must not forget Marx's acute protests about the material inequalities generated by capitalist economies. In the mid-1990s there are still obscenely rich capitalist owners and absurdly poor proletarian toilers. One calculation, which is admittedly a function of the bull markets in the 1990s, shows the world's 400 richest individuals owning nearly as much personal wealth as the poorest half of the whole planet's human population—over 2.5 billion people. See Hans-Peter Martin and Harald Schumann, *The Global Trap: Globalization and the Assault on Democracy and Prosperity* (London: Zed, 1997), 23.

6. For a useful example of this sort of Marxian-inspired analysis, see Jeremy Rifkin, *The End of Work: The Decline of the Global Labor Force and the Dawn of the Post-Market Era* (New York: Putnam's, 1994).

7. Derrida, *Specters of Marx,* 85.

8. Ibid.

9. Ibid.

10. Ibid., 92.

11. For example, see Ernesto Laclau and Chantel Mouffe, *Hegemony and Socialist Strategy* (London: Verso, 1985).

12. For some examples of social critique in these terms, see Ben Agger, *Fast Capitalism* (Urbana: University of Illinois Press, 1989); and Timothy W. Luke, *Screens of Power: Ideology, Domination, and Resistance in Informational Society* (Urbana: University of Illinois Press, 1989).

13. See Manuel Castells, *The Rise of the Network Society,* vol. 1 of *The Information Age: Economy, Society, and Culture* (London: Blackwell, 1996).

14. See, for example, Rudolf Hilfering, *Finance Capital* (London: Routledge and Kegan Paul, 1981); Georg Lukács, *Marxism and Human Liberation* (New York: Dell, 1973); Max Horkheimer, *The Eclipse of Reason* (New York: Seabury, 1974); Herbert Marcuse, *One-Dimensional Man* (Boston: Beacon, 1964); Serge Mallet, *Essays on the New Working Class,* ed. Dick Howard and Dean Savage (St. Louis: Telos, 1974); Lucien Goldmann, *Cultural Creation in Modern Society* (St. Louis: Telos, 1972); Harry Braverman, *Labor and Monopoly Capital* (New York: Monthly Review Press, 1974); and Ernest Mandel, *Late Capitalism* (London: Verso, 1978).

15. See, once again, Fukuyama, *The End of History,* 291, 300–301.

16. For a preliminary discussion of the USSR in terms of the informational revolution, see Timothy W. Luke, "Technology and Soviet Foreign Trade: On the Political Economy of an Underdeveloped Superpower," *International Studies Quarterly* 29 (Sept. 1985): 327–53.

17. See, for example, Zbigniew Brezinski, *The Grand Failure: The Birth and Death of Communism in the Twentieth Century* (New York: Collier, 1990).

18. For more discussion, see Timothy W. Luke, "Yeltsin's Progress: On Russia's Pilgrimage to the West," *Soviet and Post-Soviet Review* 21, no. 1 (1994): 2–11; and idem, "Postcommunism in the USSR: The McGulag Archipelago," *Telos* 84 (Summer 1990): 33–42.

19. Cited in Alan Sheridan, *Michel Foucault: The Will to Truth* (London: Tavistock, 1980), 31.

20. For the sources of this move, see Hannah Arendt, *Origins of Totalitarianism* (New York: Harcourt Brace Jovanovich, 1966); and Carl J. Friedrich and Zbigniew K. Brezinski, *Totalitarian Dictatorship and Democracy* (Cambridge, Mass.: Harvard University Press, 1965).

21. Michel Foucault, *The Order of Things: An Archaeology of the Human Sciences* (New York: Vintage, 1973), xv.

22. For samples of such arcane categorizations, see the standard Sovietological journals, including *Soviet Studies, Slavic Studies, Post-Soviet Affairs, Problems of Communism, Studies in Comparative Communism,* and *Soviet and Post-Soviet Review.* Similar doubts are raised by Walter Lacquer, *The Dream That Failed: Reflections on the Soviet Union* (New York: Oxford University Press, 1994), 96–129.

23. Foucault, *Order of Things,* xv.

24. Bruno Latour, *We Have Never Been Modern* (London: Harvester Wheatsleaf, 1993), 4.

25. Ibid., 6.

26. See Karl Marx, "Marx on the History of His Opinions," *The Marx-Engels Reader,* ed. Robert C. Tucker, 2d ed. (New York: Norton, 1978), 4. Beck's acute analysis of the collectives binding people and things together in the contemporary macroenvironments of global capitalism, however, flips this equation. He holds that the conflicts between new class experts and local communities in the environment reverse Marx's formula. That is, "*consciousness (knowledge) determines being.* . . . the degree, the extent, and the symptoms of people's endangerment are fundamentally *dependent on external knowledge*" (Ulrich Beck, *The Risk Society* [London: Sage, 1992], 53).

27. Latour, *We Have Never Been Modern,* 13.

28. See Robert V. Daniels, *The Conscience of the Revolution* (New York: Simon and Schuster, 1960); John H. Kautsky, *Communism and the Politics of Development: Persistent Myths and Changing Behavior* (New York: Wiley, 1968); Andrei Amalrik, *Will the Soviet Union Survive to 1984?* (New York: Harper and Row, 1970); Bernard Kerblay, *Modern Soviet Society* (New York: Pantheon, 1983); and Tony Cliff, *State Capitalism in Russia* (London: Bookmarks, 1988).

29. For further discussion, see Timothy W. Luke, "The Proletarian Ethic and Soviet Industrialization," *American Political Science Review* 77 (Sept. 1983): 588–601.

30. Murray Feshbach, *Ecocide in the USSR: Health and Nature under Seige* (New York: Basic, 1992).

31. Karl Marx, *Capital,* vol. 1 (New York: International, 1967), 72.

32. Ibid.

33. Ibid.

34. Georg Lukács, *History and Class Consciousness: Studies in Marxist Dialectics* (Cambridge, Mass.: MIT Press, 1971), 83.

35. Ibid., 86.

36. Ibid., 83.

37. Ernest Mandel observes that "far from representing a 'post-industrial society' late capitalism thus constitutes generalized universal industrialization for the first time in history. Mechanization, standardization, over-specialization and parcellization of labor, which in the past determined only the realm of commodity production in actual industry, now penetrate into all sectors of social life" (*Late Capitalism,* 37).

38. Max Horkheimer and Theodor W. Adorno, *Dialectic of Enlightenment* (New York: Seabury, 1972), 121.

39. For more discussion of the opposition of the "biosphere" and "technosphere," see Barry Commoner, *Making Peace with the Planet* (New York: Pantheon, 1990), 3–40.

40. Certain passages in Marx's *Economic and Philosophical Manuscripts, The German Ideology,* the *Grundrisse,* and *Capital,* vol. 1, as well as *The Communist Manifesto* (with Engels), contain useful observations on nature and human activity in the environment, but there is no systematic consideration of "ecological" concerns per se. Engels is more attentive to nature in *Anti-Dühring* and *The Dialectics of Nature,* but these writings too do not really center Marxian critique on environmentalistic themes of analysis. For additional consideration, see Andrew Light, *A Green Materialist Reader* (Minneapolis: University of Minnesota Press, forthcoming); and Alfred Schmidt, *The Concept of Nature in Marx* (London: New Left, 1971), 102.

41. See Enrique Leff, *Green Production: Toward an Environmental Rationality* (New York: Guilford, 1994).

42. Karl Marx, "Economic and Philosophic Manuscripts," *Karl Marx: Selected Writings,* ed. Lawrence H. Simon (Indianapolis: Hackett, 1944), 64.

43. Ibid., 63.

44. Ibid.

45. Harold Perkin, *The Third Revolution: Professional Elites in the Modern World* (London: Routledge, 1996), 1–27.

46. See Klaus Eder, *The New Politics of Class: Social Movements and Cultural Dynamics in Advanced Societies* (London: Sage, 1993), 101–96.

47. See Luke, *Screens of Power,* 207–39.

48. Beck, *The Risk Society,* 20–50.

49. Ibid., 52.

50. Derrida, *Specters of Marx,* 84.

51. Ibid., 85.

52. Ibid., 85–88.

53. Marx, *Capital,* 1:35.

54. Marx, "Economic and Philosophic Manuscripts," 64.

55. Marx, *Capital*, 1:372.

56. See also Lewis Mumford, *The Myth of the Machine: The Pentagon of Power* (New York: Harcourt Brace Jovanovich, 1970).

57. Andrew Goudie, *The Human Impact on the Natural Environment*, 4th ed. (Cambridge, Mass.: MIT Press, 1994).

58. See Eder, *The New Politics of Class*, 17–62; and Alvin W. Gouldner, *The Future of Intellectuals and the Rise of the New Class* (New York: Seabury, 1979), 11–47.

59. For early efforts to articulate this point, see Murray Bookchin, *Post-Scarcity Anarchism* (Berkeley: Ramparts, 1971); and Barry Commoner, *The Closing Circle: Nature, Man, and Technology* (New York: Knopf, 1971). More indirectly, one also sees this stance in Herbert Marcuse, *One-Dimensional Man: Studies in the Ideology of Advanced Industrial Society* (Boston: Beacon, 1964).

60. See William Greider, *One World, Ready or Not: The Maniac Logic of Global Capitalism* (New York: Simon and Schuster, 1997).

61. See David Remnick, *Lenin's Tomb: The Last Days of the Soviet Empire* (New York: Random House, 1993).

62. For a parallel argument, see Lester W. Milbrath, *Learning to Think Environmentally, While There Is Still Time* (Albany: State University of New York Press, 1996).

63. This stance is articulated well in Edward N. Luttwak, *The Endangered American Dream: How to Stop the United States from Becoming a Third-World Country and How to Win the Geo-Economic Struggle for Industrial Supremacy* (New York: Simon and Schuster, 1993); as well as in James Fallows, *Looking at the Sun: The Rise of the New East Asian Economic and Political System* (New York: Pantheon, 1994).

64. See David Helvarg, *The War against the Greens: The "Wise Use" Movement, The New Right, and Anti-Environmental Violence* (San Francisco: Sierra Club Books, 1994).

65. For additional consideration, see Robert Gottlieb, *Forcing the Spring: The Transformation of the American Environmental Movement* (Washington, D.C.: Island, 1993).

66. To begin this analytical task, see Lewis Mumford, *Technics and Civilization* (New York: Harcourt, Brace, 1934); Andrew Pickering, *The Mangle of Practice: Time, Agency, and Science* (Chicago: University of Chicago Press, 1995); and David Ashley, *History without a Subject: The Postmodern Condition* (Boulder, Colo.: Westview Press, 1997).

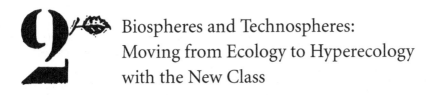

2 Biospheres and Technospheres: Moving from Ecology to Hyperecology with the New Class

The complicated cycles of production and consumption, which are inextricably interwoven through everyday technological and economic practices in contemporary transnational commerce, are verging on almost complete chaos. Highly planned programs for corporate construction systematically generate completely unplanned outcomes of environmental destruction, creating ecological risks of immense proportion. Any steps taken to mitigate these risks cannot be executed with any certainty of success. Doing anything might make everything worse; doing nothing might make something better.

At this historical juncture, political theorists and ecologists should work out shared intellectual frameworks for building an ecological society. Unfortunately, most academic disciplines, such as ecology and political theory, invoke disciplinary practices to ensure that everyone's imagination fits the approved scope and correct method of normal disciplinary inquiry. When Eugene Odum, for example, asserts that ecology is a "major interdisciplinary science that links together the biological, physical, and social sciences,"[1] political theorists rarely count themselves among even these broad interdisciplinary ranks. More ironically, although political theorists routinely address questions of values, power, and the state, ecologists see their science as one that "does not ask what kind of society would be best for maintaining a particular ecosystem—that is considered a question for value theory, for politics, for ethics."[2] Ecologists leave ethical and political angles in "scientific ecology" open, hoping perhaps that others will cover them. Yet political theorists ignore the ecological implications of their reasoning, believing that these scientific concerns are beyond their expertise. Consequently, the prevailing intellectual division of labor, once again, divides and domesticates critical thinking about the collectives of human and nonhuman beings with normalizing disciplinary constraints.

This division and docility must end. Without sinking into a green foundationalist stance, which would replace the materialist-reductionistic foundationalism of technological operationalist science with the idealist-holistic foundationalism of antitechnological earth wisdom, political theorists should weave their analyses of power, politics, and the state into a critical appreciation of scientific ecology's sense of sustainability, survival, and the environment. Such interdisciplinary efforts should be able to develop an ecological contextualism that would integrate a clear sense of the manner in which ecological constraints frame social, political, economic, and cultural practices within the technological and environmental context of the present. In turn these critiques of environmental destruction should open broader dialogues over the methods by which individuals, as both citizens and consumers, could intervene as defenders of their habitats in today's global ecology. More important, these interpretations would reveal how nonelite human beings who want to take new aesthetic, economic, political, or social paths to more ecologically responsible ways of living might revolutionize their everyday economic activities by changing their environmental sensibilities. To begin, this theoretical review asks two questions: First, how did this chaotic environmental regime begin? Second, what role did capital, science, and art play in its creation?

Mediating the Biosphere and Technosphere

To preserve the planet's ecologies at a global level, the inhabitants of each human community must rethink the entire range of their economic and technological interconnections to their local habitats in terms of their interconnections with the regional, national, and international exchange of goods and services.[3] Such a review of these collectives brings up the question of existing "bioregions" in first nature, or the larger biosphere of the planet, within which the ecologies of any and all human communities are rooted. Modern societies virtually ignore their members' positions in such bioregions in organizing everyone's ecological reproduction.[4] This approach is misguided, because bioregions are the key setting of social connections to specific places, water sources, plants, animals, peoples, and climates from which communities culturally constitute their meaningful place in the first nature of the natural biosphere.

The "domination of nature" is not so much the total control of natural events as it is the willful disregard of local ecological conditions in building human settlements. Mechanical heating and refrigeration systems enable virtually identical houses to be built in frigid Buffalo, New York, and torrid

Brownsville, Texas. Environmentally appropriate shelter could be built in both locations using earth berms, passive solar features, local materials, site-specific special vegetation, and unconventional design to create quite acceptable interior climate control cheaply and nonmechanically. Technical fixes, which imply expensive dependencies on corporate power grids, national energy markets, and complex mechanical technologies, allow builders to construct houses that suit design criteria set by models in *Metropolis* or *Southern Living* and thereby ignore the environments of upstate New York or river delta Texas. In turn, homeowners are encouraged to see themselves living amid the cultural imagineering of architectural designs celebrated in Sunday paper real estate sections, which also push the symbolic packages of high-status acts and artifacts celebrated in *Metropolis* or *Southern Living* rather than the natural confines of their immediate bioregions. Stylistic tropes, pirated from cozy Adirondack villages or quaint Mexican pueblos, become the contextual codes anchoring popular and professional expectations in home construction. The balloon-frame, three-bedroom, two-bath mechanical house provides the technological intervention; a forest cottage's shingle siding or a hacienda's stucco walls complete the symbolic imagineering system that almost utterly ignores the environment. Becoming more mindful of local environments, histories, and communities in the ecological regime of every contemporary society could awaken individuals to the importance of developing their own sustainable, self-reliant ecological society within that ecological context. For at least a century, however, the changing forms and values of advanced capitalist society have prompted their inhabitants to become less and less mindful of ecological concerns.

Creating an ecological society, which could be tied sensibly to its bioregional context, would involve making many major changes. It should become, as Porritt asserts, a "permaculture." The rules of reproducing such a self-sustaining social-ecological order would differ, qualitatively and quantitatively, from those behind the current environmental practices of advanced corporate capitalism. At a minimum, a permaculture should meet four basic ecological requirements: "It must produce more energy than it consumes; it must not destroy its own base through misuse of soil or water resources; it must meet local needs, not serve some mass-produced, processed and packaged market; and it must find all the necessary nutrients on site. . . . Its success depends on very careful design, the use of a very large number of plant and animal species, the recycling of all materials, and hard work."[5] Permaculture, then, should be guided by larger social-ecological agendas of caring for the immediate and global environment. Its constituents would need to accept the goals of conserving energy as well as allocating its useful power to everyone in more accessible, decentralized forms of application. Being an economy rooted in values tied to ecological caring, as the introduction asserted, its economic processes would not "mine" its habitat with unsustainable forms of agriculture, forestry, industry, or fishery. Rather, it would tend toward "minding" its habitat by using low-impact technics for producing the food, fiber, energy, shelter, and artifacts needed by its inhabitants. It would be much more localistic and self-reliant within the resource base of a particular bioregion. Instead of consuming huge amounts of nonrenewable energy and resources from elsewhere around the planet, the members of a permaculture would resist the unconscious bargain that has been struck with transnational business, which presumes the indirect colonization of other outside bioregions to produce products for the enjoyment of a handful of people living at a few core capitalist sites in nation-states that are capable of structuring export flows for their advantage.

Such permacultural transformations, therefore, would presume a thoroughgoing reconstruction of the substance and form given to ideal and material culture.[6] Only a radical rebuilding of almost everything that now exists in the collectives made by corporate exchange into our built environment, social landscape, and material culture could begin to create a sustainable permacultural mode of production from some of the salvageable fragments fabricated by the unsustainable commerce of transnational capitalism. The concept of ecology should create concern for the total pattern of all relations between natural organisms and their environment. The totality of advanced corporate capitalist ecologies, however, with their superexploitation of eons-old stocks of nature's resources over the spans of only two or three human generations, operate at levels beyond and above the rough natural balance of the biosphere. In fact, these interactions outstrip the capabilities of ecology, as a scientific system and technical regime, to comprehend or cope with them. The established patterns of market-driven ecological relations are so excessive and so destructive that new accounts are needed to record how they cause such immense environmental devastation in many biomes all over the Earth. Why has this happened, and why does it continue?

Abstract technoregions in the built environments of second nature, or the always emergent technosphere of the planet within which modernized human communities are embedded, operate by virtue of environmental transactions that are over, beyond, or outside rough equilibria of their natural habitats. These transactions create a new ecological context that is an artificial hyperecology of an ultimately unsustainable type. In core capitalist states a great deal of time and energy may be expended on environmental regulations, resource surveys, ecological studies, and conservation policies, but these vain attempts to reform and regulate the flow of goods and services through today's hyperecologies in second nature have failed. At best they only postpone the ultimate day of environmental reckoning. As a result, and despite the agency of these environmental protections, the ecological situation in the United States and many other advanced industrial countries is deteriorating markedly year by year.

Beginning with their instrumentally rational categories of accounting for the economic processes of commodity production and consumption, transnational hyperecologies ignore almost all concrete communal ties between local land, water, plants, animals, climate, and peoples. Instead they respecify the characteristics of ecological exchange in technoeconomic terms. Inside these artificial social spaces, hyperecologies compound their demands through abstract mathematical functions, measuring gains or losses by the density, velocity, intensity, and quantity of goods and services being exchanged.[7] With little regard to biotic diversity, geographic place, or historical tradition, essentially similar kinds of urbanized, suburbanized, or ruralized zones of consumption have emerged at many different sites by using standardized energy, natural resources, food, water, and population inputs drawn from all over the Earth through transnational commodity, energy, and labor markets. State power and market clout provide the requisite force needed to impose these costs on the many for the benefit of the few. By substituting "Earth Days" for real ecological transformation, the hyperecologies of transnational exchange are repackaged in a green wrapper of ecological concern, but they simply continue the profligate waste of energy, resources, and time to maintain the abstract aggregate subjectivity of "an average consumer" enjoying "the typical standard of living" in developed cities and suburbs.[8]

These superintensive trends of factor utilization are completely dedicated to reproducing the collectives of late capitalism, and this hyperecology continuously sustains advanced capitalist social relations by increasingly drawing in the necessary inputs from increasingly farther recesses in the biosphere. It becomes an "ephemeraculture" in that it uses far more energy than it produces, it destroys its own ecological base, it does not meet local needs in local habitats, it destroys multiculture in favor of monoculture, and it promotes chaotic carelessness.

High-tech and Hyperecologies

Conventional empirical analyses of economic consumption regard the creation and appropriation of consumable objects as the most refined sign of humanity's technological relationship to the environment. Possessing innate needs for material goods and services, people supposedly manipulate their environment in first nature technologically and socially to create objects and processed materials in second nature that will satisfy those needs. In actuality, however, this entire theory of consumption, if such discursive constructs are indeed a scientific economic theory and not pure political ideology, still follow the original tautology celebrated by Adam Smith as the essence of markets. That is, available *objects* (material goods and services) produced for modern markets are defined completely by the existing *subjects* (individual people with "innate" needs) who buy, sell, or barter for them in the marketplace. What is produced allegedly is what is consumers want, and what consumers want is what is produced.

As chapter 3 suggests, this story may have been true in feudal markets, but it rapidly mutated into myth with the advent of today's high-tech economy. The myth holds that GM, Toyota, BP, Sony, IBM, or NEC produce what their consumers really want and not what their new class managers design for delivery to them. Even in our supposedly "more complex" modern world, the myth continues to hold. Large capitalist corporations are believed to be today's most appropriate tool for getting customers what they want, not individual entrepreneurs working to truck, barter, or exchange with individual customers. The real substantive issues of who dominates whom in the contemporary global ecology are submerged from the beginning in the primitive assumptions of political economy as commodification co-modifies everything around monetized exchange. The intervention of special corporate, political, technological, and social interests in the fabrication of marketized desires for individual subjects are almost totally ignored. Instead, the identities of the human subjects in any ecology or economy are apprehended solely in the terms of their personal desire for material objects or their commodified attributes. In complex economies, then, the discourses of economic rationality and political power assume that persons conveniently realize that they "need" exactly what is manufactured and delivered to be "sold" in the markets of free enterprise. At the same time, the marketing department of any free enterprise amazingly designs, produces, and ships precisely those objects and services that fulfill "the needs" of their buyers. Buyers and sellers thus co-modify each other's preferences and products in the commodity nexus.

Such economic parables mystify the psychosocial codes of desire that unfold behind these ideological veils. The explanatory convention of sociological, psychological, or economic needs, as Jean Baudrillard argues, "naturalizes the processes of exchange."[9] Thus the mode of consumption, which is *always* a contingent social construct that is historically contrived, culturally guided, and economically controlled for the benefit of one group at the expense of other groups, is reduced in the industrial ecologies of ephemeracultures to an ahistorical, noncultural, and extra-economic "natural" process. Just as one must breathe, one must consume goods and services to satisfy needs that are as innate, unchanging, and uncontrollable as the body's need for oxygen. Nothing could be farther from the truth. To counter such naturalizing explanations of the social process behind commodity exchange, however, one must indicate how politically fabricated systems of exchange instead commodify the material satisfactions of human desire while ideologically transforming them into the irresistible outcome of natural processes.[10] In particular, corporate capital has reconstituted consumption itself. As an ideology and a politics of consummativity, consumption now pivots on an entirely new bioeconomics of transnational economic production and social reproduction in today's hyperecologies.

Entrepreneurial capitalism, which decisively transformed much of Western European and North American society through the creation of modern commerce and industry after the Reformation, largely fueled its productive cycles by drawing the products of many diverse bioregional ecologies into the urban ecology of capitalist core cities. A second nature of human artifice has plainly existed within but apart from first nature as far back as the Neolithic Revolution, when human groups became permanent sedentary inhabitants of agricultural towns and trading cities. However, an enduring tie to self-created use values of goods and services kept most human cultures apart from the modernizing impetus first provided by early modern European capitalism, which began to privilege, exhaustively and exclusively, the exchange value of goods and services over those of use value. Entrepreneurial capital, as it emerged in the modern bourgeois city, transformed economic and social relations by extending a rationalizing logic of commercial exchange into many economic activities, social institutions, or geographic regions that were hitherto precapitalist. As this exchange-based logic of commodification from the market place penetrated the living place and working place, so too did the city penetrate the countryside, the market dominate the farm, the mind worker subordinate the handworker, and the capitalist metropole imperialize the precapitalist periphery.

The dynamic of this productive cycle implied its own inherent limits in pushing commercial exchange into new geographic spaces. Beginning in the fourteenth and fifteenth centuries, capitalist entrepreneurs acquired power by extending the grasp of their markets outside their commercial cities into the adjacent villages, farms, and regions. Essentially, they grew by creating or expanding stretches of second nature in first nature. With the growth of nation-states, entrepreneurial traders trekked across continents to win new conquests in Asia, Africa, and the Americas. By the late nineteenth century, however, the easy pickings in the richer bioregions of precapitalist societies of the Western and Southern Hemispheres had been largely divided among the competing entrepreneurs and nation-states of Western Europe and North America. In the 1880s and 1890s capitalist entrepreneurs found fewer and fewer precapitalist bioregions in first nature to penetrate commercially, loosening the essential underpinnings of this model's extensive reproduction logic. The decisive shift to intensive industrialization from the extensive entrepreneurial mode of capitalism, therefore, did not become general until the discovery and exploitation of new external bioregions tapered off to nearly nothing.

As the next chapter suggests, the shift to megatechnics embodied the technological possibilities of superintensive modes of commodity production but threatened capitalist owners and managers with overproduction and underconsumption in their global markets. New sites of economic exploitation had to be fabricated. To respond the production planners of North American and Western European capitalist societies from the 1880s to the 1980s in a sense invented such sites, using scientific management, industrial design, and professional development to draw them out of the workings of second nature, or the abstract technoregions generated by intensifying exchange in existing cultural settings and established social space. Conjuring these new virgin territories from existing cultural space as the terrains of a new urban consumer society was a brilliant but fundamentally anti-ecological solution to the crisis of extensive production in the 1880s and 1890s.[11] Thus the final encirclement of nature in the closing of naturally limited bioregional frontiers in first nature opened up artificially unlimited technoregional zones of conquest in second nature for mass consumption–based industrial capitalism.

The Geographies of Bioregions and Technoregions

The geographic codes of entrepreneurial capital gradually rewrote the surface of the planet, extending outward in the fourteenth and fifteenth centuries from the original Eurocentric orbits of commercial exchange and capturing the inhabitants of numerous non-European zones of terra incognita until every frontier was closed and all unexplored territories were mapped. Every bioregion from the Arctic to the Antipodes was soon catalogued to its fullest extent for any economic utility or ecological possibility. Entrepreneurial capital met its "limits to growth" in the encirclement of the planet and the containment of diverse precapitalist modes of production from various bioregions within a single system of commodity production tied to a national geographics of production in the core capitalist powers' imperialism. Transnational corporate capital, on the other hand, gradually reinscribed the economic and ecological realities in such national geographics of production as a transnational geographics of consumption in its diverse, new-found technoregions of socioeconomically reengineered cultural space.[12]

Every craft and science, each industry and trade—all with their own disciplines and discourses—rapidly fabricated its own technical geography to map and develop new worlds held out by the intensive expansion of global exchange. No longer content to reproduce "the European world" merely by defining and dominating the otherness found in what was labeled metaphorically "the world of nature," as well as "the Oriental world" or "the Islamic world" or "the New World," "the modern world" mostly relegated this extensive colonial geography of entrepreneurial capitalism to "the traditional world" as it iterated its own new logics of endless growth through the evolving terrains of artificial technoregions defined in the intensive postimperial geography of corporate capitalism. Here, entirely new transnational topographies and transcultural territories emerge sui generis from the interactivity of international communication, manufacturing, travel, commerce, and transportation.

No longer grounded to one planetary place, one ethnonational location, or one environmental site, these semi-imaginary, semiconcrete technoregions in many ways are the cultural homelands of most modern individuals and groups. Technoregions generally position the practical placement of economic interactions within global networks from which communities instrumentally fabricate their shared strategies for occupying space in the second nature of the artificial technosphere. Some of their names are taken and passed as metaphors, yet technoregions are the technified commons of transnational society. Like the different partially imagined and partially engineered territories of Disneyland's "Tomorrowland," "Fantasyland," or "Frontierland," these feats of imagineering are simultaneously real and unreal. Contemporary workers and modern corporations, for example, no longer set out to prosper in "the New World" or "the colonial world." Instead they labor to make their marks in the thematic territories, market possibilities, spatial expanses, or resource reserves of the banking world, the scientific world, the art world, the literary world, the financial world, the auto world, the fashion world, the business world, the music world, the advertising world, the military world, the medical world, the aerospace world, the computer world, or the professional world, to name only a few transnational zones in the now worldwide webs of economic production, social consumption, and cultural reproduction defined by such new geographics in the nominal nationality of the world's countries.

These technoregional settings form the everyday lifescapes of contemporary individuals and society. Every human household imports and exports from these various technoregions the pieces and parts needed for its members' lives, the commodified goods, packaged services, and coded practices of a new material existence that envelopes all in the lifeworld of modernity.[13] In these international socioeconomic and intertextual cultural spaces of the technosphere, entire hyperecologies of domination and resistance continually form and re-form collectively apart from, but still dependent on, the biosphere of nature. Ironically, however, the technoregions' intensive and interdependent use of resources in second nature is also rapidly destroying the natural planetary balance of bioregions in first nature.

Each new technology and discourse of modernity projects its own concrete imaginary spaces to be conquered and mastered through scientific or technical means. The closing of the natural frontiers in the 1880s and 1890s simply saw the colonizing impulse displaced into new realms for competitive activity defined by geographies of more abstract economic, technological, and social spaces rather than existing geological, biological, and oceanic regions. Fernand Braudel asks, when capitalist economies faced the potential for endless growth, was it merely coincidence that "the future was to belong to the societies fickle enough to care about changing the colors, materials and shapes of costume, as well as the social order and the map of the world—societies, that is, which were ready to break with their traditions? There is a connection."[14] Therefore, ecology as such can no longer be understood through the concrete biogeography of naturally evolved bioregions in first nature; it becomes instead a double for the hyperecologies of abstract technogeographics, tracing out naturalized histories for artificially constructed technoregions in second nature. Nature becomes, as Marx claims, humanity's inorganic body.

Defining, developing, and defending these socioeconomic topologies with their own unstable but dynamic cultural properties have been central concerns behind the ephemeraculture of corporate capital for over a century. Getting corporate capital first to decamp from such zones and then finding the means to reclaim an ecological style of human life from the technoregions will be immensely difficult, if not impossible. The raison d'être of advanced technologies and the economic survival of corporate capital are tied to keeping these artificial territories continuously producing by constantly rediscovering new realms to collectivize as commodities in second nature. If change is to be attained, everything developed over the last century, all that is commonly called "civilization," "modernity," and "progress" in the technosphere of second nature, will need to be totally rethought. To stay within the limits of permacultural living in the bioregions of the now ravaged biosphere, some means of scaling back ephemeracultural life in the megatechnical technoregions of transnational enterprise must be accepted.

Mumford's insights into different regimes of technics are quite perceptive. Given the tremendous productivity of high-tech firms, the more progressive commercial and industrial elites of modern entrepreneurial capital recognized that extensive capitalist expansion into nature's bioregions, with its emphasis on individual accumulation, moralistic productivity, and the construction of the "supply side" on traditional discourses of need, had to be strongly augmented, if not entirely replaced. The decisive shift to intensive capitalist industrialization from the extensive entrepreneurial mode of capitalism did not become common until U.S. and European firms developed high-tech apparatuses for national markets and constituted the new urban consumer society as their structural response to the great depression of the 1890s. By mobilizing the scientific research capabilities of new technics to technically inform and managerially guide industrial production, entrepreneurs slowly concentrated their market shares and capital holdings through oligopolistic organization into large capital combines that could increasingly obviate market forces by creating more plannable circuits of production.[15] Hence, new forms of intensive capitalist administration in artificial technoregions placed a new stress on formal organization, designed consumption, and the management of the "demand side" of industry in national polyarchies with new discourses of style, modernity, or fashion. This niche ecology in turn presented itself as the most rational path for moving beyond the confusing maze of slow or absent growth raised by meeting entrepreneurial capital's ecological limits.[16]

Just as entrepreneurial capital slowly developed world markets by integrating disparate points of individual production into a unified commercial whole, so did corporate capital under the guidance of new class elites attain even more total command over individuals' and families' ecological relations with nature in its artificial technoregions. As Horkheimer suggests,

> Mastery of nature has not brought man to self-realization; on the contrary, the status quo continues to exert its objective compulsion. The factors in the contemporary situation—population growth, a technology that is becoming fully automated, the

> centralization of economic and therefore political power, the increased rationality of the individual as a result of his work in industry—are inflicting upon life a degree of organization and manipulation that leaves the individual only enough spontaneity to launch himself onto the path prescribed for him.[17]

In the workplace and living place, new class professional managers divorced skill from activity, planning from doing, theory from practice, and thought from action to find the paths prescribed to individuals. By integrating capital, technique, material, energy, labor, and markets into large corporate concentrations, the managerial classes and owners purposely alienated the workers from their family-accumulated property and personally acquired skill as well as from their often more ecological use of basic natural materials, simple energy, communal crafts, and local markets of precapitalist society through which the commerce of entrepreneurial capitalism had tied them into world trade. With this economic reconstitution of individuals' and families' interactions with nature, moving from a less bioregional to a more technoregional basis, corporate capital could intensify its rationalization of everyday life by means of increased state regulation, the technical reorganization of labor, and the scientific management of all spheres of social interaction.

As large firms claimed a monopoly on planning purposive-rational action in the workplace, individuals and families also increasingly accepted the disciplinary definitions given by the new class, which by this time managed most state and corporate agencies, to their individual ecological wants and private material goals. The organic need for air, drink, food, clothing, shelter, and productive labor, hitherto defined by the homespun organic crafts of the precapitalist or entrepreneurial capitalist household, underwent rapid commercial redefinition through many artistic transformations to constitute the incessantly commodified needs beneath everyone's purchasing of corporate products. These rationally designed corporate interventions into the ecological reproduction of society in turn enabled the aggregate planning system of corporate production "to organize the entire society in its interest and image" in the diverse technoregions of corporate design.[18]

Having made the real decisions about the ways in which these satisfactions would be provided, the planning system of megatechnics embedded within corporate capital turned to the state to make acceptance of this exchange-based mode of social reproduction compulsory through coercion, education, and legislation. Horkheimer notes that, as a result of this collaboration,

> for all their activity men are becoming more passive; for all their power over nature they are becoming more powerless in relation to society and themselves. So-

> ciety acts upon the masses in their fragmented state, which is exactly the state dictators dream of. "The isolated individual, the pure subject of self-preservation," says Adorno, "embodies the innermost principle of society, but does so in unqualified contrast to society. The elements that are united in him, the elements that clash in him—his 'properties'—are simultaneously elements of the social whole. The isolated individual is a monad in the strict sense, that is, it reflects the whole with all its contradictions but it is not aware of the whole."[19]

Starting in the affluent upper-class core and middle-class suburbs of the major industrial cities and then spreading into more marginal market zones in the inner-city ethnic neighborhoods, racial ghettos, small towns, and rural areas, the corporate forms of personality and society favored by the new class first emerged on the diverse terrains of technoregions from within the bioregional wreckage of the precapitalist and bourgeois social orders. The managers of corporate capital and the state decided the ground rules of this new ecology. They planned what particular material packages and behavioral scripts could be produced and provided in the technoregions along multiple spectra of limited quality- and quantity-graded alternatives to the masses of consumers. Consumers would simply exercise their "free choice" in the markets of corporate hyperecology. In turn, individuals would not look beyond these packaged material alternatives. They deliver the commodified need-satisfactions required to fulfill individual need-definitions as each consumer might have imagined them. Through this developmental path, the individual personality becomes an integral part of the collective means of high-tech production, and the modern family becomes yet another service delivery node in the hyperecologies of the ephemeraculture.

Coding Consummativity

This co-modifying circuit of commodified reproduction elaborates the essential logic of "consummativity," which anchors this entire system. Instead of maintaining the irreducible tension between the public and private spheres that liberal economic and legal theory accept as true to accept the individual contingency of rational living, the public and private have collapsed into co-modifying circuits of identity all across the technosphere in the coding systems of corporate-managed consummativity. The collective imperatives of the firm or the state are in turn internalized by individuals in the form of personalized tastes of consumption in the family, firm, and mass public. Such identity linkages allow the state and firm to regulate the economic and ecological existence of individuals closely, inasmuch as most persons now desire the "needs" extended to them as rewarding reified scripts of normal behavior written by the media, mass education, or professional experts and as the packages of mass-produced material goods made available by corporate commerce.[20] Yet these individual "needs" also are simultaneously required by the contemporary state and corporate firm as co-modifying forces of organization, direction, and value. The aggregate possibility for economic growth and the specific quality of commodity claims implied by these individual needs taken en masse are the productive forces guaranteeing further development in today's transnational corporate system of capitalist production.

The underlying codes of technified consummativity in corporate capitalism rarely manifest themselves openly. They are masked instead as democratic social and economic revolutions "rooted in the democratic alibi of universals," like convenience, modernity, growth, utility or progress. As Baudrillard suggests, consummativity presents itself "as a function of human needs, and thus a universal empirical function. Objects, goods, services, all this 'responds' to the universal motivations of the social and individual anthropos. On this basis one could even argue (the leitmotiv of the ideologues of consumption) that its function is to correct the social inequalities of a stratified society: confronting the hierarchy of power and social origins, there would be a democracy of leisure, of the expressway and the refrigerator."[21] In a sense, then, as the inchoate mass demands for a better "standard of living" in the "velvet revolutions" of Eastern Europe during 1989–91 illustrate, corporate capital can still pose successfully as a revolutionary vanguard for those who want more bananas, autos, oranges, and washing machines. Speaking on behalf of deprived consumers, and challenging the apparently more oppressive stratification, inequality, and material deprivation of all other forms of precapitalist or anticapitalist society, the new class offers the promise of complete economic democracy, social equality, and material abundance. This pledge is legitimated by the expansive corporate collateral of sparkling new material goods, exciting cultural events, and satisfying social services.

Under corporate capitalism the plannable life course of all individuals qua consumers becomes a capital asset in that the consummative mobilization of production in any given technoregion directly boosts the productivity, profitability, and power of corporate capital's increasingly automated industries.[22] With the hyperecology of second nature, corporate capital finds in consummativity

> the ultimate realization of the private individual as a productive force. The system of needs must wring liberty and pleasure from him as so many functional elements of the reproduction of the system of production and the relations of power that

> sanction it. It gives rise to these private functions according to the same principle of abstraction and radical "alienation" that was formerly (and still today) the case for his labor power. In this system, the "liberation" of needs, of consumers, of women, of the young, the body, etc., is always really the mobilization of needs, consumers, the body. . . . It is never an explosive liberation, but a controlled emancipation, a mobilization whose end is competitive exploitation.[23]

As a result the disciplinary managerial planning of corporate expertise can generate new hierarchies of status, power, and privilege in the economic democracy of mass consumption by developing different "consumption communities"[24] around distinct grades of material objects and professional services. Creating and then serving even newer modes of desire in these technoregions perpetually drives their hyperecologies of endless growth. Allegedly competing capitalist firms produce similar goods and services using similar techniques and structures planned out on a massive scale to satisfy the desires of individual subjects that their "competing lines" of products now necessarily presume will exist. Subjectivity is encoded directly and indirectly in manufactured materiality. The increasingly homogenized object world of corporate ephemeracultures is concomitantly invested with rich, heterogeneous symbolic or imaginary differentiations to provide individual subjects with plenty of codes with which they and others can distinguish the various relative status grades of community and personality across and within the collectives of people and things constituting these consumption communities.

This highly politicized process of differentiating identical goods and services wholly preoccupies the imaginative reengineering of personal consciousness and collective consumption in corporate capitalist production. As Baudrillard observes: "Thus the fetishization of the commodity is the fetishization of a product emptied of its concrete substance of labor and subjected to another type of labor, a labor of signification, that is, of coded abstraction (the production of differences and of sign values). It is an active, collective process of production and reproduction of a code, a system, invested with all the diverted, unbound desire separated out from the process of real labor."[25] Just as exchange value outstripped and mastered use value, so too has sign value now overcome exchange value in contemporary corporate hyperecologies. Hence "fetishism is actually attached to the sign object, the object eviscerated of its substance and history, and reduced to the state of marking a difference, epitomizing a whole system of differences."[26] Under the profit horizon of globalized corporate production, the consciousness-engineering industries of art, design, and advertising spend millions of dollars and hours to carefully construct codes that differentiate the sign values of commodified objects. In addition, the varying psychodemographic means of steering individuals to these artificially defined and symbolically differentiated manufactured goods and packaged services—through direct mail, magazine ads, television dramas, radio giveaways, peer pressure, fashion discourse, or public education—conduct the power of capital through the symbolic codes of consumption.

By fabricating different, distinctive consumption communities, new class managers and designers also use personal desires and their commodified satisfactions as the means of distinguishing between

> those for whom the prestige of consumption is in a way the usufruct of their fundamental privilege (cultural and political), from those who are *consecrated* to consumption, triumphantly resigning themselves to it as the very sign of their social relegation, those for whom consumption, the very profusion of goods and objects, marks the limit of their social chances, those for whom the demands for culture, social responsibility, and personal accomplishment are resolved into needs and absolved in the objects that satisfy them.[27]

Consumption communities absorb and recast the symbolic differentiations propagated by corporate capital in the familial, social, and cultural understandings of the community. In these mythological spaces, "all are free to dance and enjoy themselves, just as they have been free, since the historical neutralization of religion, to join any of the innumerable sects. But freedom to choose an ideology—since ideology always reflects economic coercion—everywhere proves to be the freedom to choose what always is the same."[28] In accepting ephemeral ideologies of identity and purpose by living hyperecologically, people consign themselves to "finding their salvation in objects, consecrated to a social destiny of consumption and thus assigned to a slave morality (enjoyment, immorality, irresponsibility) as opposed to a master morality (responsibility and power)."[29] In internalizing the expectations of these packaged choices of imposed consumption, which have been tied to "discretionary income" and "leisure time" in ephemeraculture, individuals purposely accept new kinds of responsibilities. In an important sense individual subjects occupy a key niche in contemporary hyperecologies in that they closely control their own behavior (or serve as complements of the administrative state) and ceaselessly consume products (or function as predictable units of production for the corporate sector).

Desire: Economic Asset, Ecological Liability

New class managerialism purposely stimulates the propagation of consumption, not only as the rewards of accepting a life of material abundance in an affluent society, but also as a constant investment in a new productive force. "The *consumption* of individuals," Baudrillard notes, "mediates the *productivity* of corporate capital; it becomes a productive force required by the functioning of the system itself, by its process of reproduction and survival. In other words, there are only these kinds of needs because the system of corporate production needs them. And the needs invested by the individual consumer today are just as essential to the order of production as the capital invested by the capitalist entrepreneur and the labor power invested in the wage laborer. It is *all* capital."[30] Under the hyperecological imperatives of ephemeraculture, individuals as consumers become essential capital assets in that their consummative mobilization directly boosts the productivity, profitability, and power of advanced corporate firms' increasingly intensive industries. On the horizons set by corporate capitalism's consummative order, the social affirmation of increasing individualistic permissiveness, whose codes always accelerate the rationally organized exploitation of desire to increase productivity, acquires as much importance in maintaining social cohesion as the values of ascetic self-discipline, personal frugality, and individual sacrifice once did in the productivist order of entrepreneurial capital.[31]

In the anti-ecological codes of consummativity, the individual's private space is redrawn into flexible sets of brief, limited entitlements to small, impermanent technoregional tracts. New technified forms of community, immediacy, and subjectivity are invented in the consumption of highly coded commodities whose proper social and personal administration allows new class experts simultaneously to manage, effectively or ineffectively, the communal, emotional, and psychological stability of hyperecological consumers in the technosphere. Corporate capital, when it began to develop its present globalized hegemony, did not need to immediately expand farther into the first nature bioregions of peripheral areas, such as India, China, or Africa, as did entrepreneurial capital in its quest to sell simple consumer goods to satisfy one set of unchanging "organic needs" in those areas' permacultures for every individual there. Instead, it refocused itself on limited segments of second nature technoregions at home, recapitalizing the more "artificial needs" of affluent North American and European individuals by selling them three times, five times, or even ten times what they might materially need to survive as humane beings in the unending cycles of ephemeraculture.

Talking in terms of countries is always problematic, given the serious inequalities in resource consumption and distribution that exist inside the borders of all nation-states. Nonetheless, in the hyperecologies of the most affluent nations, the top 20 percent of the world's nations consume 85 percent of the world's timber resources, 75 percent of metal production, and 70 percent of its energy resources as they are extracted every year from nature, because everyday needs there have been "liberated" by ephemeracultural advertising, planned obsolescence, organized waste, and regulated fashion to be five, six, or seven times as intensive as they might be in strictly permacultural terms. Material benefits from these hyperecologies are still reserved for the enjoyment of only a few hundred million people, mainly in Japan, Europe, and America, while the Earth's other billions continue living in comparative poverty and squalor.

The ephemeraculture of global business runs on volatile streams of new class codes. The manifold arts of the consciousness-management and design industries spend millions of dollars and thousands of hours to carefully differentiate objects in the marketplace, objects that are artificially defined and symbolically differentiated but often essentially identical materially. The discourses of market rewards and punishments constantly float around these rich imaginary visions, providing the disciplinary impetus to choose, desire, and possess the flow of objects valorized by aesthetic signs. By the same token, such code-intensified products of corporate capital produce and reproduce the larger symbolic codes of new class social privilege and political power in each act of consumption. Most important, much of the money and labor spent on such symbolic coding now is invested on various continents of the art world and design world at various levels of aesthetic creation.

On another level so-called high artists might claim that such allegations pertain only to the allegedly "low artists" working in the genres of popular culture, commercial art, or industrial design. Still, in a more indirect sense, high art too is totally involved in the reproduction of late-capitalist technoregions, for it has become simply one more segment of the "leisure industry" or "entertainment business," one that simply happens to be tied to high-prestige museums, schools, or galleries.[32] Individuals who are often seen as autonomous artists working as painters, sculptors, poets, dancers, actors, singers, musicians, broadcasters, filmmakers, artisans, or writers, may believe that they constitute a critical, politicized avant-garde. In reality, however, they often act like nothing more than the privileged labor force of an important industry, turning out another line of products for various small elite markets.

Even so, it is clear that design and the arts—both as "high art" and "low art" forms—play the key role in the production and reproduction of these coded abstractions by investing them with unbound desire. The revolutionary development of the commercial arts over the past century parallels in lockstep the emergence of corporate capital and its consummative systems of social integration. Commercial art and commercialized artists are, in one sense, another new class formation, one more professional-technical articulation in vocational, institutional, and functional terms of the aestheticized commerce resting at the core of late capitalism. Sign value as exchange value is expressed in aesthetic terms in immense systems of visual, auditory, and tactile communication centered on defining differences in material objects, stylized behaviors, and industrialized images to constantly revalorize commodities in consummative cultures.[33]

Each segment of an individual's life has been sliced up scientifically by marketing analysts and reconstituted as innumerable slabs of desire on an aestheticized field of consumer objects contained in different technoregions—such as the auto world, the food world, the urban world, the medical world, the fashion world, or the housing world—to energize the respective industries established to produce the requisite objects of satisfaction for the ephemeraculture. "*In the process of satisfaction,*" then, as Baudrillard maintains, each individual "valorizes and makes fruitful his own potentialities for pleasure; he 'realizes' and manages, to the best of his ability, his own 'faculty' of pleasure, treated literally like a productive force."[34] In the final analysis, aesthetic means of cultivating passive consumption, through the controlled emancipation of personal self-seeking and sensual fulfillment, serve at least partly as the material basis of late capitalism's hyperecological cycles of accumulation and reproduction. The logic of consummativity entails the entire global hyperecology of excess and waste, with corporate firms and service states planning the level of aggregate demand suitable for many technoregions and then managing the scope of any individual's specific demand for goods and services as his or her consummative codes continuously turn the psychic need for new material satisfactions into a dynamic productive asset.

Consummative codes promote the practices of "one-dimensional" modes of thinking and behaving in ephemeracultures:

> The productive apparatus and the goods and services which it produces "sell" or impose the social system as a whole. The means of mass transportation and communication, the commodities of lodging, food, and clothing, the irresistible output of the entertainment and information industry carry with them prescribed attitudes and habits, certain intellectual and emotional reactions which bind the consumers more or less pleasantly to the producers and, through the latter, to the whole. The products indoctrinate and manipulate; they promote a false consciousness which is immune against its falsehood. And as these beneficial products become available to more individuals in more social classes, the indoctrination they carry ceases to be publicity; it becomes a way of life. It is a good way of life—much

> better than before—and as a good way of life, it militates against qualitative change. Thus emerges a pattern of one-dimensional thought and behavior in which ideas, aspirations, and objectives that, by their content, transcend the established universe of discourse and action are either repelled or reduced to terms of this universe. They are redefined by the rationality of the given system and of its quantitative extension.[35]

When put in this light, consummativity implies the containment of desires, transforming them into a dynamic productive force. Their increasingly sophisticated imagineering ramifies into new dimensions of goods and services that communicate the consummative ideology to new consuming groups. These new groups are in turn discursively disciplined by restructuring domestic reproduction to reveal "supplies" in new markets for the new objects and services "demanded" by these new consumers.

Within the corporate commodity system, commodified desires, as they are defined within this disciplinary regime, ultimately draw the boundaries comodifying the psychosocial profiles of individuals benefiting from transnational capitalism. That is, the necessity of corporate production and the freedom of individual consumption fuse in millions of standard variations as "personality." Hence we gain the latest "historical concept of a social being who, in the rupture of symbolic exchange, autonomizes him/herself and rationalizes his desire, his relation to others and to objects, in terms of needs, utility, satisfaction and use value."[36] Contemporary permissiveness can be closely equated with this psychosocial tendency for individuals to jettison the more symbolic moral exchange of the traditional bourgeois family in favor of corporate society's encouragements to "think of yourself," autonomizing the self and rationalizing its desire for ephemeral types of material goods and services. As the disciplinary code of contemporary subjectivity, consummativity permits the new class to mobilize simultaneously almost all human instincts in "a kind of totally consuming immorality in which the individual finally submerges himself in a pleasure principle entirely controlled by production planning."[37]

For many people in most technoregions, fresh desires first come to light in artistic sign value differentia, liberating new wishes and mobilizing fresh wants, both to justify corporate capitalist firms' wasteful consumption of natural resources and to provide substance for new mass-produced products fabricated from these natural resources. Such recombinantly imagineered needs are transnational enterprises' only truly "renewable resource" of any importance. This constant revitalization of human wants with fresh images and objects of desire drives the hyperecologies of transnational environmental destruction.

Once produced, the sign values of consummativity continue affirming and concretizing the hyperecological order of late capitalism in the objects and images of the consumer goods themselves.[38] The material culture of corporate capitalism makes consummative culture material by accelerating product turnover in the hyperecology made manifest in the acts and artifacts of mass consumption. As a result consumer goods provide a vitally important field for putting cultural meanings into public and private discourses as forces of social change or cultural continuity, which artists and designers always exploit in valorizing commodities with their instrumental imagination.[39] Such manifest and latent meanings, on the other hand, can also give artists and designers tremendous opportunities to challenge the object codes of late capitalism, questioning both the media and the messages that the hyperecology of late capitalism uses to integrate individuals and society into its reproduction.[40]

It is through these object codes and their aestheticized means of mass propagation that art and design shape the ecology of advanced global capitalism. The real facticity of corporate capitalism gains continuous expression through the style, design, shape, and color of mass-produced material objects adduced by the instrumental imagination of commercialized arts and design. The codes of desire, need, and want are denominated artistically in aesthetic terms first to attract individuals and then to keep them recoding their personal aspirations in terms of scientifically designed and organizationally produced material satisfactions. Without design and the arts, the consummative society could not endlessly redynamicize its unrelenting production of newer goods, trendier products, and fresher images. Moreover, it would not be grounded on the superexhaustive use of nature and its resources. The destruction of nature begins in part in the design salons and artistic studios of every individual artist whose instrumentalized imagination has been mobilized by the market or the firm to make individuals desire more, want everything longer, and wish it to be better in purely consummative terms.

This peculiar developmental ethic of "looking out for number one" could not be farther from autonomy. Developing a unique personal identity or purpose in these cultural collectives boils down to reassembling the prepackaged purposes imputed by the aestheticized codings of one's income level, occupation, residence, or material possessions into an individual behavioral map for loosely programmed personal development. General Motors, for example, produces cars, and it wants to dominate the auto world of global automotive markets. Through focus group research, it discovers what one or more demographic blocs of buyers now desire. In concretizing their desire for "freedom," "excitement," or "practicality," it fulfills its purposes of producing profits by selling the identity/commodity of Oldsmobiles, Pontiacs, or GMCs to individuals who "succeed" by coding themselves effectively in or with these products. This process goes far beyond automobiles; all psychosocial development in any person's life is defined increasingly in terms of accumulating standardized objects or consuming conventionalized experiences produced within the marketplace. "Far from the individual expressing his needs in the economic system," Baudrillard claims, "it is the economic system that induces the individual function and parallel functionality of objects and needs."[41] The individual subject—whether the original emancipated one of liberal bourgeois "male liberation" or one cast in the more corporate capitalist forms of "minority group" liberation—ultimately remains a disciplinary construct that is perhaps no more than "an ideological structure, a historical form correlative with the commodity form (exchange value), and the object form (use value)."[42]

The disjunction between political theory and ecology highlights the paradoxes and problems of linking any analysis of power and the state to a concern for ecology and the environment. Political theorists have not systematically addressed the concerns of ecology. When they have dealt with ecology, the important links between the dynamics of first and second nature have typically been ignored. Beyond the hermit kingdoms of political theory, the environmental problems of the last four or five decades—soil erosion, industrial pollution, rampant overpopulation, resource scarcity, wasteful inefficiencies—have sparked the formation of many different environmental protest and pressure groups. Yet these populist resistances in new social movements have raised questions about power, society, and the state without much guidance from political theorists.

Consumeristic hyperecologies constitute an entirely new system of objects on the terrains of second nature. Baudrillard maintains that this second nature has a fecundity or vitality of its own:

> Could we classify the luxuriant growth of objects as we do a flora or fauna, complete with tropical and glacial species, sudden mutations, and varieties threatened by extinction? Our urban civilization is witness to an ever-accelerating procession of generations of products, appliances and gadgets by comparison with which mankind appears to be a remarkably stable species. This pollulation of objects is no odder, when we come to think about it, than that to be observed in countless natural species.[43]

Finding rationality and systematicity in hyperecology's quickening procession of products, Baudrillard believes that technified taxonomies for every object (products, goods, appliances, gadgets, etc.) of the system permit us to plumb the system of objects propounded by contemporary economies of mass production and mass consumption. To do so, however, one must push past the silences of the silent majorities and decipher the meanings of mass consumption as the consuming masses reveal them. Exploring the consumption of objects discloses "the processes whereby people relate to them and with the systems of human behavior and relationships that result therefrom," thereby allowing anyone to reach "an understanding of what happens to objects by virtue of their being produced and consumed, possessed and personalized."[44]

Here is where habitus forms from the systems of objects and objects of systems compounded with the technosphere. Bourdieu asserts that it is out of "the capacity to produce classifiable practices and works, and the capacity to differentiate and appreciate these practices and products (taste), that the represented social world, i.e., the space of life-styles [habitus], is constituted."[45] Yet the dual dimensionality of habitus as a structured and structuring structure parallels the properties of habitat, which when taken in environmental terms provides another schema for deciphering collectives generating ecological practices by comprehending them within specific settings. Anthropogenic ecological habitats of second nature in the technoregionalized ranges of the biosphere are formed from hyperecological habitus, the system of distinctive signs in practices and works driving lives styled by the system of objects. In these new spaces, as chapters 3 and 4 suggest, hyperecologies can be monitored to judge their relative success or failure in terms of abstract mathematical measures of consumption, surveying national gains or losses by the density, velocity, intensity, and quantity of goods and services being exchanged in mass consumption. Here one finds geo-economists, as chapter 5 maintains, pushing for wiser uses of any biotic assets in all anthropogenic exchanges.

To preserve the hyperecological political economy of high-technology liberal capitalism, many offices of the U.S. state and transnational firms must function as environmental protection agencies. They hope to fuse a green geopolitics of national security with a gray geo-economics of continual growth to sustain existing industrial ecologies of mass consumption with a wise use of nature exercised through private property rights. Habitus is habitat, but habitat now also defines or directs habitus. Conservationist ethics, resource managerialism, and green rhetorics, then, congeal as an unusually cohesive power/knowledge formation whose hyperecologies become an integral element of this new regime's codes of social normalization.

Paradoxically, however, almost every threat posed by these environmental risks has not diminished; instead, their damage has largely escaped effective containment and control. Consequently, various elements within the environmental movement have begun to question the effectiveness of ordinary political responses to the environmental crisis and to advance new programs for launching a fundamental moral transformation in contemporary advanced capitalist economies and societies.[46] Such agendas of ethical revitalization, however, often tie back to simplistic foundationalist readings of nature. Nature in these ethical rereadings becomes some type of suprahuman subjectivity that is discovered or deployed discursively to legitimate various ecological policies, because as such it is being read, constructed, or understood as having a truly univocal program for guiding human efforts of moral transformation.[47] This chapter has taken an alternative position, arguing in favor of a more contextual, historical, and social reading of nature—both first nature and second nature—that captures more accurately the high-tech complexities of contemporary technoregional exchange in natural settings. The next two chapters explore some of the new institutional politics and rhetorical debates over methods to sustain development by adopting more managerialist approaches toward minding the Earth's bioregions.

Notes

1. Eugene Odum, *Ecology: The Link between the Natural and Social Sciences,* 2d ed. (New York: Holt, Rinehart and Winston, 1975), 398.

2. Bill Devall and George Sessions, *Deep Ecology: Living As If Nature Mattered* (Salt Lake City: Peregrine Smith, 1985), 74–75.

3. Although they take an extremely technocratic and fairly alarmist form, as chapter 4 suggests, the annual *State of the World* reports from the Worldwatch Institute provide one example of this sort of thinking. For recent examples, see *State of the World 1998* (New York: Norton, 1998), *State of the World 1997* (New York: Norton, 1997), and *State of the World 1996* (New York: Norton, 1996).

4. See Kirkpatrick Sale, *Dwellers in the Land: A Bioregional Vision* (San Francisco: Sierra Club Books, 1985); Jonathon Poritt, *Seeing Green* (London: Blackwell, 1984); and, perhaps most important, Thomas Berry, *The Dream of Nature* (San Francisco: Sierra Club Books, 1988). For more extended discussions of the crisis facing the Earth's bioregions, see Lester Brown, Christopher Flavin, and Sandra Postel, *Saving the Planet* (New York: Norton, 1991); Barry Commoner, *Making Peace with the Planet* (New York: Pantheon, 1990); and Lester Brown, *Building a Sustainable Society* (New York: Norton, 1981).

5. Porritt, *Seeing Green,* 180.

6. These reconstructions are beginning. For more examples, see Berry, *The Dream of Nature,* as well as Murray Bookchin, *The Philosophy of Social Ecology* (Montreal: Black Rose, 1990); Suzi Gablik, *The Re-Enchantment of Art* (New York: Thames and Hudson, 1991); and Donna J. Haraway, *Simians, Cyborgs, and Women: The Reinvention of Nature* (New York: Routledge, 1991).

7. For a comprehensive critical overview of this hyperecological cycle that focuses on its implications for the Earth's atmosphere and biosphere, see Bill McKibben, *The End of Nature* (New York: Random House, 1989).

8. In this regard, radical ecologists such as Bookchin, for example, have grave doubts about the shift to the hyperecological logic of late capitalism. "This all-encompassing image of an intractable nature that must be tamed by a rational humanity has given us a domineering form of reason, science, and technology—a fragmentation of humanity into hierarchies, classes, state institutions, gender, and ethnic divisions. It has fostered nationalistic hatreds, imperialistic adventures, and a global philosophy of rule that identifies order with dominance and submission. In slowly corroding every familial, economic, aesthetic, ideological, and cultural tie that provided a sense of place and meaning for the individual in a vital human community, this antinaturalistic mentality has filled the awesome vacuum created by an utterly nihilistic and antisocial development with massive urban entities that are neither cities nor villages, with ubiquitous bureaucracies that impersonally manipulate the lives of faceless masses of atomized human beings, with giant corporate enterprises that spill beyond the boundaries of the world's richest nations to conglomerate on a global scale and determine the material life of the most remote hamlets on the planet, and finally, with highly centralized State institutions and military forces of unbridled power that threaten not only the freedom of the individual but the survival of the species" (Murray Bookchin, *The Modern Crisis* [Philadelphia: New Society, 1986], 52–53).

9. Jean Baudrillard, *For a Critique of the Political Economy of the Sign* (St. Louis: Telos, 1981), 72.

10. See John Kenneth Galbraith, *The New Industrial State,* 3d ed. (New York: New American Library, 1978); Eli Zaretsky, *Capitalism, the Family, and Personal Life* (New York: Harper and Row, 1976); Immanuel Wallerstein, *The Modern World System* (New York: Basic, 1974); Ralf Dahrendorf, *Class and Class Conflict in Industrial Society* (Stanford, Calif.: Stanford University Press, 1958); Harry Braverman, *Labor and Monopoly Capital: The Degradation of Work in the Twentieth Century* (New York: Monthly Review Press, 1974); and David Noble, *America by Design: Science, Technology, and the Rise of Corporate Capitalism* (New York: Basic, 1977).

11. See Siegfried Giedion, *Mechanization Takes Command* (Fairlawn, N.J.: 1948); and James Burnham, *The Managerial Revolution* (Bloomington: Indiana University Press, 1960).

12. As Edward W. Soja suggests, modernity is always composed out of "both con-

text and conjuncture. It can be understood as the specificity of being alive, in the world, at a particular time and place; a vital individual and collective sense of contemporaneity. . . . spatiality, temporality, and social being can be seen as the abstract dimensions which together comprise all facets of human existence. More concretely specified, each of the abstract existential dimensions comes to life as a social construct which shapes empirical reality and is simultaneously shaped by it. Thus, the spatial order of human existence arises from the (social) production of space, the construction of human geographies that both reflect and configure being in the world. . . . the social order of being-in-the-world can be seen as revolving around the constitution of society, the production and reproduction of social relations, institutions, and practices" (*Postmodern Geographies: The Reassertion of Space in Critical Theory* [London: Verso, 1989], 25).

13. For additional discussion, see Stephen K. White, *The Recent Work of Jürgen Habermas: Reason, Justice, and Modernity* (Cambridge: Cambridge University Press, 1988), 90–123.

14. Fernand Braudel, *Capitalism and Material Life, 1400–1800* (New York: Harper and Row, 1973), 323.

15. See Noble, *America by Design;* Gabraith, *The New Industrial State;* and Giedion, *Mechanization Takes Command.*

16. For more elaboration, see Ernest Mandel, *Late Capitalism* (London: Verso, 1978).

17. Max Horkheimer, *Critique of Instrumental Reason* (New York: Seabury, 1974), 4.

18. Herbert Marcuse, *Counter-Revolution and Revolt* (Boston: Beacon, 1972), 11.

19. Horkheimer, *Critique of Instrumental Reason,* 27.

20. See Sut Jhally, *The Codes of Advertising: Fetishism and the Political Economy of Meaning in the Consumer Society* (New York: St. Martin's, 1987).

21. Baudrillard, *Critique,* 58.

22. Ibid., 82.

23. Ibid., 85.

24. Daniel Boorstin, *The Americans: The Democratic Experience* (New York: Vintage, 1973), 89–166.

25. Baudrillard, *Critique,* 93.

26. Ibid.

27. Ibid., 61.

28. Max Horkheimer and Theodor W. Adorno, *Dialectic of Enlightenment,* trans. John Cumming (New York: Seabury, 1972), 167.

29. Baudrillard, *Critique,* 62.

30. Ibid., 82.

31. See Stuart Ewen, *All Consuming Images: The Politics of Style in Contemporary Culture* (New York: Basic, 1988).

32. For a parallel argument, see Brian O'Doherty, *Inside the White Cube: The Ideology of the Gallery Space* (Santa Monica, Calif.: Lapis, 1986); and Suzi Gablik, *Has Mod-*

ernism Failed? (New York: Thames and Hudson, 1984). For examples of the ways in which artists and art collaborate in the rationalization of capitalist commodity production, see Adrian Forty, *Objects of Desire* (New York: Pantheon, 1986); Bevis Hiller, *The Style of the Century, 1990–1980* (New York: E. P. Dutton, 1983); Thomas Hine, *Populuxe* (New York: Knopf, 1986); Bryan Holme, *Advertising: Reflections of a Century* (New York: Viking, 1982); Richard Gray Wilson, Dianne H. Pilgrim, and Dickran Tashjan, *The Machine Age in America, 1918–1941* (New York: Harry N. Abrams, 1988); or Chester H. Liebs, *Mainstreet to Miracle Mile: American Roadside Architecture* (Boston: Little Brown, 1985).

33. Wolfgang F. Haug, *Critique of Commodity Aesthetics: Appearance, Sexuality, and Advertising in Capitalist Society* (Minneapolis: University of Minnesota Press, 1986). Even the leisure pursuits contrived by new class product designers provide little relief from toil, because they too are engineered to maximize consummativity. Although Wendell Berry romanticizes the virtues of work, his take on consummative relaxation rings true: "Their leisure is a frantic involvement with salesmen, illusions, and machines. It is an expensive imitation of their work—anxious, hurried, unsatisfying. As their work offers no satisfactions in terms of work but must always be holding before itself the will-o'-the-wisp of freedom from work, so their leisure has no leisurely goals but must always be outside of itself, in some activity or some thing typically provided by a salesman." See Wendell Berry, *A Continuous Harmony: Essays Cultural and Agricultural* (San Diego: Harcourt Brace, 1972), 118–19.

34. Baudrillard, *Critique,* 136.

35. Herbert Marcuse, *One-Dimensional Man: Studies in the Ideology of Advanced Industrial Society* (Boston: Beacon, 1964), 10.

36. Baudrillard, *Critique,* 136. On this point Marcuse plainly identifies the dangers of reducing the social understanding of liberty to personal choice in the marketplaces of hyperecology: "Under the rule of a repressive whole, liberty can be made into a powerful instrument of domination. The range of choice open to the individual is not the decisive factor in determining the degree of human freedom, but what can be chosen and what is chosen by the individual. The criterion for free choice can never be an absolute one, but neither is it entirely relative. Free election of masters does not abolish the masters or the slaves. Free choice among a wide variety of goods and services does not signify freedom if these goods and services sustain social controls over a life of toil and fear—that is, if they sustain alienation. And the spontaneous reproduction of superimposed needs by the individual does not establish autonomy; it only testifies to the efficacy of the controls" (*One-Dimensional Man,* 7–8).

37. Marcuse, *One-Dimensional Man,* 85.

38. Marshall Sahlins, *Culture and Practical Reason* (Chicago: University of Chicago Press, 1976), 178.

39. There are few precedents for such a revolutionary turn in art or popular culture. Although they clearly were not ecologically minded, challenges against the ob-

ject codes of mass consumption can be found in some aspects of dadaism, futurism, or surrealism in Europe prior to 1945. A few artists, designers, and cultural producers working in these movements called into doubt, from both progressive and reactionary political positions, the established social codes of appropriation, interpretation, and reception of consumer goods with their radical recasting or counterstylization of mass-mediated images and mass-circulated object codes. Similarly, the situationists in the 1950s expressed a radical critique of everyday life and the consummative society's cultivation of spectacle as a mechanism of social integration. See Elisabeth Sussman, ed., *On the Passage of a Few People through a Rather Brief Moment in Time: The Situationist International, 1957–1972* (Cambridge, Mass.: MIT Press, 1989); and Sadie Plant, *The Most Radical Gesture: The Situationist International in a Postmodern Age* (London: Routledge, 1992).

40. See Timothy W. Luke, *Screens of Power: Ideology, Domination, and Resistance in Informational Society* (Urbana: University of Illinois Press, 1989), 19–58. There are not many models for such a broad politico-aesthetic reformation of society. The aesthetic and political designs of William Morris, which was soon reduced from a revolutionary challenge to a stylish affirmation, are perhaps the best example of such a comprehensive attempt to provide new, thoroughgoing "re-visions" of art, politics, and society as a whole in modern consumer economies. See E. P. Thomson, *William Morris: Romantic to Revolutionary* (New York: Pantheon, 1977); and Holbrook Jackson, *William Morris: Craftsman Socialist* (London: A. C. Fifield, 1908).

41. Baudrillard, *Critique,* 183.

42. Ibid.

43. Jean Baudrillard, *The System of Objects* (New York: Verso, 1996), 3.

44. Ibid., 4–5.

45. Pierre Bourdieu, *Distinction: A Social Critique of the Judgement of Taste* (Cambridge, Mass.: Harvard University Press, 1984), 170.

46. See, for example, Devall and Sessions, *Deep Ecology;* John Seed, Joanna Macy, Pat Fleming, and Arne Naess, *Thinking Like a Mountain: Towards a Council of All Beings* (Santa Cruz, Calif.: New Society, 1989); and Arne Naess, *Ecology, Community, and Life-Style,* rev. and trans. David Rothenberg (Cambridge: Cambridge University Press, 1989). An ethic of ecological responsibility, despite the invention of "green consumerism," runs directly counter to consumerism in the United States. A consumer is someone who uses things up to the point of despoilation. Many ecological populists in economic and environmental justice movements realize that waste, obsolescence, and disposability are one more source of new class empowerment. To revitalize individual discretion and local choice, "a more realistic and creative vision of ourselves would teach us that our ecological obligations are to use, not use up; to use by the standard of real need, not fashion or whim; and then to relinquish what we have used in a way that returns it to the common ecological fund from which it came" (Berry, *A Continuous Harmony,* 111).

47. On this point see Christopher Manes, *Green Rage: Radical Environmentalism and the Unmaking of Civilization* (Boston: Little, Brown, 1990); Rupert Sheldrake, *The Rebirth of Nature: The Greening of Science and God* (Rochester, Vt.: Park Street Press, 1994); and Carolyn Merchant, *Earthcare: Women and the Environment* (New York: Routledge, 1995).

5 The Dangers of Discourse: Polyarchy and Megatechnics as Environmental Forces

The inadequacies of language quickly cloud political discussions of contestable concepts. As chapters 1 and 2 suggest, the meanings of basic terms, such as *ecology, populism, bureaucracy, technology, liberal, democracy, crisis,* or *the environment,* are unstable, variable, and unfixed. Elaborate debates must develop their meanings in particular ways to promote specific goals. Consequently, this chapter starts across uncertain ground, acknowledging that the discursive terrain will continue shifting as the argument ironically teases meanings out of these concepts in rethinking the contradictions between popular autonomy and bureaucratic administration in the struggle over ecological reform.

To construct an ecological critique, some concepts, such as that of liberal democracy, will intentionally be read out of focus, destabilizing their apparently stabilized meanings. At the same time, other notions, such as that of ecological populism, will be reinterpreted in a sharper focus, fixing some of their more unfixed connotations in a new interpretive register. Most important, this chapter will reconsider how liberal democratic systems produce their peculiar understanding of nature as humanity's inorganic body and create the environmental crisis as an integral part of every one of their products. In addition, this chapter also examines how such polyarchical regimes can inventively use "green" agendas to adapt this crisis in their own operations. Turning habitus into habitat can easily become "ecologized." By rebuilding biospheric ecologies as technospheric hyperecologies, the new class forges the narrow technocratic regime of control that underpins liberal capitalist democracies.[1]

Ecological critiques thrive on developing a discourse of dangers, but they are not attuned to other dangers of discourse that arise out of naively accepting mainstream environmental categories. Following President Reagan's denials that there was a problem with the environment, even though President Nixon had first proclaimed a "crisis" in the 1970s to capitalize on the ecological concerns of voters at that time, in 1989 the United States came under the control of George Bush, the "Environmental President," who cynically adopted this label in stand-up campaign spots at the Grand Canyon and Boston Harbor to win voters in the 1988 election.[2] This green president was succeeded in 1992 by an allegedly even more environmental president, Bill Clinton, and the nation's most environmental vice president ever, Al Gore. As chapter 5 considers in more detail, Gore is the author of an archetypical bureaucratic green manifesto, *Earth in the Balance: Ecology and the Human Spirit.* This tract invites liberal democratic state functionaries everywhere "to conceive of a plan to heal the global environment" while billing such reconceptualizations as the quintessence of contemporary political realism, since "public attitudes are still changing—and . . . proposals which are today considered too bold to be politically feasible will soon be derided as woefully inadequate to the task at hand."[3] With this invitation to stay ahead of the curve in public opinion, Gore shows how established administrators in the state apparatus would stay in control simply by going "green." Therefore, any radical democratic resistance of ecological populists that seeks to create something truly new and different within the prevailing modes of political economy must define how and why its "alternatives" depart from the environmentalized forms of rule touted by Gore and other born-again bureaucratic greens. Likewise, radical ecological thinkers must be cautious about the policy injunctions they recommend to their communities as plausible responses to the environmental crisis, lest they become another domesticated expression of artificial negativity to rerationalize an already irrational regime.[4] Danger lies perhaps not in being ignored but rather in being accepted too literally and too soon.

Liberal Democracy = Polyarchy + Megatechnics

Even now, democracy remains an essentially contested concept. The social construction of both what it *is* and how it *should be* still preoccupies the energy and intelligence of many political scientists, sociologists, media pundits, and economists. Since the 1960s entire literatures about the most desired new qualities for a radical participatory democracy have been written and rewritten in some detail. Nonetheless, once the dust raised in these writings settles, the general consensus about existing democracies endorses Joseph Schumpeter's reduction of democracy, as it is practiced by modern liberal democracies in Western capitalist economies, to "a political *method,* that is to say, a certain type of institutional arrangement for arriving at political—legislative and administrative—decisions."[5] This method is centered mainly on using periodic open elections to choose and legitimate a group of experts who will make these decisions. Such democracies typically arrange all major communicative, economic, political, and social institutions around supporting the formal mechanisms "for arriving at political decisions in which individuals acquire the power to decide by means of a competitive struggle for the people's vote."[6] Most significantly, these mechanisms should include "competing" political leaders, parties, or alliances that allegedly offer clear choices between different candidates, values, or policies in more or less open and free elections to mass electorates. Moreover, just as they freely choose between various consumer products in the open marketplace, voters presumably can freely decide to pick from many alternative electoral choices by endorsing one or another with their ballots.

Polyarchy

This peculiar vision of democracy embodies most modern social and political scientists' efforts to account for the technocratic managerialism of many advanced capitalist states by improving on what Schumpeter labeled a classical theory of democracy. Classical democracy supposedly rested on a maximal level of continuous participation by every citizen, as well as on a moral ideal of a rational, active, informed, and engaged citizenship that guaranteed the implementation of wise policies guided by civic virtue. Various images of this sort of democracy are at the heart of the participatory democracy literature written since the 1960s. Advocates of democratic populism, such as Murray Bookchin or Christopher Lasch, frequently invoke such activist ideals as their best vision of a more participatory democratic society.[7] Regarding classical democracy as an arrangement for realizing direct democracy in small-scale, face-to-face settings, Schumpeter somewhat problematically defines it as "that institutional arrangement for arriving at political decisions which realizes the common good by making people decide issues through the election of individuals who are to assemble in order to carry out its will."[8] To work well, classical democratic systems allegedly require everyone to know precisely "what he wants to stand for"; moreover, "a clear *and prompt* conclusion as to particular issues would have to be derived according to the rules of logical inference"; and finally, "all this the model citizen would have to perform for himself and independent of pressure groups and propaganda."[9] Since such conditions of popular rule via direct democracy no longer hold true, if indeed they ever did, this classical theory of democracy must give way, along with the image of self-rule by rational, active, informed, and engaged citizens, to the more realistic practices of modern liberal democracies, where much less rational, active, informed, or engaged voters periodically disapprove or approve of different expert elites competing for governmental offices in systems of indirect rule via representative democracy.

Participation for the vast majority of citizens in modern liberal democracy therefore boils down to a routinized process of periodically giving electoral affirmation to this or that set of contending programs, policies, and politicians. To protect their positions, voters supposedly vote for leaders who publicly espouse programmatic solutions that can be seen as fulfilling the voters' assessments of their own interests.[10] Inactive or apathetic voters, according to the theory, either see their interests already being served or at least see them as not being severely threatened by incumbent governments. Robert Dahl argues that this model of governance requires all citizens to have unimpaired opportunities to formulate their preferences, signify their preference to their fellow citizens and the government by individual and collective action, and have their preferences weighed equally in the conduct of government without regard to their content or source.[11] Associated sets of parallel institutional arrangements—such as the freedom of expression, the right to vote, the freedom to organize, eligibility for office holding, access to alternative information in a free press, the guarantee of free and fair elections, the right to compete for votes, and the linkage of voting to policy implementation—are all centered on closing the preference-forming, preference-signifying, preference-registering circuits between voting publics and competing elites.[12]

Organized on a territorialized basis in modern nation-states, such democratic institutional arrangements allow for competing elites at the local, regional, and national level to gain or lose authority in response to the votes cast by the voters inhabiting any particular national territory. On this foundation, then, liberal democracies are seen as providing stable, equitable, and responsive levels of popular governance, which Dahl renames "polyarchy." Polyarchy's combination of competing elites, trusting publics, and moderating civic norms is something much less than the classical model of democracy described by Schumpeter, but it is seen as better adapted to today's political context. As Dahl observes, when matched with a basic consensus of the ruling elites on what are the legitimate social norms as well as the popular majority's general acceptance of the ruling elites' expertise, these institutional arrangements provide "a relatively efficient system for reinforcing agreement, encouraging moderation, and maintaining social peace."[13]

The criticisms of such polyarchical arrangements in contrast to classical normative democratic theories, as both are identified in modern empirical, descriptive, or formal theories of democracy, are numerous and wide ranging.[14] The criticism is often compelling, particularly inasmuch as the critics assail the reliability of the voter-leader preference-to-policy circuit. Such attacks challenge the practices of democratic elitism, doubt the responsiveness of polyarchy, or dispute the rationality of such collective choice structures. These critiques, however, overlook the ecological foundations undergirding polyarchical versions of modern liberal democracy. The way that polyarchies work in the political sphere parallels megatechnic practices prevailing in their industrial ecologies and social technologies. In fact, the megatechnical economy coincides closely with a polyarchical polity in contemporary capitalist systems. Its particular preference constrictions, lack of responsiveness, and collective irrationalities are quite comparable to their polyarchical analogues.

The main elites competing to control contemporary polyarchies are essentially recruited from the new class, and their ranks are filled by people with the educational competence that provides training in complex, technical decision making. Once again, they are the symbolic analysts and the professional-technical intelligentsia that Reich identifies as the knowledge-generating and symbol-manipulating classes, who articulate and apply their expertise in both state bureaucracies and corporate enterprises.[15] Under their charge, the overall substantive ends of polyarchies have been tied to ensuring greater technical efficiencies in these networks of instrumental rationality to provide various "public goods," including social welfare services, political stability, economic growth, and mass consumption. The instrumental rationality of megatechnics, which has grown to a transnational scale, now intrudes into many more areas of everyday life.[16] As these constant interventions fuse political administration with economic management, however, they begin undercutting their substantive ends. Megatechnics confounds its own means-ends efficiencies. The transaction costs of instrumentally rationalizing everyday life on a global scale increasingly limits the benefits of making the transactions. More and more "public evils"—pollution, rising prices, resource scarcities, national conflicts, great-power competition, domestic violence, unemployment, or service shortages—are created in a process of providing fewer and fewer "public goods." Up to this point, the existing forms of polyarchy have not discovered effective solutions for this "rationality crisis," especially since they remain preoccupied with answering the still pressing challenges of the "distribution crisis" feared in polyarchical politics.[17]

With regard to the environment, many individual members of these elites may be highly reflective agents who are very worried about ecological questions. Many support the Sierra Club, the Nature Conservancy, the Audubon Society, or the World Wildlife Fund, but such affiliations merely mystify the brutality and irresponsibility implicit in their systems' megatechnic production by draping green ribbons around the incredible bounty of material goods, cultural benefits, and social services that the presently unsustainable rates of exploiting nature now provide for a lucky few with the income to gain access to them.[18] Such ideological predilections in the professional-technical classes' practices, as well as their political interests in maintaining the existing structures of new class power and knowledge, must be reexamined against the backdrop of other, more concrete alternatives (such as those raised in chapters 7, 8, and 9) for resisting megatechnics beyond supporting environmental pressure groups run by other professional greens who would regulate corporate interests managed by less environmentally minded new class managers. By reducing citizens, who often want to be more economically and politically autonomous, to dependent consumers and clients, the megatechnical economy increasingly consolidates more power in the hands of professional-technical experts in state agencies and private firms.[19]

The reign of polyarchical elites is rationalized rhetorically as a democratic process by citing the competitive struggle for votes among the competing blocs of political elites. Continuous, face-to-face arrangements of participatory democracy, these elites argue, cannot work on a vast national scale with the territorial diversity of modern welfare states. Rather than explore how smaller political systems on a nonnational scale might supplant this regime, these technocratic elites push for sustaining this bloc of political institutions, because many of its members concur with one another about the alleged unworkability of direct democratic systems. Such reasoning, however, only echoes the dubious social scientific legitimation discourses used to justify preserving megatechnics as a economic, social, and technological formation.

Megatechnics

In many respects the key organizing principle of polyarchy is economic growth: creating it, managing it, and distributing its costs and benefits on a national scale in particular territorialized states. All voters, it is claimed, want more material goods and social services, so technocratic elites compete to control the government offices that allow them to implement various policies to serve these ends. As Bill Clinton explained during the 1992 U.S. presidential elections, when it comes to modern liberal democracy, the bottom line of polyarchical administration is clear: "It's the economy, stupid!" The peculiar technical complex that underpins the economy, however, has been under continual redevelopment for over sixty years, beginning in the global economic crisis of the 1930s, even though its roots might be traced, as Lewis Mumford argues, back to the French Revolution, European absolutism, or even Oriental despotism:

> Up to 1940 it was still possible to regard the continuation and acceleration of modern technology as, on the whole, favorable to human development; and so firmly has this conviction been implanted, so completely has the Myth of the Machine taken hold of the modern mind, that these archaic beliefs are still widely regarded as well-founded, scientifically accredited, indubitably "progressive"—in short, practically unchallengeable.
>
> Not that anyone, at the beginning of the twentieth century, could have been unaware that profound changes were being made in every aspect of daily life. These changes were invigorated and abetted, not merely by a great access of energy, but by a network of transportation systems and communications systems that had never existed before on anything like the present scale. The growth of capitalism, however uneven in its distribution of benefits, nevertheless appeared to many observers as the necessary preparation for a more equitable, socialized system. The seemingly ordained extension of political democracy, through responsible party government, at least in industrially advanced countries, supposedly guaranteed a smooth transition, by an accretion of measures that provided for social security and social welfare.[20]

Even as these apparently benign technological developments took hold, Mumford asserts, the mechanisms of a new megatechnics were being designed by corporate capital in the national marketplace; "indeed, the great industrial corporations and cartels were working models" for all social planning as part of "*a profound re-orientation of human habits, efforts, and goals*" that added up to "dictatorship by a scientific elite"[21] through the planned consumption and engineered production discussed in chapter 2.

The struggles of World War II and the ensuing four decades of the cold war provided the formative context for a new megamachinery, or a megatechnic complex, to begin operating with essentially unlimited access to the ancient assets of autocratic authority: power, speed, and control.[22] After 1939,

> the necessary components of the megamachine were not merely enlarged in scope but brought into close coordination and cooperation, so that in each country they functioned increasingly as a single unit. Every part of the daily routine was placed directly or indirectly under governmental control—food rationing, fuel rationing, clothes production, building—all obeyed regulations laid down by the central agen-

> cy: the system of conscription applied in effect, not only to the armed forces, but to the entire country.
>
> Though industry at first moved reluctantly into this new orbit, the growth of cartels, trusts, and monopolies which had taken place during the previous century equipped these organizations for active collaboration under government control—lured naturally by the huge financial incentive for accepting such integration, namely, costs plus a large guaranteed profit. This ensured both maximum production and maximum financial return. As the war progressed this megatechnic assemblage functioned increasingly, despite corporate jealousies and local antagonisms, as a single working unit.[23]

When combined with the White House's centralized command and control of nuclear weapons and the Pentagon's mobilization of science and technology as national security assets, a megatechnical political economy took hold within the United States, as well as among the other Western capitalist democracies, in the 1950s and 1960s. At the same time, the officially sanctioned waste of the affluent society made possible by megatechnics made possible as well Schumpeter's minimalist vision of democratic politics—or choosing between two leaders, parties, or coalitions competing to manage the polyarchical state and megatechnical economy.

As Mumford observes, megatechnics works on several levels. Competing elites of professional-technical workers, high-tech scientists, and symbolic analysts first create growth and then reallocate its material payoffs to the larger society.

> Given these "ideal" conditions—power-machines, centralized control, and unlimited waste and destruction—there is no doubt about the immense productivity of megatechnics, or about the fact that a larger part of the population than ever before stands to benefit from its methods; for industry itself can compensate for higher wages by passing on the increase in costs to the expanding body of consumers, sedulously conditioned by advertising and "education" to ask only for those mass products that can be profitably supplied. Judged purely in terms of fabricated goods, there is no doubt that an economy of abundance is already in partial operation. . . . Though the total result of the economy of abundance leaves a far smaller net gain than its proud exponents are usually willing to admit, it has nevertheless introduced one significant factor that outweighs many of its deficiencies. This factor is doubtless responsible for the unguarded way in which it has been embraced: namely, in order to work at all, the megatechnic system must not merely increase the rewards but distribute them throughout the whole population. Implicit in mass production are two notions that have the effect, if not the intention, of a humane moral principle. First, the basic goods of production, being a product of our total culture, should, once they exist in abundance, be distributed

> equally to every member of the community; and second, efficiency should be maintained, whenever work depends upon human effort, not by deprivation, coercion, and punishment, but mainly by adequate differential rewards.[24]

Granted this megatechnical system of creating abundance, the institutional arrangements of polyarchy provide voters with electoral mechanisms for satisfying their preferences about economic growth by selecting political leaders capable of realizing this material abundance.

Megatechnics works much like polyarchy, but it shifts its methods of legitimation to the so-called marketplace. In markets megatechnics can be seen as an economic-social-technological method or a set of institutional arrangements for making and enforcing decisions that are essentially ecological—energy, resource, land, water, and labor use in economic-social-technological structures. What should be political decisions made by affected publics become subpolitical decisions framed by technocratic experts. These methods arrange most communicative, economic, political and social institutions around technological mechanisms for making ecological decisions in which competing groups of new class operatives, or those professional-managerial-technical workers who manage firms and invent technologies, struggle for affirmation in people's purchases. Megatechnics, in this sense, often represents itself as a permanent election or perpetual poll in which economic, social, and technological blocs of businesses, services, and utilities offer a wide array of choices between easily differentiable products, services, and policies in more or less open markets. In the same manner that voters choose between candidates in elections, buyers, clients, and users "vote for" or "choose among" these alternatives with their purchases.

Just as classical democracy supposedly can no longer work in polyarchies, to retrace Schumpeter's somewhat contestable claims, megatechnical operatives also argue that classical economic self-reliance in communities of independent producers cannot fit into today's context. Such classical forms of economic self-reliance assume as an ideal of economic freedom a maximal level of continuous individual labor, unceasing family capital accumulation, and arduous personal skill acquisition by every household. Typically seen as a system of self-management, autonomous ownership, and polytechnical virtuosity in small-scale face-to-face settings, economic self-reliance stood for everyone's having a demonstrated ability to produce and consume material satisfactions for his or her own needs independently of many exogenous sources of supply. Economic self-reliance among rational, active, informed, and engaged ecological-technological actors, therefore, must give way in megatechnics to much less rational, active, informed, and engaged buyers, clients, and users continually approving or disapproving the small subsets of prepackaged alternatives offered by different corporate organizations hustling after their purchases with competing products.

For the vast majority of consumers served by modern megatechnics, autonomy is nothing more than the minor ambit of their tightly confined purchasing behavior, which affirms this or that set of competing products, packages, or professionals. To serve and protect their needs, consumers supposedly buy the products that are branded with those attributes that they attach to their needs. Inattentive or apathetic consumers continue to buy whatever they buy because either they believe their interests are being served or at least they are not being severely threatened. Like polyarchy, a megatechnical system also pretends that all consumers have an unimpaired opportunity to formulate their preferences, signify them to others and the market, and get them weighed equally in the mix of marketplace products without regard to their content or source. Other associated institutional arrangements, such as legislation pertaining to equal employment, free trade, open markets, enterprise incorporation, patent rights, service guarantees, and technical standards, are all directed at rationalizing preference-forming, preference-signifying, and preference-registering circuits between buying publics and competing economic elites.

Also organized mostly in markets drawn along territorial lines inside modern nation-states, megatechnic institutional arrangements enable these competing elites to gain or lose profits in response to buying decisions made by consumers. With the appropriate intervention of state authorities to rationalize economic growth, megatechnical systems are seen as providing stable, equitable, and responsive levels of widespread material abundance. By mixing this combination of competing economic elites, trusting consumer publics, and moderating marketplace norms, one can never emulate the economic self-reliance of classical economies. But this arrangement is supposedly well suited to today's economic settings, because it allegedly matches the basic consensus shared by the masses and elites on what ecological forms legitimately should be. They also embody a general acceptance of the managing elites' experience in running the entire system, generating—as Dahl might say—a relatively efficient order for informing agreement, promoting exchange, and sustaining economic, social, and technological stability.

Consequently, many new class professionals today would argue that the battle against scarcity in agricultural production has been won forever. The development of corporate agriculture in the United States promises to deliver increasingly larger amounts of food to increasingly larger groups of consumers with increasingly smaller contributions of human labor. Yet this entire mode of megatechnical agriculture is arguably unsustainable and doomed to collapse precisely because it has substituted so much energy, capital, and organization for labor.[25] The farm belts around U.S. cities are increasingly paved over for suburbia, shopping malls, and new service industries. The food production of the nation is concentrated in a few areas, so that it takes six calories of nonrenewable fossil fuel energy to produce one calorie of renewable food energy, and as much as one bushel of good topsoil is lost for every two bushels of corn produced under these energy-intensive means of production. Meanwhile, billions of gallons of fuel are expended shipping fruit and vegetables from heavily irrigated, semiarid California fields to temperate zone cities in the North and East, which have lost their agricultural support networks to overdevelopment of land for housing or industry.

In less than a century, nearly half the topsoil in the plains states has been lost to erosion. Nearly one-sixth of all known reserves of fossil fuels have been dissipated. Nonetheless, these losses are counted as "gains" by advanced technological society because the external invisible costs of accumulating existing stocks of petroleum energy and topsoil enter into modern megatechnical models as "free" natural resources, simply awaiting development into goods ready to be exploited at a profit.[26] In fact, advanced megatechnic technologies work because of their users' increasingly sophisticated ability to socialize costs while privatizing benefits by ignoring or discounting such invisibles, intangibles, and externals as topsoil, petroleum deposits, weather patterns, biome ecologies, and water resources, even though they are essential capital inputs needed to maintain industrial and agricultural production.

As a result, Mumford notes, megatechnics survives as long as its clients and customers ratify the prepackaged choices presented to them in "the marketplace" by the competing elites of corporations, laboratories, and utilities. In other words:

> At least one thing should soon become clear: once the majority of any nation opts for megatechnics, or passively accepts the system without further question, no other choices will remain. But if people are willing to surrender their life completely at the source, this authoritarian system promises generously to give back as much of it as can be mechanically graded, quantitatively multiplied, scientifically sorted, technically conditioned, manipulated, directed, and socially distributed under supervision of a centralized bureaucracy. What held at first only for increasing the quantity of goods, now applies to every aspect of life. The willing member of megatechnic society can have everything the system produces—provided he and his

> group have no private wishes of their own, and will make no attempt personally to alter its quality or reduce its quantity or question the competence of its "decision-makers."[27]

No one can, in a sense, legitimately challenge the "method" of megatechnics, for the entire productive system embodies a systemic ideology favoring growth, efficiency, and technique. Instead, buyers who become dissatisfied with one set of services or goods must buy another product or find an alternative source—which are, of course, only the expressions of technical decisions made by other, perhaps more competent, elite decision makers to serve their economic interests differently. Questioning whether the services actually "serve" or whether the goods are "good" is beyond the logic of the megatechnical system. Once again, political choices are rendered down to subpolitical options.

Just as citizens forsake more authentic political autonomy for polyarchy, producers give up their ecological freedoms in forsaking economic self-reliance. Mumford sums up the condition of consumers and clients under megatechnics thus:

> For the sake of material and symbolic abundance through automated superfluity, these machine-addicts are ready to give up their prerogatives as living beings: the right to be alive, to exercise all their organs without officious interference, to see through their own eyes, hear with their own ears, to work with their own hands, to move on their own legs, to think with their own minds, to experience erotic gratification and to beget children in direct sexual intercourse—in short, reacting as whole human beings to other whole human beings, in constant engagement with both the visible environment and the immense heritage of historic culture, whereof technology itself is only a part.[28]

These tradeoffs of freedom for security, however, often prove hollow, even on their own terms. Polyarchy does not actually protect all voters' interests, and megatechnics does not truly fill all consumers' needs. Competing elites, once in power or with dominant market share, push their interests on the voting and buying public to shape the mass of all individual preferences. In the end, the short-run social benefits of creating, managing, and distributing the fruits of economic growth that the polyarchical state's megatechnical economy produces are being overwhelmed by long-run, ecological costs intrinsic to this entire mode of political economy. As Mumford concludes: "The gain seems on paper to be larger than it actually is; for this reckoning leaves out the negative abundance that has accompanied this feat: the depleted soils and mineral supplies, the polluted air and water, the rusting auto graveyards, the mountains of waste paper and other rubbish, the poisoned organisms, the millions of dead and injured on the highways, all of which are inevitable by-products of the system. These are the poisonous effluents, as it were, of our affluent society."[29] Not surprisingly, then, megatechnical living is increasingly redefined in languages of biohazards, environmental dangers, or ecological risk.

Community and Bureaucracy: Ecological Battles

Community as an organizing concept can and does have many meanings. In the polyarchical elitist frameworks of new class bureaucracies, however, community degrades into the most "minimal" or "thinnest" attributes of association. Collective life has little popular form or populist content, for the managerial regime simply seeks the support of highly mobile individual voters and loosely defined interest groups in periodic elections and daily purchases. As clients and consumers, today's communities of human beings in many highly developed nation-states are little more than infrastructural artifacts. They can be described either as some indistinct population interacting functionally as individuals at a given location (such as the suburban households in tract housing developments or the patrons and salespeople at the same local shopping centers) or as a stable population of businesses and households organized into discrete geographic-legal units (such as the circulating sets of firms and families sited temporarily or permanently in some city, county, or town). Granted the extraordinary personal, economic, geographic, and social mobility of contemporary U.S. society, the ecological relationships between workplace and residence, production and consumption, and administration and allocation have become extremely fragmented in the abstract individualism behind many new class designs for advanced industrial society. The division of group interests, loss of common historical consciousness, weakening of shared beliefs, and lessening of ecological responsibility in these minimal thin communities are in turn what require us to turn our attention to alternative categories for understanding community.

The traditional stability of premodern communities provides a legitimating writ for imposing far more fluid, mobile, and variable forms of everyday life, such as those produced and managed by new class experts, in the diverse voluntary associations of modern contractual society. If modernity boils down to "the change to change," then lacking this kind of change becomes a prima facie pretext for imposing changes from above or without. Instead of the supposed security of traditional solidarity, organic identity, and communal purpose, the dynamism of modern societies allegedly brings the putative benefits of possessive individualism, situational rationality, and instrumental self-interest favored by new class bureaucrats and managers. The new class, then, reimagine their values and institutions as the sine qua non of "modernity," while all forms of resistance to them become "tradition." Once community is framed by these discursive categories, its meaning becomes even more problematic because new class analytic assumptions shield against adopting thicker or maximal understandings of it, which typically have populist undertones. In fact, modern canons of social theory can usually cope conceptually with these alternative visions of community only in distorted forms that support new class criticism of populist activities.

Rethinking the reorganization of communal life, then, is a threatening endeavor in contemporary polyarchies. Few of the apparent dangers in a more maximal form of community are guaranteed to occur, but new class experts are always ready to block any proposal favoring more populist visions of community. Unless one accepts the thinnest, most minimal constructions of community, which means the polyarchical and megatechnical solutions favored by the new class in their managerial organization of clients and consumers, some faction of privileged interests among the new class will feel aggrieved. Precapitalist communities, as modern social theory tries to understand them, probably never existed and would be impossible to revitalize even if they did, and their now unknown collective practices cannot heal the many different forms of individualized injury that contemporary community continues to create. Nonetheless, the populist impulse to reconstitute thin, minimal communities—which capitalist megatechnics now continuously reshape to suit the requirements of new class polyarchical management—as new populist forms of thicker maximal community under popular democratic control still draws stern indictments for its disciplinary "deviations." Because of these disruptive proclivities, then, democratic populist projects continue to be attacked by new class experts eager to prevent lay people from causing any unplanned changes from below.

New disciplinary discourses about democracy, such as rational choice theory or collective decision-making models, work to enforce thin community by using instrumentally rational mechanisms of regulation to reduce all possible forms of thick community to massive aggregations of individual choice acts.[30] In one sense, at any given moment of decision making, voters and leaders might be seen as rationally choosing or collectively deciding between this *x* or that *y*. In another sense, however, *x* or *y* also are often elaborate mystifications overlaid with innumerable prepackaged decisions and overdetermined possibilities. Thus, an instance of individual rational choice may be not so much a choice by rational individuals as a decision to implement this or that rationalized administrative theory; in turn, the system of collective decision making is typically a choice between empowering this or that decision-making bureaucratic collective. In the end individuals do not realize their preferences as individuals as much as they actualize the authority of various bureaucratic agents, who either rationalize theory as policy or program administrative routines as decision-making collectives.[31]

In the last analysis, polyarchy must be stood on its head if it is to be read accurately. Schumpeter and Dahl envision the institutional arrangements of modern liberal democracy as mechanisms allowing the voters to form their preferences, signal these preferences to one another and their leaders, and register such preferences in policy without considering their content and origin. More often than not, however, it works the other way around. Highly organized corporate and institutional groups with a clear awareness of their interests register their preferences in the process of governance, signifying their preferences to one another and to elected leaders and forcing the voters to form their preferences within the narrow compass of preprocessed options as they have been marked out by such institutional arrangements.[32]

This new class reading of democracy in modern liberal regimes obviously presents any communitarian, populistic, or participatory reading of democracy in a very negative light. By constructing the myth of classical democracy as an impossible set of unattainable democratic practices oriented toward maximal popular participation, communal engagement, and substantive civic virtue, the scientific scripts of modern polyarchy tend to anachronize, ironize, or patronize any contemporary efforts to revitalize communitarian behaviors or institutions that its empirical-descriptive findings have attributed to the classical mythos. Knowledge about polyarchy becomes a power to prevent democracy. Participatory democracy cannot succeed, because Susie Shopper and Joe Six-Pack, not Antigone or Pericles, would be in charge of making decisions. And "everyone knows" that they could not do as well as the existing ranks of new class managers, engineers, and administrators already apparently competently in charge. Consequently, advocates for any insurgent vision of democratic populism as the basis for living in ecological communities of independent producers start out with two strikes against them.

Different choices, however, can be made about the ways in which power, knowledge and wealth are defined and exercised. And perhaps they should be made mainly by nonelites at the immediate local level, grounded in their concrete ecological settings, rather than by various polyarchical elites working in distant government and corporate offices.[33] Similarly, by fabricating many expert-oriented narratives about modern democracy as an archive of institutionalized necessity that empowers perpetually competing elites to govern often inattentive voters with little interest in or knowledge about politics, many social science discourses legitimate the operations of a new system of administrative power in which permanent formations of bureaucratic expertise are periodically directed toward or redirected away from certain policy preferences by voters as they make changes in the elected leadership. Nominally charged to implement particular policy packages by the voters and their elected leaders, these bureaucratic experts recognize how inattentive and unknowledgeable the voters actually are, as well as how self-interested and competitive the elected officials always will be. Hence such administrative specialists will use the existing institutional arrangements to serve enduring preferences as they see them formed, signified, and registered by organized social forces or economic blocs in the larger society, which also compete as lobbies, pressure groups, or issue coalitions to win electoral support from voters and support leaders in electoral competitions. Modern democratic theory, then, normalizes a fairly stable regime for new class elite governance of the experts, by the experts, and for the experts as the outcome of preferences expressed by the voters.

Although insurgent new social movements may begin as expressions of democratic populists, the dynamics of power in modern liberal democracies, if we can trust the narratives of reality adduced by such empirical-descriptive theories of polyarchy, select only small blocs of competitive elites to compete in the leadership cycle of the existing regime. Anyone supporting democratic populist alternatives is often treated as an anachronism or irrelevance. In accepting the options of electoral competition, however, one complies with the regime, shelving a vision of popular participation and accepting voter apathy as the price of winning access to leadership sites through this type of electioneering. Indeed, the existing institutional arrangements are designed to screen out movements by destabilizing extranormal movements of popular democrats in favor of maintaining stable blocs of normalizing bureaucrats.

Instead of developing *real* alternative modes of living, working, thinking, and acting that do not presume the input of many megawatts of electrical power, millions of gallons of water, or thousands of tons of matériel simply to sustain a typical small suburban neighborhood, new class functionaries in city hall and in corporate headquarters often look to high-tech science for new large-scale "techno-fixes" to maintain the economy in the slow worsening of the ecological crisis. This thinking may provide a pretext for bureaucratic greens to tinker with some of the unprofitable and underproductive practices that are responsible for producing ecological irrationality, but it is not a radical reengineering of prevailing industrial metabolisms that will preserve a pristine ecology.

Most new class professionals and managers refuse to recognize, as the radical ecologists have for many years, that an unanticipated development, "the entropy state," has risen unexpectedly from the concatenation of managerially rational designs working in each corporate enterprise. More concretely, "the entropy state is a society at the stage when complexity and interdependence have reached the point where the transaction costs that are generated equal or exceed the society's productive capabilities."[34] Ecological resistance movements argue that advanced industrial capitalism—working in part within the territorial nation-state and in part within post-Fordist transnational networks—has reached a turning point in its development. The apparently necessary costs of maintaining the necessary throughput of goods, services, and information for these corporate metabolisms at least matches if not surpasses the input potentials of the environment's carrying capacity. This excessive demand not only endangers megatechnical polyarchy's satisfaction of its human clients' output expectations; it now also threatens to wreck entire natural biomes for centuries. By intensifying the inputs of nonrenewable energy, management, advanced technological expertise, and capital, many transnational industries have transformed the material life of a small minority of humanity. Unfortunately, the true costs of these innovations are never calculated or even considered. Instead, the invisible and external costs of advanced technologies' visible, tangible, and internal benefits are continually charged off because they cannot be adequately accounted for under nonecological modes of thinking.[35] At most they too become commodified as pollution rights to be swapped in commodity markets, along with pork bellies or wheat futures, which does not end their destruction but rather valorizes waste by permitting it to be concentrated or constrained by markets at different locations.[36]

The vaunted rational efficiency of advanced capitalist firms actually hides the gross irrationalities, such as Love Canal, acid rain, the Exxon *Valdez,* forest death, Three Mile Island, and ozone depletion, that are an *integral* and not an *accidental* part of modern life. These ecological disasters would arguably be worthwhile tradeoffs if the material utopia of abundance for all that advanced megatechnical capitalism once promised were a reality. But it is not. Instead there are still only a relative handful of highly developed regions enjoying privatized commodity consumption in Western Europe, East Asia, and North America that have based their urban industrial ecologies over the past century on despoiling the material resources of thousands of millennia. Megatechnics does not have the technical answers for developing the planet's finite fund of material, intellectual, and cultural resources for everyone in the world at levels enjoyed by the more affluent classes of the OECD countries. The miseries of Rwanda, Somalia, Bangladesh, Cambodia, Haiti, and Bolivia appear to be inescapable links of the megatechnical commodity chains now encircling the globe to sustain suburban affluence.[37]

In addition to the real scarcities that existed prior to the spread of megatechnical industrialization around the world in the 1880s, artificial scarcities are continually created by the productive processes of advanced megatechnics as it has restructured the world economy up to the 1990s. Deforestation has caused massive desertification, irrigation has led to tremendous salination of agricultural land and fresh water supplies, fossil fuel combustion has altered weather patterns and activities, chemical fertilizers and pesticides have broken food chains, cheap energy has given way to expensive energy, and corporate farm mechanization has depleted once immense stocks of arable soils.[38]

Informationalization need not serve transnational corporate firms exclusively. It also carries the potential to advance the empowerment of lay people in their everyday lives. The current order of megatechnics embedded in cold war polyarchical regimes has presupposed the increasing disempowerment of people by creating endless dependencies on technocratic experts among citizens, forcing them to become consumers and clients.[39] With the progressive colonization of more and more corners of daily life over the past century, restricted state and corporate grammars of ordinary life have been generated in the corporate commodity's and the state entitlement's "one-dimensionalization" of existence. This grammar of governmentality has stressed passivity, dependency, supervision, and uniformity as technocratic experts have packaged material goods and scripted social roles for the increasingly uniform masses of contemporary consumers, clients, and citizens. Other contragovernmental informationalized grammars of living, however, could revitalize personal activity, independence, autonomy, and diversity among many more democratic groups of ecologically empowered individuals by resisting the conduct of conduct brought to life by the new class.

In certain respects the "distribution crisis" of the last century, which has underpinned polyarchy's mass electoral politics for the last sixty years, has been "solved" only in some ways for a few effectively organized political blocs. Large and now growing pockets of poverty remain obvious in many polyarchies, and material want is a bitter fact of life outside a handful of powerful nation-states in the Northern Hemisphere. This global poverty beyond the planet's affluent zones is inextricably linked to plenty within the powerful advanced industrial countries. Distribution is still a daunting challenge, but now a key concern of polyarchies and megatechnics, "after two centuries of economic growth, is no longer the adequacy of resources or their 'efficient' allocation for maximum output."[40] Along with distribution, another basic problem for megatechnics today is connected to rationalization, or "the way that output is produced, the definition of what constitutes output, what is produced, and who decides development policy."[41]

After over a century of rapid economic growth, some of the technical and organizational challenges of struggling against material necessity under megatechnics have been met: given any set (a) of operational conditions, many industries can produce and distribute virtually any range (b) of products. However, the polyarchical leaderships of advanced megatechnic economies often are unmindful of the tough questions coming before and after that distributional problem: Who rightly should decide what *a* or which *b*? Why produce *b* with *a*? What do the production and consumption of *b* mean? How might the costs of the *a* conditions be measured? Who guarantees the "givens" and "operational conditions"? And for whose benefit is *b* produced and at what cost? Such questions about choosing ends and applying means arise from popular doubts about the overall rationality of the conduct of conduct provided by advanced corporate capitalism. The ecological populist resistance focuses on, as Marcuse proposed, "the system of profitable domination" that underlies such productivity.[42] The old logic of misconstrued economic efficiency and misstated distributional equity has not provided a completely satisfactory criteria. In addition, tremendous risks are often produced now as easily as great rewards. The existing lines of consensus on substantive ends of polyarchy and instrumental means of megatechnics, then, are no longer regarded as universally true or trustworthy.

The overall opposition of ecological populism—in different ways and on diverse levels—centers on rationalization problems, and many populist movements are driven largely by a quest to renew a communal politics around these issues. Localistic populism stands for new groups of people applying the query "Who and for whom?" to hitherto occluded aspects of contemporary megatechnics. Civilian nuclear power production is a prime case in point. The problems with rationality and equity here are multidimensional: Who says we need so much energy? For what purposes are they saying this? Who decides, and why choose this way of producing energy? Who will benefit? How will the relevant indicators of output be defined—as kilowatt hours, radiation leaks, fewer hydrocarbon pollutants, more jobs, extra cancer deaths, more electrified conveniences, or more tons of poisonous wastes that remain dangerous for centuries? What happens to these wastes? Who pays the unanticipated costs? Are the "benefits" truly beneficial? Can these costs and benefits be accurately documented or fully accounted? And who decides which criteria or discourses will define what is rational, reasonable, fair, efficient, hazardous, or safe? Here the ecological populists, like local activists in the antinuclear movement, are correct in arguing that narrow, business-biased, far-away bureaucratic forces have all too often imposed bad decisions, arrived at through faulty means, on millions of citizens, clients, and consumers who had little democratic input into those decisions or legal recourse to their unfair or harmful outcome. This kind of anonymous authoritarianism and the largely illegitimate rationalization without representation that it implies are now targeted by many circles of democratic resistance and ecological populism.

New antimegatechnic or antipolyarchical grammars of everyday life, vaguely outlined in the politics of many environmental movements, propose other, alternative futures for informationalizing societies. Local democratic movements, such as the environmental justice movement, are trying to substantively justify—in terms of procedural democratic norms and immediate economic impact—who should decide what is produced, how output is measured, and why production should be undertaken. And they seek to increase the voice, access, and control of the people who will suffer or benefit after corrective policy steps are taken. In many cases, ranging from Italy's Northern League to North America's bioregionalists, they are questioning the institutions of the modern nation-state, finding their polyarchical logic to be a major part of the problem behind megatechnics. On the one hand, the struggle against scarcity and all the problems surrounding the challenge of fair distribution are clearly not settled; on the other hand, many ecological populists are addressing new issues: the local defense of their communities' ecologies as those communities defend their cultures, lifestyles, and values against continuing corporate colonization by the megatechnical cultures of the new class.[43] In other words, most democratic populist opposition to contemporary states and firms transcends old-line labor-versus-capital conflicts within the national welfare state—it is much more ecological, populist, and localistic, making it also often more postproletarian, postindustrial, and postdistributional.

Community and Modernity: Populists versus the New Class

In the final analysis, populist critiques of new class thinking and practice bear traces of truth, but few push their doubts far enough. Instead, a thoroughgoing political critique today must return to the volatile issues of ecology. Although Lasch indicates how populism might provide an alternative political basis for new collective associations of people and things, he ignores those populist initiatives in American thought and politics that have often approximated what he hopes to realize, namely, communally grounded ecological thinking and environmental activism.[44] Different collective choices about ways in which power, knowledge, and wealth are exercised, defined, and shared can be made. Local democratic groups in ecological populist movements are one means by which changes could be made by nonelites in their immediate local context, grounded in their concrete ecological settings, rather than by new class experts working in distant government and corporate offices with little real sense of what the costs and benefits of their decisions might be.[45]

This other form of life could unfold when communities realize that many, if not almost all, of the material and symbolic foundations of new class power, and therefore popular communal powerlessness, rest on the results of technocratic choices made by distant bureaucratic and corporate agencies. The hyperecologies of megatechnics interpose specialized technical expertise and complex hierarchical organization between the production of most goods and services and the sites of their final consumption, disempowering people in their families, neighborhoods, and cities.[46]

In the 1990s the conflicted and contradictory practices of polyarchy and megatechnics have become much more obvious.[47] The cold war constellation of permanent mobilization, nuclear confrontation, and ideological competition, which anchored so much of Mumford's accounts of megatechnics, now is dissipating in the chaotic flows of the new world order. Polyarchical regimes have been under assault by new social movements since the 1960s, and megatechnical economies have been in crisis since the oil shocks of the 1970s. Nonetheless, the deep structures of both formations persist, and new initiatives to rejuvenate them, as chapters 4 and 5 argue, are always being developed.

In the eight decades since 1918, much has changed in the acts and artifacts created by modern industry, liberal democracy, and secular culture. Cultural identities that unfolded within industrial society—male wage work outside the home and female shadow work at home, bourgeois ownership and proletarian dispossession, public administration and private enterprise, national states and civil societies, scientific methods and traditional values, collective goods and individual benefits, welfare states and war machines, class conflict and national community, nature conservation and social consumption, instrumental rationality and religious morality, international relations and domestic politics—are disappointing their adherents, disintegrating in everyday use, and disrupting shared prospects for survival. Yet the intellectual frameworks commonly used for appraising these massive shifts remain trapped within categories propounded by Comte, Darwin, Durkheim, Marshall, Marx, Mill, Walras, and Weber during the seven decades before 1918, as industrial society matured into the dominant modern economic form. The choices defined by those classic accounts of economy and society centered on the imperatives of modernization: the either/or tradeoffs of progress versus stasis, modernity versus tradition, industry versus agriculture, science versus religion, nature versus culture, and civilization versus barbarism. In many ways these tradeoffs have already been made. As a result, contemporary learned debate and policy deliberations are stymied by antiquated understandings, carried away on exhausted trends, and confused before arrested revolutions because they presume these tensions remain in play.

For better or worse, many forms of populist resistance in the United States implicitly have opposed accepting categories of interpretation rooted in the workings of industrial modernity. Unlike many other political interests in the United States, most populists have recognized that today's political challenges are not explicable in the settled simplicities of either/or terms. Modernity has overcome tradition in most respects, and the syncretic hybrid aftermath of this process leaves us in a much more ambiguous time and place of neither/nor situations.

In his quest to map the contours of late capitalism, Jameson sees it operating where "the modernization process is complete and Nature is gone for good."[48] At this juncture it seems that Jameson is right: the modernization process, at least as it was understood by Durkheim, Marx, or Weber, is over, and there is no going back to what they knew and understood to be true. Thus the special sciences of economics, sociology, anthropology, philosophy, or politics, which have been built on modernization narratives of either/or, now face the entirely transformed terms of neither/nor. Here the choices are between neither unfettered modernity nor untrammeled tradition; instead, they arise out of many alternative coexisting modernities and traditions developing both globally and locally.

Since the two world wars, virtually nowhere in the world holds on to traditional formulas of authority: democracy is spreading everywhere. Since the cold war, nowhere in the world seriously holds forth as a real alternative to the market: capitalism is everywhere. These realities cannot be separated from any new critique responding to this general situation, because they are, strangely enough, key components of the contemporary environment. Anticipating perhaps the dawning of the millennium in 2000, some also see this moment as a decisive series of great endings: the end of nature, the end of history, the end of otherness.

The eclipse of otherness, history, and nature by megatechnics and polyarchy on a global scale might be misread in triumphalist terms as the foundation of Fukuyama's "coherent and directional Universal History of mankind."[49] On the other hand, it could simply indicate how these artificial forces now surround all living and nonliving things as their environment. Accordingly, Fukuyama's vision of "accumulation without end"[50] now culminates in the "omnipolitanization" of the planet seen during the past two or three decades of global economic and social development. Omnipolitanization develops, as Virilio asserts, from the hyperconcentration of urbanized values and practices in a "*world-city*, the city to end all cities," and "in these basically eccentric or, if you like, *omnipolitan* conditions, the various social and cultural realities that still constitute a nation's wealth will soon give way to a sort of 'political' *stereo-reality* in which the interaction of exchanges will no longer look any different from the—automatic—interconnection of financial markets today."[51]

Omnipolitanization may be what remains when polyarchies nearly complete the modernization process and megatechnics confirm that most of wild nature is gone for good. Economy and society, culture and politics, and science and technology acquire significant new quiddity as an artificial second nature with its own operational times and functional spaces within, over, or beyond the now lost autochthonous verities of first nature's geophysical time and space. The figures of nature, history, and otherness once guided people toward industrial modernity, but the integrative subsumption of these terms into modern industrialization now forces all beyond the old boundaries of modern industrial democracy. To see only the end of nature, history, and otherness, one falls into another either/or trap in which opposites overcome each other, annihilating, displacing, or erasing their contrapoles. In fact, opposites tend to coexist, intermingle, or meld, allowing us to see the beginning of new arrangements that come from these terms but no longer can be understood through them. Beck notes that modernization must become reflexive at this juncture: a reality that has been reaffirmed by many populist political movements of the past generation.

This discussion of populism, as a systemic critique of the new class and a critical reappraisal of technology within everyday life, implicitly endorses Beck's vision of "the risk society." Under the command, control, and communication systems of the new class, "the social production of *wealth* is systematically accompanied by the social production of *risks*," and as a result, "the problems and conflicts relating to distribution in a society of scarcity overlap with the problems and conflicts that arise from the production, definition, and distribution of techno-scientifically produced risks."[52] Modernization is forced to become reflexive in the struggles of the new class to manage people's everyday lifeworld, because it is making, and it already has remade, polyarchical megatechnics into humanity's new global environment. Although the classical narratives of rationalization underpinning modernization presume that greater command, control, communication, and intelligence will come to all from the new class's applying more rationality to life, the experiences of living amid past, ongoing, and planned exercises of such professional-technical rationalization bring many consequences beyond anyone's command, control, communication, or intelligence. The growing calculability of instrumental rationality brings along with it new measures of incalculability—unintended and unanticipated—out of instrumental irrationality. Populism, then, is a new type of popular reformation in modernity's terms and conditions. Attacking megatechnics and polyarchy is not a neo-Luddite reaction; instead, it means "the radicalization of modernity against its limitations and division in industrial society."[53]

Megatechnical living forces all of us, or everyone who is part of the vast collectives associating all people with nonhuman subjects and objects, to recognize how much the allegedly neutral technologies that many associate with "progress" are, in fact, highly political: their materialized *technē* shapes the moral praxes of politics and carries the productive effects of power as discipline, discourse, and domination. Outside the polyarchical state, the system of megatechnics is also an ethicopolitical system. This reality resonates behind all populist challenges to the megatechnical systems that form the building blocks of everyday life. When the collectives of polyarchical megatechnics become environment, a new awareness of the "rules specifying the purposes of the technology, its appropriate applications, the appropriate or legitimate owners and operators, how the results of applying the technology will be distributed and so on"[54] must be developed by people to sustain their freedoms. Each of these concerns is now being contested in populist politics, as ordinary individuals and professional-technical groups struggle with the demands of living well on the Earth and the difficulties of the Earth's well-being.

What is compelling about contemporary megatechnics is the everchanging messiness of complicated techno-economic infrastructures running just beneath, behind, and beside any nation's great, but still quite different, urban places. These turbulent world wide webs move matter, energy, and information from everywhere to anywhere while at the same time piling up much more of these goods and their services in a few places to the detriment of many other places. They work underneath, above, and apart from the polis, but they are also structures of power, systems of exchange, and signs of culture constructed by authoritative experts to operate authoritatively beyond much popular control. These subpolitical realms, as Beck indicates, are often misrepresented by locking them up within the black boxes of science and technology, but their power effects, social values, and cultural practices continue to be quite destructive and nondemocratic. These subpolitical collectives in turn constitute a "subpolis" that emerges from the imbrication of people and things as "the possibilities for social change from the collaboration of research, technology, and science accumulate," particularly when unchanging territorial jurisdictions and paralyzed political institutions ensure that the real organizational power activated by technology "*migrates from the domain of politics to that of subpolitics.*"[55]

The subpolis can be seen as the determinate point where modern technology, new class authority, and contemporary populism interlace. It is the materialized assembly of rationalization strategies under the control of the new class that "preprograms the permanent change of all realms of social life under the justifying cloak of techno-economic progress, in contradistinction to the simplest rules of democracy—knowledge of the goals of social change, discussion, voting, and consent."[56] It represents the continuous workings and fixed works of megatechnical collectives, whose operational powers are layered under politics, occluded by technologies from ordinary political understandings, and hidden from politicians by the mechanics of markets but also vested in the professional labor of new class experts to serve the needs of everyone as clients and consumers. Like the polis, the subpolis is a built environment, but its constructs are all too often depoliticized by the professional-technical rhetorics of civil engineering, public health, corporate management, scientific experiment, technical design, and property ownership. It houses the quasi objectivity of polyarchical subjects embedded in megatechnical activities, but it cannot be separated from the quasi subjectivity of objects circulating en masse in globalized economies of scale. This is also where populist resistances can strike at new class power prerogatives.

Beneath, behind, and beside the workings of polyarchical megatechnics as an environment, new populist movements belie the importance of the subpolis as a new collective, combining the coevolution of human and nonhuman life. In those contexts, the workings of modern technics and markets are "institutionalized as 'progress'" but remain subject to the dictates of "business, science, and technology, for whom democratic procedures are invalid."[57] Unlike the national-statal polis, which has been seen as a community of people situated in a specific geographical locality or particular nation-state, the subpolis is an ever-shifting assembly of ordinary people and extraordinary technics interoperating locally and globally with many other technical assemblies and people elsewhere along multi-, trans-, and supernational lines as well as within inter-, infra-, and intralocal spaces.

The realities of megatechnical living, then, should move everyone to think about and act out new political projects as the old modernizing faith of the masses in elites decays amid populist resistances against expertise. What was political no longer captures how power works; what was a-, non-, pre-, or subpolitical is where most critical decisions now are made. Populists say this, contest the rules of its operations, and push these systems for new rights, obligations, and institutions.[58] Some populism is pitched at states, parties, and bureaucracies to revitalize their workings, but much more of it is centered on the subpolis underpinning the polity. New class expertise, with its routinization of life, erasure of choice, and rationalization without representation, is what must be challenged now by populism. Instead of letting technology in the service of capital decide things, populists want to decide, putting technics in service for the people, by the people, and of the people.

On one level both polyarchy and megatechnics are being challenged by populist resistances, which stand for revitalizing classical democratic practices and economic self-reliance on a more localized, bioregional level beneath megatechnics' hyperecologies. On a second level, however, polyarchy and megatechnics, in responding to such democratic populist resistance movements, are not beyond adapting "environmental concerns" into their systems of collective administration for the subpolis. As chapters 4 and 5 also indicate, the shift to more "environmentalized" conceptions of space, time, power, and control so as to regulate the structures of consummativity could easily bring natural bioregions and artificial technoregions more closely together. On a third level, the acceptance of environmentalized discourses of stability and security, which shift from an exclusive focus on political-military "sovereignty" to a more expansive concern for economic-ecological "sustainability," may simply mark the advent of bureaucratic greens rising to prominence in the administrative apparatus of contemporary polyarchical states. So we must be cautious about current debates over ecology and politics. Agendas that sound like those of an ecological democratic populism may in fact serve as a disciplinary primer for environmentalizing bureaucratic greens. The invocation to rule "environmentally" in response to an "ecological crisis" must be seen as an interesting but potentially threatening project. As chapter 4 discloses, in addition to articulating its professed ecological goals, this project imparts tremendous powers, determines important roles, and defines major challenges to blocs of bureaucratic greens as they elaborate new knowledge, new perceptions, and new attitudes to fix a new basis for their authority over "the environment" in the polyarchical state apparatus.

Notes

1. Peter Bachrach, *The Theory of Democratic Elitism: A Critique* (Boston: Little Brown, 1967).

2. For the U.S. government's initial alarmist analysis of the environmental crisis, see the Council on Environmental Quality, *Environmental Quality: The First Annual Report of the Council on Environmental Quality* (Washington, D.C.: U.S. Governmental Printing Office, 1970).

3. Albert Gore, *Earth in the Balance: Ecology and the Human Spirit* (Boston: Houghton Mifflin, 1992), 304–5.

4. See Timothy W. Luke, *Social Theory and Modernity: Dissent, Critique, and Revolution* (Newbury Park, Calif.: Sage, 1990), 159–82.

5. Joseph A. Schumpeter, *Capitalism, Socialism, and Democracy* (London: Allen and Unwin, 1943), 242.

6. Ibid., 269.

7. See Murray Bookchin, *The Rise of Urbanization and the Decline of Citizenship* (San Francisco: Sierra Club Books, 1987); and Christopher Lasch, *The True and Only Heaven: Progress and Its Critics* (New York: Norton, 1991).

8. Schumpeter, *Capitalism, Socialism, and Democracy,* 250.

9. Ibid., 253–54.

10. Robert Dahl, *Preface to Democratic Theory* (Chicago: University of Chicago Press, 1956).

11. Robert Dahl, *Polyarchy: Participation and Opposition* (New Haven, Conn.: Yale University Press, 1971), 2.

12. Ibid., 3–4.

13. Dahl, *Preface,* 149–51.

14. See Kenneth Arrow, *Social Choice and Individual Values* (New Haven, Conn.: Yale University Press, 1951); Anthony Downs, *An Economic Theory of Democracy* (New York: Harper and Row, 1957); C. Wright Mills, *Power, Politics, and People: Collected Essays* (New York: Oxford University Press, 1963); Christian Bay, "Politics and Pseudo-Politics," *American Political Science Review* 59 (March 1965): 1–18; Bachrach, *Theory of Democratic Elitism;* Brian Barry, *Sociologists, Economists, and Democracy* (Chicago: University of Chicago Press, 1970); and Carole Pateman, *Participation and Democratic Theory* (Cambridge: Cambridge University Press, 1970).

15. See Robert B. Reich, *The Work of Nations: Preparing Ourselves for Twenty-first Century Capitalism* (New York: Knopf, 1991).

16. See Timothy W. Luke, "Liberal Society and Cyborg Subjectivity: The Politics of Environments, Bodies, and Nature," *Alternatives: A Journal of World Policy* 21, no. 1 (1996): 1–30.

17. See Jürgen Habermas, *Legitimation Crisis* (Boston: Beacon, 1975).

18. For more on this view of the new class, see Christopher Lasch, *The Revolt of the Elites and the Betrayal of Democracy* (New York: Norton, 1995), 3–49.

19. See Ben Agger, *Discourse of Domination* (Evanston, Ill.: Northwestern University Press, 1992).

20. Lewis Mumford, *The Myth of the Machine: The Pentagon of Power* (New York: Harcourt Brace Jovanovich, 1970), 236–37.

21. Ibid., 237, 236, 245.

22. Ibid., 259.

23. Ibid., 253–54.

24. Ibid., 324.

25. See Wendell Berry, *Meeting the Expectations of the Land: Essays in Sustainable Agriculture and Stewardship* (San Francisco: North Point, 1984); and idem, *The Unsettling of America: Culture and Agriculture* (New York: Avon, 1977).

26. D. J. McMichael, *Planetary Overload: Global Environmental Change and the Health of the Human Species* (Cambridge: Cambridge University Press, 1993); Herman Daly, *For the Common Good* (Boston: Beacon, 1990).

27. Mumford, *Myth of the Machine,* 322.

28. Ibid.

29. Ibid.

30. See James Coleman, *Foundations of Social Theory* (Cambridge, Mass.: Harvard University Press, 1990).

31. Timothy W. Luke, "Reason and Rationality in Rational Choice Theory," *Social Research* 52 (Spring 1985): 65–98.

32. See Susan Herbst, *Numbered Voices: How Opinion Polling Has Shaped American Politics* (Chicago: University of Chicago Press, 1993); Stanley A. Deetz, *Democracy in an Age of Corporate Colonization* (Albany: State University of New York Press, 1992); John R. Zaller, *The Nature and Origins of Mass Opinion* (Cambridge: Cambridge University Press, 1992); Benjamin Ginsberg, *The Captive Public* (New York: Basic, 1986); and Elisabeth Noelle-Neumann, *The Spiral of Silence: Public Opinion—Our Social Skin* (Chicago: University of Chicago Press, 1984).

33. See, for example, Murray Bookchin, *Toward an Ecological Society* (Montreal: Black Rose, 1980); as well as William Foote White and Kathleen King White, *Making Mondragon: The Growth and Dynamics of the Worker Cooperative Complex,* 2d ed., rev. (Ithaca, N.Y.: Institute of Labor Research Press, 1991); and Roy Morrison, *We Build the Road as We Travel* (Philadelphia: New Society, 1991).

34. Hazel Henderson, "The Entropy State," *Creating Alternative Futures: The End of Economics* (New York: Berkley Windhover, 1978), 83.

35. For further discussion, see Richard J. Barnet and John Cavanaugh, *Global Dreams: Imperial Corporations and the New World Order* (New York: Simon and Schuster, 1994); Richard J. Barnet, *The Lean Years: Politics in the Age of Scarcity* (New York: Simon and Schuster, 1980); William Ophuls, *Ecology and the Politics of Scarcity*

(San Francisco: Freeman, 1977); and Leopold Kohr, *The Breakdown of Nations* (New York: Dutton, 1957).

36. For some consideration of this commodification of pollution, see Frances Cairncross, *Costing the Earth: The Challenges for Governments, the Opportunities for Business* (Boston: Harvard Business School Press, 1991); and Robert Costanza, ed., *Ecological Economics: The Science and Management of Sustainability* (New York: Columbia University Press, 1991).

37. Widening and deepening inequality is now the hallmark of economies and societies under the managerial charge of new class experts. Indeed, 85 percent of the planet's overall gross national product, 85 percent of world trade, and 85 percent of domestic savings are accounted for every year by only the wealthiest fifth of all nation-states. The other 80 percent of the world's countries limp along on the leftovers of this tremendous material inequality. See Hans-Peter Martin and Harald Schumann, *The Global Trap: Globalization and the Assault on Democracy and Prosperity* (London: Zed:, 1997), 29. For more discussions of environmental consciousness and ecological exploitation around the world, see Winthrop P. Carty and Elizabeth Lee, *The Rhino Man and Other Uncommon Environmentalists* (Washington, D.C.: Seven Locks, 1992); and John McCormick, *Reclaiming Paradise: The Global Environmental Movement* (Bloomington: Indiana University Press, 1989).

38. Additional consideration can be found in Andrew Goudie, *The Human Impact on the Natural Environment*, 4th ed. (Cambridge, Mass: MIT Press, 1994).

39. For more analysis of this point, see Timothy W. Luke, *Screens of Power: Ideology, Domination, and Resistance in Informational Society* (Urbana: University of Illinois Press, 1989).

40. Martin Carnoy, *The State and Political Theory* (Princeton, N.J.: Princeton University Press, 1984), 3. Addressing this issue, Herbert Marcuse claims, "In the contemporary era, the conquest of scarcity is still confined to small areas of advanced industrial society. Their prosperity covers up the Inferno inside and outside their borders; it also spreads a repressive productivity and 'false needs.' It is repressive precisely to the degree to which it promotes the satisfaction of needs which require continuing the rat race of catching up with one's peers and with planned obsolescence, enjoying freedom from using the brain, working with and for the means of destruction. The obvious comforts generated by this sort of productivity, and even more, the support which it gives to a system of profitable domination, facilitate its importation in less advanced areas of the world where the introduction of such a system still means tremendous progress in technical and human terms" (*One-Dimensional Man* [Boston: Beacon, 1964], 241).

41. Carnoy, *The State*, 3.

42. Marcuse, *One-Dimensional Man*, 241.

43. See Klaus Eder, *The New Politics of Class: Social Movements and Cultural Dynamics in Advanced Societies* (London: Sage, 1993), for sociological class analysis of such popular resistance movements.

44. Lasch, *True and Only Heaven,* 509–32.

45. See, for example, Paul Piccone, "Paradoxes of *Perestroika,*" *Telos* 84 (Summer 1990): 3–32; Paul Piccone and G. L. Ulmen, "Schmitt's 'Testament' and the Future of Europe," *Telos* 83 (Spring 1990): 3–34; and Harry C. Boyte and Frank Riessman, eds., *The New Populism: The Politics of Empowerment* (Philadelphia: Temple University Press, 1986), 111–73.

46. For these points in another register, see Daniel Bell, *The Coming of Post-Industrial Society* (New York: Basic, 1973); and Zbigniew Brzezinski, *Between Two Ages: America's Role in the Technetronic Era* (New York: Viking, 1970).

47. For additional discussion, see Kevin Phillips, *The Politics of Rich and Poor: Wealth and the American Electorate in the Reagan Aftermath* (New York: Random House, 1990), 3–32; and Reich, *The Work of Nations.*

48. Fredric Jameson, *Postmodernism, or The Cutural Logic of Late Capitalism* (Durham, N.C.: Duke University Press, 1991), ix.

49. Francis Fukuyama, *The End of History and the Last Man* (New York: Free Press, 1992), xxiii.

50. Ibid., 89–97.

51. Paul Virilio, *Open Sky* (London: Verso, 1997), 75.

52. Ulrich Beck, *The Risk Society: Towards a New Modernity* (London: Sage, 1992), 19.

53. Ulrich Beck, *The Reinvention of Politics* (Cambridge: Polity, 1997), 60.

54. Beck, *Risk Society,* 209.

55. Ibid., 223.

56. Ibid., 184.

57. Ibid., 14.

58. See Christopher H. Foreman Jr., *The Promise and the Peril of Environmental Justice* (Washington, D.C.: Brookings Institution Press, 1998), for more critical discussion of these issues.

4 On Environmentality: Geopower and Ecoknowledge in Contemporary Environmental Discourse

This chapter continues exploring how discourses of nature, ecology, or the environment, as disciplinary articulations of "ecoknowledge," can be mobilized by professional-technical experts in contemporary polyarchies to generate "geopower" over nature (but also within and through it) for the megatechnical governance of modern economies and societies. The thought of Michel Foucault, particularly his vision of productive power operating in discursively formed discipline through many variegated regimes of truth, provides a basis for advancing this reinterpretation, because many of the operational practices associated with "the environment" are perplexing until one puts them under a critical lens. Such dynamics have been at play for nearly 130 years, or since self-conscious ecological discourses were formulated by George Marsh and Ernst Haeckel in the nineteenth century, but their effects are increasingly apparent today.[1]

Many examples might be mobilized here, but this examination of geopower systems as new governmental codes, or a regime of "environmentality," will center on one illustrative case, the work of the Worldwatch Institute. The continuous attempt to reinvent the forces of nature in the economic exploitation of advanced technologies, linking biophysical or geophysical structures to the rational management of their energies as geopower, seems to be an ongoing supplement to the disciplinary construction of various modes of biopower in promoting the growth of human populations.[2] Directed at generating geopower from the more rational insertion of natural and artificial bodies into the machinery of production, discourses of environmentality can be seen refabricating natural environments as those sites where power/knowledge operates as ensembles of geopower and ecoknowledge.

In and of itself, nature is meaningless until humans assign meanings to it by interpreting some or all of its many apparent signs as meaningful. The outcomes of this activity, however, are indeterminate. Because different human beings will observe its varying patterns with different emphases, accentuating some while ignoring others, nature's meanings always will be multiple and unfixed.[3] These interpretive acts, then, can construct only contestable textual fields, which will be read on various levels of expression for their many manifest and latent meanings. Before technologies turn its matter and energy into products, nature is already transformed discursively into "natural resources." Once it is rendered intelligible through such semantic reactions, it can be used to legitimize almost anything.

Some caution, however, is essential. Over the past three decades, natural places and processes (a.k.a. "the environment" or "ecology," or sometimes even still "nature") have been portrayed as suffering from extraordinary new abuse at the hands of humans. The natural environment is often cast as either being completely engulfed by economic crises or becoming the material spoils at the center of the most pressing political struggles of this era. Such discourses typically maintain that the struggles to amend these abnormalities with corrective countermeasures, such as sustainable development, balanced growth or ecological responsibility, are the most "meaningful" human project of our time.

Just as we might doubt claims made by Aristotle, Hobbes, Smith, Rousseau, or Spencer when their respective rhetorics of nature are deployed to legitimize particular programs for attaining unjust cultural values, economic institutions, or political choices, so too must we critically reread contemporary accounts of nature caught up in describing the challenges of "the environmental crisis." We must reexamine the discursive uses and conceptual definitions of some common theoretical notions, such as the environment, environmentalism, and environmentalist, to reconsider the ways in which many contemporary environmentalists are giving a new look to the concept of the environment by transforming its meaning in the practices of "environmentality." Finally, additional doubts must be raised about the apparently benign intentions of most environmental actions, given the disciplinary propensities in this environmentality regime.

To justify such caution, this study of geopower and ecoknowledge will look again at the work of the Worldwatch Institute. Established in 1974 amid the economic and political panic sparked by the OPEC oil crisis of 1973, the Worldwatch Institute might be dismissed as just another nest of D.C. policy wonks turning out position papers on water scarcity, reforestation, windmill economics, and overpopulation. Even though this image of the Worldwatchers is accurate, it is incomplete. Given such incompleteness, "worldwatching" ought not to be quickly ignored or easily dismissed, because these activities often disclose the workings of power/knowledge formations. Consequently, this chapter also briefly unpacks a recent Worldwatch Institute publication, *Saving the Planet: How to Shape an Environmentally Sustainable Society,* by Lester Brown, Christopher Flavin, and Sandra Postel, to illustrate how the ecoknowledge generated by the Worldwatch Institute can be reinterpreted as a multilayered mediation of this new regime of geopower.[4]

Ecodiction: Making Nature Speak as "Environment"

Many individuals who are intent on making the world into "a better place to live" often turn to nature to make their improvements. Believing that they must do anything to protect the environment, they transform this undertaking into a moral crusade. Their struggles are often hobbled by a fundamental lack of clarity about what the environment *is,* because the exact meaning of this term remains elusive, vague, or even nonexistent. *Environment, environmentalism,* and *environmentalist* are accepted so broadly now that it is difficult to remember how recently they came into such wide currency. Before 1960 their use in ordinary discussion of policy issues was quite rare. More suggestive terms, such as *nature, conservation,* or *ecology,* were deployed typically in references about the characteristics of the environmental. A generation, later in the 1990s, nature in these discourses might occasionally appear as *nature,* but its presence increasingly is marked as the *environment.* This twist is interesting inasmuch as the various meanings of *nature,* while remaining fully contestable, are somewhat more clear. The meanings of *environment,* on the other hand, usually are essentially uncontested, but they remain very unclear. Finding a documentary register of this shifting usage is not an exact practice, but to start, one might look back through newspaper indexes, dictionaries, or expert discourses to develop a sense of the shifts.

The yearly index for the *New York Times* begins to suggest something about the term *environment.* In 1960, the year when Rachel Carson's *New Yorker* essays first drew broad public attention to the manner in which pesticides were despoiling wildlife, there is only one story in the index about environmental science, and it ties the topic to astronautics. Five years earlier, in 1955, the word is not even registered in the index, but by 1965 there are four entries for *environment,* one of them about an LBJ speech on the need for greater efforts at conservation and beautification in preserving the environment. By 1970 there are almost two and a half pages of citations. More important, the concept remains a significant feature in the index during every year after 1970: one and two-thirds pages in 1975, one and a third in 1980, two pages in 1985, and three and a third in 1990. Even though more attention is being allotted in the *New York Times* to what is broadly labeled as "environmental" or "environmentalistic," what *environment* means in the index is less clear. It encompasses nature, conservation, and ecology as well as pollution, deforestation, and contamination.

Dictionary definitions rarely provide any definitive diction, but they do register drifting variations in textual expressions as words accumulate new uses over time. Even though *environment* is cited as a framing influence or constraining force in hard sciences such as biology and geology as far back as Darwin, Haeckel, Malthus, or Marsh, an ecological construction of these dimly understood relations surfaces only in the 1960s. Even then, it does not become wholly articulate in the current senses of the term until the 1980s. In *Webster's Collegiate Dictionary,* fifth edition (1948), for example, the environment is "that which environs; surroundings; the aggregate of all the external conditions and influences affecting the life and development of an organism, etc., human behavior, society, etc." These allusions to the totality of influences impinging on a person, organism, or society as the general meaning of *environment* are also marked fifteen years earlier in the *Oxford English Dictionary* (1933). The environment is understood there as "the conditions under which any person or thing lives or is developed," as well as "the sum-total of influences which modify and determine the development of life or character." In other words, the definition of the environment as everything and anything that influences the existence of some entity is cast as having a biological quality or zoological dimension, but an ecological spin is not easily documented in this mix of meanings.

The *Oxford American Dictionary* in 1979 defines *environment* as "surroundings, especially those affecting people's lives"; it provides an adjectival form, *environmental,* and frames a new noun with an ecological spin: *environmentalist,* "a person who seeks to protect or improve the environment." The 1984 *Webster's II New Riverside University Dictionary* echoes and amplifies these understandings by noting that *environment* means "surroundings" but extending this to include "the combination of external or extrinsic physical conditions affecting and influencing the growth and development of organisms," as well as "the complex of social and cultural conditions affecting the nature of an individual or community." Fifteen years after the first Earth Day, which recast environmentalism as the political agency of environmental (used here in the sense of nature) protection, environmentalism remains defined in dictionaries as primarily a variation in epistemological doctrines. Only in *Webster's Ninth Collegiate Dictionary* (1990) does *environment* get defined as "the complex of physical, chemical, and biotic factors . . . that act upon an organism or an ecological community and ultimately determine its form and survival," whereas *environmentalism* is identified more fully as "advocacy of the preservation or improvement of the natural environment; *esp:* the movement to control pollution."

Despite the talk about its importance, the environment escapes exacting definition. References to it in professional discussions also show that its meanings are not clearly articulated in expert "environmentalist" discourses. For almost any given ecological writer, the significance of the environment and environmentalism is now apparently assumed to be so obvious that precise definitions are superfluous. Penelope and Charles ReVelle, in their text *The Environment: Issues and Choices for Society,* for example, name their book after the environment, but they fail to include any definition of what it means in their book's glossary or analysis.[5] Rogene Buchholz, in *Principles of Environmental Management: The Greening of Business,* does not define the environment as a vital concept in ecology, even though he recounts standard dictionary definitions, presenting it as the surroundings that are natural organisms' ecological settings.[6] When the environment is defined by experts, then, it basically comes to encompass everything. Bernard Nebel, for example, in his *Environmental Science: The Way the World Works,* follows this fashion by identifying the environment as "the combination of all things and factors external to the individual or population of organisms in question."[7] Given such nonexistent, derivative, or vague understandings of *environment,* it becomes more interesting as to how and why *nature, biosphere,* or *ecological systems* can easily circulate in rough and ready exchange as conceptual equivalents for the term.

This tendency marks the work of explicitly political analyses of the environment. Even Barry Commoner, whose political thinking on environmental problems from the 1960s through the 1990s has won wide respect, takes this path. Commoner does not directly confront the concept of the environment; instead he divides nature into "two worlds: the natural ecosphere, the thin skin of air, water, and soil and the plants and animals that live in it, and the man-made technosphere," which now has become "sufficiently large and intense to alter the natural processes that govern the ecosphere. And in turn, the altered ecosphere threatens to flood our great cities, dry up our bountiful farms, contaminate our food and water, and poison our bodies—catastrophically diminishing our ability to provide for basic human needs."[8] Commoner depicts these two worlds as being "at war." As humans in the technosphere disrupt the ecosphere, the ecosphere responds with equally or more disruptive secondary effects in the technosphere. In some sense the environment is nature for Commoner, but it is also society, or perhaps more accurately, a new composite of nature-as-transformed-by-society. The prospect of something like geopower emerging from expert intellectual interventions is foreshadowed by his critiques. In fact, geopower might be seen as the technified means of productively fusing the technosphere with the biosphere through the right codes of ecoknowledge. Commoner stresses this interpretation in *The Closing Circle* when he claims that "the environment is, so to speak, the house created on the earth *by* living things, *for* living things."[9] This representation of the environment as life's house, however, does little more than reduce it to a biophysical housing of all living things—or, again, the setting that surrounds organisms. Hence environmentalism becomes the practice of more rationally or justly running this house created by living things for living things.

This curiously unclear situation can be tracked past Commoner to Carson's original call for greater environmental awareness. *Silent Spring,* which appeared in *The New Yorker* in 1960 and as a book in 1962, largely directed its analysis at "the web of life" rather than "the environment."[10] In reexamining how unregulated application of chemical pesticides adversely affected biotic communities in the world's overlapping and interconnecting food chains, Carson constructed a provisional reading of the environment. Some substances from the technosphere, chemical pesticides, were invented to kill something in the biosphere, animal pests. Although their application was intended to control only those animals that ate crops, carried disease, and infested dwellings, their impact was much broader. Pesticides soon spread through everything in the ecosphere—both human technosphere and nonhuman biosphere—returning from the "out there" of natural environments and moving into plant, animal, and human bodies situated in the "in here" of artificial environments with unintended, unanticipated, and unwanted negative effects. By using zoological, toxicological, epidemiological, and ecological insights, Carson generated a new sense of how the environment might be seen. However, she never posed her analysis directly on a formalized notion of the environment or environmental damage.

The absence of the environment as a concept in well-respected analyses of nature, ecology, and environmental discourse also appears in Donald Worster's *Nature's Economy: The Roots of Ecology.*[11] By centering his presentation on ecology and nature, Worster stresses how thermodynamic and bioeconomic paradigms have gradually moved most schools of ecological reasoning away from organicist outlooks. The book includes social notions of ways in which environmental damage, environmental impacts, and environmental concern have changed, but all these phrases are used without any clearly articulated differentiation of the terms' meanings. This vacuum fills immense expanses in many more recent considerations of environmental politics, policy, and problems. Anna Bramwell's careful analysis *Ecology in the Twentieth Century: A History* does not explicitly refer to the environment in the text or the index, even though it liberally uses the term to account for social approaches to ecology.[12] Robert Paehlke's *Environmentalism and the Future of Progressive Politics* (1989) spends nearly three hundred pages discussing environmentalist politics, ideology, and movements but never really gets around to defining what the environment actually is.[13] Max Oelschlaeger's *Idea of Wilderness* (1991) elaborately explores the notions of wilderness, nature, and ecology, yet it too does not explicitly articulate the identity and meaning of the environment.[14] Even Robyn Eckersley's *Environmentalism and Political Theory: Toward an Ecocentric Approach* (1992), which frets about environmental degradation as it reexamines environmentalism as political theory, never directly addresses what the environment is or even how the notion is used.[15] What *environment,* or *environmental,* means for these authors remains occluded by undisclosed assumptions.

The environment also preoccupies the reasoning in deep ecological narratives. *Deep Ecology: Living As If Nature Mattered,* by Bill Devall and George Sessions, consciously sets deep ecology at the center of the environmental movement, while it also attempts to fabricate an ecological position that is deeper, broader, and more profound than that allegedly propounded by mere "reform environmentalism."[16] In the face of environmental degradation, they urge readers to embrace the merits of wilderness consciousness and ecotopian alternatives against contemporary transnational capitalist economies. Nevertheless, their understanding of the environment remains an elusive notion, packed haphazardly into the notions of wilderness, bioregion, and nature advanced by deep ecology. Warwick Fox's *Toward a Transpersonal Ecology: Developing New Foundations for Environmentalism* also centers its discussions on environmentalist struggles to halt environmental damage.[17] Fox evades the issue by doubting that definitions of *environment* can even be made in terms representing it as "the *external* conditions or surroundings of organisms," because these "rigid distinctions that we tend to draw between ourselves and our environment" need to be replaced by an integrative ecological consciousness interrelating the two.[18] One wonders whether we ought to know what we are integrating before we actually fuse ourselves with it.

Roderick Nash, in *Wilderness and the American Mind,* does discuss environmentalism. He indexes the topic of environment in the book, but the entry recommends that the reader see also *conservation* and *ecology* to frame the concept. The environment is not explicitly defined in the analysis of wilderness, even though Nash records how the U.S. concern for conservation in resource use or preservation of beautiful scenery shifted policies toward worrying about "the survival of the ecosystem" and "the health of the total environment."[19] In *The Rights of Nature: A History of Environmental Ethics* (1989), Nash's title belies his definition of environment.[20] The index reads "environment. *See* Nature," and the elaboration of environmental ethics boils down to "the idea that morality ought to include the relationship of humans to nature."[21] This implicit conflation of the environment with nature or ecology in Nash's thinking is indicative of most discussions of the environment, at least those where any effort is made to define it. The environment is considered to be so immediately obvious that definition would be superfluous.

As these indexes, dictionaries, and experts indicate, all concepts, including those of the environment, environmentalism, and environmentalist, can be deployed loosely. As one might expect, the usages of the relevant terms show that they tend to mean various things to many people in several different contexts. Another approach to this problem might return to the term's early origins, hoping to reveal other embedded understandings of the environment that could be even more suggestive. The obvious ambiguities in *environment,* which often encompass virtually everything they can by citing a wide range of characteristics, such as *all* surroundings, *every* factor that affects organisms, the *totality* of circumstances, or the *sum* complex of conditions, need clarification.

On Environing

The separation of organisms from their environments is the primary conceptual divide cut through reality by the rhetorics of ecology.[22] This discursive turn goes back to Haeckel's initial identification of ecology in 1866 as the positive science that investigates all relations of an organism to its organic and inorganic environments. Nonetheless, there are differences among ecologists over what these environments might be. Because the expanses of the organic and inorganic environment are total, it often is defined in conceptual terms, delimiting what it *is* by looking at what it *is not.* In other words, ecologists center the organism, or biotic community, or local ecosystems within their system of study, while the environment is reduced to everything outside of, but still acting on, what is centered as the subject of analysis. With these maneuvers environments are often transformed rhetorically into silences, backgrounds, or settings.

Environmental analysis tries to reduce "everything" in nature to measures of "anything" available for measurement in metrics accepted as legitimate by society, such as temperature levels, gas concentrations, molecular dispersions, resource stocks, or growth rates, to track variations in "something," such as an organism's, a biome's or a river's responses to the variables being measured. Is it the environment that is being understood here, however, or is identity being manufactured by reducing the environment to a subset of practicable measurements? Although the term is used to characterize human relationships with their surroundings, the concept of the environment rarely captures the whole quality or entire quantity of human beings' interrelations with all the terrains, waters, climates, soils, architectures, technologies, societies, economies, cultures, or states surrounding them. In its most expansive applications, the environment becomes a strong but sloppy force: it is anything out there, everything around us, something affecting us, nothing within us, but also a thing on which we act.

Perhaps the origins of the environment as a concept, its historical emergence and original applications as a word in the English language, might prove useful here. This analytical move is not made to uncover a stable essence; it simply reilluminates qualities that accompany the term from its earliest origins. In this original sense, which is borrowed by English from Old French, an environment is the result of the action signaled by the verb *to environ.* Environing as a verb is in fact a type of military, police, or strategic action. To environ is to encircle, encompass, envelope, or enclose. It is the physical activity of surrounding, circumscribing, or ringing around something. Its use even suggests stationing guards around, thronging with hostile intent, or standing watch over some person or place. To environ a site or a subject is to beset, beleaguer, or besiege that place or person.

An environment, as either the means of such activity or the product of these actions, can now be read in a more suggestive manner, especially in the light of the methods through which environmental knowledge is produced and consumed. It is the encirclement, circumscription, or beleaguerment of places and persons in a strategic disciplinary policing of space. An environmental act is already a disciplining move aimed at constructing some expanse of space—a locale, a biome, or a planet as biospheric space, as well as some city, any region, or the global economy in technospheric territory—in a discursive envelope of policing. Within these enclosures environmental expertise can arm environmental activists, policymakers, or regulators, who all stand watch in such surroundings, guarding the rings that include or exclude forces, agents, and ideas.

The original uses of the environment give an apt account of what is happening in many environmental practices today. Environmentalized places become sites of regulatory supervision where environmentalists see from above and without through the enveloping designs of resource managerialist systems. Encircled by enclosures of alarm, environments can be disassembled, recombined, and subjected to the disciplinary designs of expert management from the state, corporations, and science. Persons who are "in authority," or some individual who might be "an authority," are the agents who define environments. Once enveloped in these interpretive frames, environments can be redirected to fulfill the ends of other new scientific scripts, managerial directives, and administrative writs. All environing actions, then, engender environmentality, which infiltrates instrumental rationalities into the productive policing of ecological spaces.

Environmentality and Governmentality

These thoughts on the meaning of the environment reframe ecology inside the practices of power. One can argue that biopower formation, as it is described by Foucault, was not focused on nature in the equations of biopolitics.[23] The controlled tactics of inserting human bodies into the machineries of industrial and agricultural production to strategically adjust the growth of human populations to the development of industrial capitalism, however, did generate biopower. Under such developmental regimes, power/knowledge systems bring "life and its mechanisms into the realm of explicit calculations," remaking many disciplines of knowledge and discourses of power into institutionalized agencies as part of the "transformation of human life."[24] Once this threshold was crossed, some more apprehensive observers began to recognize how thoroughly and continually human economies and technologies put in question the existence of humans as living beings.

Foucault notes that these industrial transformations implicitly raised ecological issues, because they disrupted and redistributed the conventional understandings provided by the classical episteme for defining human interactions with nature. Living became "environmentalized" as modernity remade human beings into modern "man," "a specific living being . . . specifically related to other living beings," whose history and biological life was sustained in new megamachinic ways from within huge artificial cities and complex mechanical modes of production.[25] That is, the "biohistory" of modernizing society "through which the movements of life and the processes of history interfere with another" coupled nature/society into a dual position "that placed it at the same time outside history, in its biological environment, and inside human historicity, penetrated by the latter's techniques of knowledge and power."[26] Foucault does not develop this insight, because he believes "there is no need to lay further stress on the proliferation of political technologies that ensued, investing the body, health, modes of subsistence and habitation, living conditions, the whole space of existence" in the economies of biopower.[27]

Perhaps this is where the organism and the environment emerge as observables for modern environmental science. Such terms provide a determinate nexus of knowledge formation or a cluster of power tactics. As human beings begin to consciously wager their life as a species on the outcomes of these biopolitical strategies and technological systems, a few saw how this "man" of modernity also was wagering the lives of other or all species as well. Foucault regards this shift as one of many interesting lacunae in his analysis of biopower, but it is clear there is much more going on here. Human biopower systems embed their operations in the biological environment, penetrating the workings of many ecosystems with the techniques of knowledge and power of "man"—the knower and doer who defines himself through progress attained by such knowledge and power. Once human power/knowledge formations become the foundation of industrial economic development, they also become a material basis on which terrestrial lifeforms survive. In other words, ecological analysis emerges as one more productive power formation, disciplinary knowledge system, or strategic political technology that reinvests human bodies—their means of health, modes of subsistence, and styles of habitation integrating the whole space of existence—with biohistorical significance by framing them within their biophysical environments filled with various animal and plant bodies. Thus Foucault divides "the environmental" into two separate but interpenetrating spheres of action: the biological and the historical. For most of human history, the biological dimension, forces of nature working in the forms of disease and famine, dominated human existence with the ever-present menace of death. Developments in agricultural technologies as well as hygiene and health sciences, however, gradually provided some relief from starvation and plague by the end of the eighteenth century. As a result the historical dimension grew in importance as "the development of the different fields of knowledge concerned with life in general, the improvement of agricultural techniques, and the observations and measures relative to man's life and survival contributed to this relaxation: a relative control over life averted some of the imminent risks of death."[28]

With the coevolution of human and nonhuman beings in the environmental, the historical began to envelope, circumscribe, or surround "the biological." Environmentalized settings became a new emergent reality: "In the space of movement thus conquered, and broadening and organizing that space, methods of power and knowledge assumed responsibility for the life processes and undertook to control and modify them."[29] Although Foucault does not explicitly define these spaces, methods, and knowledges as being "environmental," such discursive maneuvers are the point of origin for many human projects that feed into environmentalization. As biological existence is refracted through economic, political, and technological existence, hitherto natural "facts of life" pass into the force fields of artificial control in the form of ecoknowledge, creating spheres of intervention for geopower.

Environments, therefore, emerge with biopower as an essential part of the constituting of modern "man," who becomes the pretext for regulating life via biopolitics. For nearly a century of industrial revolution, Earth's ecologies apparently remained another ancillary correlate of biopower, inhabiting discourses about species extinction, resource conservation, and overpopulation. Nonetheless, until the productive power regime of biopolitics became fully globalized (because nature itself is not entirely encircled), ecology was a fairly minor voice in the disciplinary chorus organizing development and growth. Things changed around the time of World War I, however, once the extensive expansionist strategies of development and growth employed in the eighteenth and nineteenth centuries collapsed, promoting the spread of conservationist ethics in Europe and North America, which fretted over conserving resources for these new resource-driven modes of intensive capitalist production. In addition, as new mediations of development and growth were constructed after 1945, the geopower-ecoknowledge nexus of environmentalized regulation comfortably supplemented the high-technology, capital-intensive development strategies that were implemented.

The environment, if one follows Foucault, should not be understood as the given natural sphere of ecological processes that human society tries to keep under control or as a mysterious domain of obscure terrestrial events that human knowledge works to explain.[30] Instead it emerges as a historical artifact that is openly constructed by power/knowledge systems; it cannot survive as an occluded reality beyond human comprehension. In this great productive network of power effects and knowledge claims, the simulation of spaces, the intensification of resources, the incitement of discoveries, the formation of special knowledges, the strengthening of controls, and the provocation of resistances can all be linked to one another.

The immanent designs of nature, when and where they are "discovered" in environments, closely parallel the arts of government. In fact, the two begin to merge in geopower/ecoknowledge systems. As Foucault sees the arts of government, they are essentially concerned with ways to introduce economy into the political practices of the state. In the eighteenth century government became the designation of a "level of reality, a field of intervention, through a series of complex processes" in which "government is the right disposition of things."[31] Governmentality applies the techniques of instrumental rationality to the arts of everyday management. It evolves as an elaborate social formation, "a triangle, sovereignty-discipline-government, which has as its primary target the population and as its essential mechanism the apparatuses of security."[32]

Foucault shows state authorities mobilizing governmentality to bring about "the emergence of population as a datum, as a field of intervention and as an objective of governmental techniques, and the process which isolates the economy as a specific sector of reality" so that "the population is the object that government must take into account in all its observations and *savoir,* in order to be able to govern effectively in a rational and conscious manner."[33] The networks of continuous, multiple, and complex interaction between populations (their increase, longevity, health, etc.), territory (its expanse, resources, control, etc.), and wealth (its creation, productivity, distribution, etc.) are sites where governmentalizing rationality can manage the productive interaction of all these forces.

Foucault does not reduce the ensembles of modernizing development to a "statalization" of society wherein the state becomes an expansive set of managerial functions, discharging its effects in the development of productive forces, the reproduction of relations of production, or the organization of ideological superstructures. He instead investigates the "governmentalization" of the economy and society, showing how individuals and groups are enmeshed within the tactics and strategies of a complex form of power whose institutions, procedures, analyses, and techniques loosely manage mass populations and their surroundings in highly politicized symbolic and material economies. Although it is an inexact set of bearings, Foucault asserts:

> This governmentalization of the state is a singularly paradoxical phenomenon, since if in fact the problems of governmentality and the techniques of government have become the only political issue, the only real space for political struggle and contestation, this is because the governmentalization of the state is at the same time what has permitted the state to survive, and it is possible to suppose that if the state is what it is today, this is so precisely thanks to this governmentality, which is at once internal and external to the state, since it is the tactics of government which make possible the continual definition and redefinition of what is within the competence

> of the state and what is not, the public versus the private, and so on; thus the state can only be understood in its survival and its limits on the basis of the general tactics of governmentality.[34]

Because governmental techniques are the central focus of political struggle, the interactions of populations with their natural surroundings in highly developed economies compel states to redefine constantly what is within their operational competence through their command over the modernizing process. To survive in a world marked by decolonization, global industrialization, and military confrontation, it is not enough for states merely to maintain legal jurisdiction over their allegedly sovereign territories. As ecological limits to growth are either discovered or defined, states are forced to guarantee their populations' fecundity and productivity in the total setting of the global political economy by becoming "environmental protection agencies."

As a result, governmentality discourse generates "truths" or "knowledges" that constitute forms of power with significant reserves of legitimacy and effectiveness. Inasmuch as they classify, organize, and vet larger understandings of reality, such discourses authorize or invalidate the operational possibilities for particular institutions, practices, or concepts in society at large, including those pertaining to the environment. In turn, categories of ecological balance can simultaneously frame the emergence of collective subjectivities, or nations as dynamic populations, and collections of subjects, or individuals as units in such nations. Against environmentalizing practices, individual subjects as well as collective subjects can be reevaluated as the elements "in which are articulated the effects of a certain type of power and the reference of a certain type of knowledge, the machinery by which the power relations give rise to a possible corpus of knowledge, and knowledge extends and reinforces the effects of this power."[35] Therefore, an effective state regime must advance ecoknowledges to activate its environmentalizing command over geopower as well as to recalibrate many of its programs of governmentality as environmentality. Like governmentality, the disciplinary articulations of environmentality boil down to establishing and enforcing "the right disposition of things" in organizing "the conduct of human conduct."

Green Governmentality as Resource Managerialism

The discursive script of environmentality embedded in terms such as *ecology* or *environment* is rarely articulated by scientific and technical analysts. Yet there are politics here. The partisans of deep ecology and social ecology dimly perceive the political dimension of scripts when they vent their frustrations with "reform environmentalism," whose intrinsic resource managerialism has defined much of the United States' modern environmental protection thinking and natural resource conservation.[36] Resource managerialism can be read as the geopower/ecoknowledge regimen of modern governmentality. Although voices in favor of conservation could be found in Europe early in the nineteenth century, the real establishment of this stance came in the United States with the Second Industrial Revolution, from the 1880s through the 1920s, and the closing of the Western Frontier in the 1890s.[37] Whether one looks at John Muir's preservationist programs or Gifford Pinchot's conservationist codes, an awareness of modern industry's power to deplete natural resources, and hence the need for systems of conserving them against early, complete, or unrenewable exploitation, is well-established by the early 1900s. President Theodore Roosevelt, for example, addressed the 1907 Governor's Conference on this concern, inviting the participants to recognize that the natural resource endowments on which "the welfare of this nation rests are becoming depleted, and in not a few cases, are already exhausted."[38]

Over the past nine decades, the fundamental premises of resource managerialism have not changed significantly. At best this code of ecological knowledge has become only more formalized in bureaucratic applications and legal interpretations. Keying off of the managerial logic of the Second Industrial Revolution, which empowered technical experts (engineers and scientists) on the shop floor and professional managers (corporate executives and financial officers) in the main office, resource managerialism also turns to experts on ecology to impose corporate needs and public agendas on nature in order to supply the economy and provision society with natural resources held in trust by centralized state authorities.

To even construct the managerial problem in this fashion, nature must be reduced—through the encirclement of space and matter by national and global economies—to a system of systems that can be dismantled, redesigned, and assembled anew to produce resources for the modern marketplace efficiently and in adequate amounts. As a cybernetic system of biophysical systems, nature's energies, materials, and sites are redefined by the ecoknowledges of resource managerialism as manageable resources for human beings to realize great material "goods" for sizeable numbers of some people, even though greater material and immaterial "evils" also might be inflicted on even larger numbers of other people who do not reside in or benefit from the advanced transnational economies of scale that basically monopolize the use of world resources at a comparative handful of highly developed regional and municipal sites. Many ecoknowledge assumptions and geopower commitments can be observed in the discourses of the Worldwatch Institute during this organization's development of its own unique vision of environmentality as part of a global resource managerialism.

Globalizing Power/Knowledge

The Worldwatch Institute provides a useful example of the manner in which regimes of environmentality might be at work in the processes of producing a geopower/ecoknowledge formation. Seeing untrammeled industrial development as the cause of environmental crises, a recent Worldwatch Institute book by Brown, Flavin, and Postel attributes the prevailing popular faith in material growth to "a narrow economic view of the world."[39] Any constraints on further growth are cast by economics "in terms of inadequate demand growth rather than limits imposed by the earth's resources."[40] Ecologists, however, study the allegedly complex, changing relationships of organisms with their environments, and for them, "growth is confined by the parameters of the biosphere."[41] For Brown, Flavin, and Postel, economists ironically regard ecologists' concerns as "a minor subdiscipline of economics—to be 'internalized' in economic models and dealt with at the margins of economic planning," whereas "to an ecologist, the economy is a narrow subset of the global ecosystem."[42] To end this schism, the discourse of dangers propagated by the Worldwatch Institute pushes to meld ecology with economics by infusing environmental studies with economic instrumental rationality and defusing economics with ecological reasoning. Once this hybridization is complete, economic growth and ecological balance can no longer be divorced from "the natural systems and resources from which they ultimately derive," and any policy backing for an economic process that "undermines the global ecosystem cannot continue indefinitely."[43]

With this rhetorical maneuver, the Worldwatch Institute articulates its version of geopower/ecoknowledge as the instrumental rationality of resource managerialism, working on a global scale in transnationalized registers of application. Nature is reinterpreted as a cybernetic system of biophysical systems that reappears among nation-states in those "four biological systems—forests, grasslands, fisheries, and croplands—which supply all of our food and much of the raw materials for industry, with the notable exceptions of fossil fuels and minerals."[44] The performance of these ecological systems must be monitored in analytical spreadsheets written in bioeconomic terms and then judged in complex equations balancing constantly increasing human population, constantly running base ecosystem outputs, and highly constrained possibilities for increasing ecosystem output given inflexible limits on throughput and input. Looking at these four systems, the Worldwatch Institute asserts that nature is merely a system of energy-conversion systems:

> Each of these systems is fueled by photosynthesis, the process by which plants use solar energy to combine water and carbon dioxide to form carbohydrates. Indeed, this process for converting solar energy into biochemical energy supports all life on earth, including the 5.4 billion members of our species. Unless we manage these basic biological systems more intelligently than we now are, the earth will never meet the basic needs of 8 billion people.
>
> Photosynthesis is the common currency of biological systems, the yardstick by which their output can be aggregated and changes in their productivity measured. Although the estimated 41 percent of photosynthetic activity that takes place in the oceans supplies us with seafood, it is the 59 percent occurring on land that supports the world economy. And it is the loss of terrestrial photosynthesis as a result of environmental degradation that is undermining many national economies.[45]

Photosynthetic energy generation and accumulation, then, constitute the accounting standard for submitting such geopower to environmentalizing discipline. They impose upper limits on economic expansion; the Earth is only so large. The 41 percent of these processes that is aquatic and marine and the 59 percent that is terrestrial are decreasing in magnitude and efficiency because of "environmental degradation." Partly localized within national territories as politically bordered destruction, and partly globalized over the biosphere as biologically unbounded transboundary pollution, the system of systems needs global management—or a powerful, all-knowing Worldwatch—to mind its environmental resources.

Such new administrative requirements follow from the convergence of dangerous trends, namely, the estimates of such bioeconomic accounting now suggesting that

> 40 percent of the earth's annual net primary production on land now goes directly to meet human needs or is indirectly used or destroyed by human activity—leaving 60 percent for the millions of other land-based species with which humans share the planet. While it took all of human history to reach this point, the share could double to 80 percent by 2030 if current rates of population growth continue; rising per capita consumption could shorten the doubling time considerably. Along the way, with people usurping an ever larger share of the earth's life-sustaining energy, natural systems will unravel faster.[46]

To avoid this collapse of ecological throughput, human beings must stop rapidly increasing their numbers in mass national populations, halt increasingly resource-intensive modes of production, and limit increasing levels of material consumption. All these ends require a measure of state surveillance and degree of managerial navigation beyond the capabilities of many modern nation-states, but perhaps not beyond those of some postmodern institution engaged in the disciplinary tasks of equilibrating the "net primary production" of solar energy fixed by photosynthesis in the four systems. Natural resources in the total solar economy of food stocks, fisheries, forest preserves, and grasslands are rhetorically ripped from nature only to be returned as environmental resources, enveloped in accounting procedures and encircled by managerial programs. Worldwatching presumes to know all this, and in knowing it, to have mastered all its economic and ecological implications through authoritative technical analysis. By questioning the old truth regime of mere economic growth, a new truth regime seeking to attain a more sophisticated ecological economy stands ready to reintegrate human production and consumption in the four biological systems.

The Worldwatch Institute writers here are engaged in a struggle "for truth" in economic and environmental discourse. By simultaneously framing economics with the bad rap of growth fetishism and twinning ecology with the high purpose of documenting environmental interconnectedness, the Worldwatchers strive to transform fields of knowledge into bands of power. Inasmuch as today's decentered network of expert discourse about ecological knowledge operates through relations of truth about environments, it taps into power on "the multiplicity of force relations immanent in the sphere in which they operate and which constitute their own organization."[47] These are the requisite moves for prevailing in a disciplinary struggle for discursive authority. By shifting the authorizing legitimacy of truth claims used in policy analysis from the *economic* terms that have dominated public discourses about collective choices to the *ecological* terms cast in these thermodynamic allusions, the Worldwatch Institute's experts want to recast the power/knowledge systems of megatechnics in advanced capitalist societies as the operational codes of their environmentality.

The Environment as Disciplinary Space

No longer nature, not merely ecosystem, the world under this kind of watch is truly becoming "an environment," ringed by many ecoknowledge centers dedicated to the rational management of its geopowers. Being an environmentalist becomes a power expression of the ecoknowledge formations of environmentality in which the geopowers of the global ecosystem can be mobilized through the disciplinary codes of green operational planning. The health of global populations, as well as the survival of the planet itself, allegedly necessitates that bioeconomic spreadsheets be draped over nature, generating an elaborate set of accounts for a terrestrial ecoeconomy of global reach and scope. Worldwatching is environing, surrounding nature with its own managerial plans and professional-technical guards who are dedicated to protecting its health, supervising its populations, and limiting its degradation. Hovering over the world in this scientifically centered surveillance machine built from the disciplinary grids of efficiency and waste, health and disease, poverty and wealth, as well as employment and unemployment discourses, Brown, Flavin, and Postel declare "the once separate issues of environment and development are now inextricably linked."[48] Indeed they are, at least in the discourses of Worldwatch Institute, whose experts survey nature-in-crisis by auditing levels of topsoil depletion, air pollution, acid rain, global warming, ozone destruction, water pollution, forest reduction, and species extinction.

The environmentalization of nature also involves a continuous reenvironing of the economy, technology, and society. Environmentalists of many persuasions can engage in continuous global surveillance sweeps, scrutinizing patterns of energy use, artifact manufacture, food production, shelter construction, waste management, and urban design for technical, managerial, and economic inefficiencies. After these sweeps are concluded, environmentalists hope to organize a permanent project of *perestroika,* the ongoing, unending restructuring of everything artificial that extracts matter and energy from nature, to more rightly dispose of things and more conveniently arrange ends in accord with their green governmentality. Sustainability on one level has many laudable intentions driving its designs; on another level, however, its discursive framing, its intellectual articulation, and its action planning already provide a power formation, a discursive center, and a rhetorical foundation to empower these blocs of expert worldwatchers to stand guard over everything and everyone else in the environmentalized world.

Environmentality would govern through things and the ends things serve by restructuring today's ecologically unsound society through elaborate new managerial designs to realize tomorrow's environmentally sustainable economy. The shape of an environmental economy would emerge gradually from a reengineered economy of environmentalizing shapes vetted by worldwatching codes. The conduct of every individual human subject today, and all his or her unsustainable practices, would be reshaped through this new system of environmentalized conduct, redirected by fresh practices, discourses, and ensembles of administration that could more efficiently synchronize the biopowers of populations with the geopowers of environments. To police global carrying capacity, this environmentalizing logic would invite each human subject to assume the much less capacious carriage of disciplinary frugality instead of affluent suburban consumerism. As all the world comes under this watch, the global watch must police its human charges to dispose of their things and arrange their ends—in reengineered spaces using new energies at new jobs and leisures—around these environing agendas.

Sustainability, however, cuts both ways. On the one hand, it can articulate a rationale for preserving nature's biotic diversity to maintain the sustainability of the biosphere. On the other hand, it also represents an effort to reinforce the prevailing order of megatechnical development by transforming sustainability into an essentially economic project. To the degree that modern subjectivity is a two-sided power/knowledge relation, scientific-professional declarations about sustainability basically outline a new mode of environmentalized subjectivity. By becoming enmeshed in a worldwatched environing, the individual subject of a sustainable society could become "subject to someone else by control and dependence," where environmentalizing global and local state agencies enforce their codes of sustainability, while simultaneously being a self-directed ecological subject "tied to his own identity by a conscience or self-knowledge."[49] In both articulations, the truth regime of ecological sustainability draws up criteria for what sort of "selfness" will be privileged with political identity and social self-knowledge as an ecological selfhood.

Sustainability, like sexuality, has become an expert discourse about exerting power over life. What the biopower strategies of the eighteenth and nineteenth centuries helped fabricate in terms of human sexuality now must be sustained for humanity in worsening global conditions of survival. How power might "invest life through and through"[50] becomes a new challenge once biopolitical relations are established for all human and nonhuman life by making the investments permanently profitable as environmentalized systems. Sustainability more or less presumes that some level of material and cultural existence worth sustaining has been attained. This biohistorical formation, then, constitutes "a new distribution of pleasures, discourses, truths, and powers; it has to be seen as the self-affirmation of one class rather than the enslavement of another: a defense, a protection, a strengthening, and an exaltation . . . as a means of social control and political subjugation."[51] Sustainable development means developing new powers by defining new models of green knowledge organized around sustaining human subjectivities in the generation of both biopower and geopower.

The global bioaccounting systems of the Worldwatch Institute with their rhetorics of scientific surveillance exemplify one project of environmentality. How nature should be governed, especially after its envelopment in the designs of resource managerialism gels in Worldwatch's disciplinary discourse, is not a purely administrative question that turns on the technicalities of scientific know-how. Rather, it is essentially and inescapably political. The discourses of Worldwatch that rhetorically reconstruct nature as suitable for being governed through particular knowledges also assign powers to new global governors and governments, which are granted writs of authority and made centers of organization in the Worldwatchers' environmentalized writs of managerial "who-can" and political "how-to."

Instituting a Worldwatch: The Ecopanopticon

The Worldwatch Institute continually couches its narratives in visual terms, alluding to its worldwatching mission as outlining an "ecologically defined vision," "how an environmentally sustainable society would look," "contrasting views of the world," or "vision of a global economy." As Foucault claims, "whenever one is dealing with a multiplicity of individuals on whom a particular form of behavior must be imposed, the panoptic schema may be used," because it enables a knowing center to reorganize the disposition of things and redirect the convenient ends of individuals in environmentalized spaces.[52] Simply because they are organisms operating in the energy exchanges of photosynthesis, human beings can become environed on all sides by the cybernetic system of biophysical systems composing nature. The various power/knowledge systems of instituting a Worldwatch environmentality ironically appear now to be a practical materialization of panoptic power.

Worldwatching in turn refocuses the moral specification of human responsibilities in the enclosed spaces and segmented places of ecosystemic niches. In generating this knowledge of environmental impact through its relentless powers of ecological observation, the institutions of Worldwatch operate as a green panopticon, enclosing nature in rings of centered normalizing supervision as where an ecoknowledge system identifies nature as "the environment." The calculus of bioeconomic accounting not only can but must reequilibrate individuals and species, energy and matter, and inefficiencies and inequities to fit into these integrated panels of globalized observation. The supervisory gaze of normalizing control, embedded in the Worldwatch Institute's panoptic practices, adduces new behaviors to fill the environmental domain or these enclosed, segmented ecological spaces, "observed at every point, in which the individuals are inserted in a fixed place, in which the slightest movements are supervised, in which all events are recorded, in which an uninterrupted work of writing links the centre and periphery, in which power is exercised without division, according to a continuous hierarchical figure, in which each individual is constantly located, examined, and distributed among the living beings, the sick and the dead."[53] To save the planet, it becomes necessary to environmentalize it, enveloping its system of systems in new disciplinary discourses to regulate population growth, economic development, and resource exploitation on a global scale with continual managerial intervention.

Many contemporary environmental movements, particularly those inspired by the Worldwatch Institute's *State of the World* annual analyses, want to push governmentality to the next step, embedding its analytical ensembles for managing population, territory, and administration in everything surrounding and sustaining societies of politicized economy on a global rather than a national level of control. Polyarchy must be denationalized so that it can become transnational. The biosphere, atmosphere, and ecosphere must be integrated into the truth regime of political economy to serve more ecological ends, but they are also made to run along new economic tracks above and beyond the territorial spaces created by nation-states. By touting the necessity of recalibrating logics of governmentality in new spatial registers at the local and global level, the geopower politics of environmentality also aim to rewrite the geographies of national stratified space with new bioregional economic maps knitted into global ecologies—complete with environmentalized zones of "dying forests," "regional desertification," "endangered bays," or "depleted farmland."

If Foucault's representation of governmentality accounts for the practices of power mobilized by centered national sovereigns in the era of capitalist modernization and national state-building after 1648, the Worldwatch Institute's approach to environmentality foreshadows the practices of power being propounded by multicentric alliances of transnational firms or loose coalitions of highly fragmented local sovereignties following the collapse of the cold war in the 1990s. New spatial domains are being created in the world today—on the one hand, by pollution, nuclear contamination, and widespread rapid deforestation, and on the other hand, by telecommunications, jet transportation, and cheap, accessible computerization. Many nation-states are not effectively answering the challenges that these new spaces pose within their borders. Nevertheless, some contemporary expert environmental groups, such as the Worldwatch Institute, the World Wildlife Federation, and Greenpeace, are at least addressing, if not answering, how these spaces are developing, what impact they have in today's political economy, and who should act to respond to the challenge. In the bargain, they also are interposing their own environmentalizing conceptual maps, technical disciplines, and organizational orders on these contested spaces as they urge local citizen's groups or global supranational agencies to move beyond the constraints imposed by national sovereignty and construct new sustainable spaces for human habitation through a globalized polyarchy.[54]

The cybernetic system of biophysical systems, once known as nature, is reduced to "the environment" so that it might be remapped from above in policing the provinces of photosynthesis and the borders of bioeconomics that these spaces constitute. The logic of classical sovereignty, which uses governmentality to impose military-administrative jurisdiction over bits and pieces of these global systems in irrationally drawn territories, must be supplanted by a larger logic of environmentality. Even so, there are many grounds for populistic local resistances to oppose these systems of green governmentality. Chapter 5 will reconsider new nationalistic responses to the environmentality question, whereas chapter 6 investigates one of the less promising options of resisting new class authority in megatechnical polyarchy through violent direct action.

Notes

1. See George Marsh, *The Earth as Modified by Human Action* (New York: Scribner's, 1885); and, Ernst Haeckel, *Generelle Morphologie der Organismen* (Berlin: Reimer, 1866).

2. Michel Foucault, *The History of Sexuality, vol. 1: An Introduction* (New York: Vintage, 1980), 140–41.

3. For some sense of the diversity in reading nature's meanings, see Ronald Bailey, *Eco-Scam: The False Prophets of Ecological Apocalypse* (New York: St. Martin's, 1993); Daniel B. Botkin, *Discordant Harmonies: A New Ecology for the Twenty-First Century* (New York: Oxford University Press, 1990); John S. Dryzek, *Rational Ecology: Environment and Political Economy* (Oxford: Blackwell, 1987); Garrett Hardin, *Living within Limits: Ecology, Economics, and Population Taboos* (New York: Oxford University Press, 1993); Barry Lopez, *Crossing Open Ground* (New York: Vintage, 1989); Max Oelschlaeger, *Caring for Creation: An Ecumenical Approach to the Environmental Crisis* (New Haven, Conn.: Yale University Press, 1994); Gary Snyder, *The Old Ways* (San Francisco: City Lights, 1977); Edward O. Wilson, *The Diversity of Life* (Cambridge, Mass.: Harvard University Press, 1992); and Yi-Fu Tuan, *Topophila: A Study of Environmental Perception, Attitudes, and Values* (New York: Columbia University Press, 1974).

4. Lester Brown, Christopher Flavin, and Sandra Postel, *Saving the Planet: How to Shape an Environmentally Sustainable Global Economy* (New York: Norton, 1991).

5. Penelope ReVelle and Charles ReVelle, *The Environment: Issues and Choices for Society* (Boston: Jones and Bartlett, 1988).

6. Rogene Buchholz, *Principles in Environmental Management: The Greening of Business* (Englewood Cliffs, N.J.: Prentice-Hall, 1993), 29–30.

7. Bernard J. Nebel, *Environmental Science: The Way the World Works,* 3d ed. (Englewood Cliffs, N.J.: Prentice-Hall), 576.

8. Barry Commoner, *Making Peace with the Planet* (New York: Pantheon, 1990), 7.

9. Barry Commoner, *The Closing Circle: Nature, Man, and Technology* (New York: Knopf, 1971), 32.

10. Rachel Carson, *Silent Spring* (Boston: Houghton Mifflin, 1962).

11. Donald Worster, *Nature's Economy: The Roots of Ecology* (Garden City, N.Y.: Anchor Doubleday, 1977).

12. Anna Bramwell, *Ecology in the Twentieth Century: A History* (New Haven, Conn.: Yale University Press, 1989).

13. Robert Paehlke, *Environmentalism and the Future of Progressive Politics* (New Haven, Conn.: Yale University Press, 1989).

14. Max Oelschlaeger, *The Idea of Wilderness: From Prehistory to the Age of Ecology* (New Haven, Conn.: Yale University Press, 1991).

15. Robyn Eckersley, *Environmentalism and Political Theory: Toward an Ecocentric Approach* (Albany: State University of New York Press, 1992).

16. Bill Devall and George Sessions, *Deep Ecology: Living As If Nature Mattered* (Salt Lake City: Peregrine Smith, 1985).

17. Warwick Fox, *Toward a Transpersonal Ecology: Developing New Foundations for Environmentalism* (Boston: Shambhala, 1990).

18. Ibid., 8.

19. Roderick Nash, *Wilderness and the American Mind,* 3d ed. (New Haven, Conn.: Yale University Press, 1982), 254.

20. Roderick Nash, *The Rights of Nature: A History of Environmental Ethics* (Madison: University of Wisconsin Press, 1989), 282.

21. Ibid., 282, 4.

22. For a more formal definition in this vein, see Michael Allaby, *The Concise Oxford Dictionary of Ecology* (New York: Oxford University Press, 1994), 138.

23. Foucault, *History of Sexuality,* 138–42.

24. Ibid., 143.

25. Ibid.

26. Ibid.

27. Ibid., 143–44.

28. Ibid., 142.

29. Ibid.

30. Ibid., 105–6.

31. Michel Foucault, "Governmentality," in *The Foucault Effect: Studies in Governmentality,* ed. Graham Burchell, Colin Gordon, and Peter Miller (Chicago: University of Chicago Press, 1991), 93.

32. Ibid., 102.

33. Ibid., 102, 100.

34. Ibid., 103.

35. Michel Foucault, *Discipline and Punish: The Birth of the Prison* (New York: Vintage, 1979), 29.

36. Timothy W. Luke, "Green Consumerism: Ecology and the Ruse of Recycling," in *In the Nature of Things: Language, Politics, and the Environment,* ed. Jane Bennett and William Chaloupka (Minneapolis: University of Minnesota Press, 1932), 154–72.

37. See David Noble, *America by Design: Science, Technology, and the Rise of Corporate Capitalism* (New York: Knopf, 1977).

38. Cited in Henry Jarrett, ed., *Perspectives on Conservation: Essays on America's Natural Resources* (Baltimore: Resources for the Future, 1958), 51.

39. Brown, Flavin, and Postel, *Saving the Planet,* 21.

40. Ibid., 22.

41. Ibid.

42. Ibid., 23.

43. Ibid.

44. Ibid., 73.

45. Ibid., 73–74.

46. Ibid., 74. For another version of technoscientific worldwatching, see Stephen H. Schneider, *Laboratory Earth: The Planetary Gamble We Can't Afford to Lose* (New York: Basic, 1997), 114–54.

47. Foucault, *History of Sexuality,* 92.

48. Brown, Flavin, and Postel, *Saving the Planet,* 25.

49. Michel Foucault, "Afterword: The Subject and Power," *Michel Foucault: Beyond Structuralism and Hermeneutics,* 2d ed., ed. H. L. Dreyfus and Paul Rabinow (Chicago: University of Chicago Press, 1982), 212.

50. Foucault, *History of Sexuality,* 13.

51. Ibid., 123.

52. Foucault, *Discipline and Punish,* 205.

53. Ibid., 197.

54. See Daniel R. White, *Postmodern Ecology: Communication, Evolution, and Play* (Albany: State University of New York Press, 1998), 77–181.

5 Ecodiscipline and the Post–Cold War Global Economy: Rethinking Environmental Critiques of Geo-Economics

This chapter reconsiders an unusual environmental debate over the post–cold war "securitization" of global economic competition among wealthy advanced nation-states or the world's foremost megatechnic polyarchies. It does this by comparing the political programs of geo-economics as articulated by Robert Reich, Lester Thurow, and Edward Luttwak to those of ecodisciplinarians, who attempt to articulate new programmatic philosophies for an ecological opposition to geo-economic industrial society. This latter group is represented here by recent works of Andrew McLaughlin, Al Gore, and David Oates.[1] The debate is particularly interesting inasmuch as it pits opposing factions of new class experts—some speaking for economic efficiency and national discipline, and others arguing for environmental protection and global oversight—against each other in the crisis-ridden economies of the 1990s.

With the collapse of old cold war conflicts, many economists, industrialists, and political leaders are increasingly representing the strategic situation of the post-1991 world system as one in which all nations will compete ruthlessly to control the future development of megatechnic marketplaces in the world economy by developing new technologies, dominating more markets, and exploiting every national economic asset.[2] In the process of such competition, environmental protection issues—ranging from resource conservation to sustainable development to ecosystem preservation—are often given short shrift in the name of creating jobs, maintaining growth, or continuing technological development. As one response, various ecodisciplinarian ethics are being advanced to answer the challenge posed by geo-economic strategies.

The discourse of geo-economics, as it has been articulated by Reich, Thurow, and Luttwak, uses military metaphors and strategic analogies to transform what hitherto were regarded as purely economic issues into national security concerns by casting commercial ways of life conducted within national technoregions as being either under attack or in need of defense. Government manipulations of trade policy, state support of major corporations, or government aid for retraining labor become vital instruments for "the continuation of the ancient rivalry of the nations by new industrial means."[3] Geo-economics takes the relative success or failure of national economics as megatechnical hyperecologies in head-to-head global competitions to be the definitive register of waxing or waning national power, as well as of rising or falling industrial competitiveness, technological vitality, and economic prowess. In this context ecological considerations can simply be ignored or given only symbolic responses. Moreover, in more intense struggles over essential economic activities, environmental resistance can even be recast as endangering national security, expressing unpatriotic sentiments, or embodying treasonous acts.

The critique of geo-economics, as well as a populistic resistance to its policies, is being tested in the struggles of many local lifeworld-defense committees, national environmental organizations, and transnational ecological alliances, but this analysis looks at the ecodisciplinary critiques of McLaughlin, Gore, and Oates. They are critical of reducing international trade to geo-economic struggles for hegemonic supremacy between warring blocs of highly developed corporate-state alliances, and they present alternative ways of producing and consuming material wealth that would not entail massive ecological destruction. Nonetheless, the ecodisciplinarians are plagued by their own peculiar political agendas that have other limitations.

The Project of Geo-Economics

Geo-economic strategies have been a feature of public discourse for at least two decades. Arguably the oil crises of the 1970s first recentered elite and popular thinking about the ties between national economic productivity, natural resources, and nationalistic competitiveness within a global economy. After twenty-five years of cold war conflict in which virtually everything was organized to conduct an East-West struggle between two military blocs centered on nuclear deterrence, geopolitical maneuvering, and ideological confrontation, many nation-states were caught short by the oil crises of 1971, 1973, and 1979. In the discourse of geo-economics, Japan's response, in particular, to its "oil *shokku*" was highly prescient inasmuch as the Japanese state refined its geo-economic strategizing: defining economic production as power creation, market building as empire creation, technological innovation as strategic initiative, and labor docility as nationalistic discipline. Here economics is seen as war conducted by other means, and all natural resources thus become strategic assets to be mobilized not only for growth and wealth production but for market domination and power creation. To oppose growth is not only to oppose economic prosperity; it is to oppose the political future, national interest, and collective security of the nation-state.

Richard Barnet illustrated many of these positions in his early geo-economic treatise *The Lean Years: Politics in the Age of Scarcity*, which systematically explores the connections between political power and physical resources during the 1970s. Arguing that "whoever controls world resources controls the world in a way that mere occupation of territory cannot match,"[4] Barnet asked, first, whether that decade's resource scarcities were real and, second, whether control over natural resources was changing the global balance of power. After surveying the struggles to manipulate access to oil, minerals, water, and food resources, he did see a geo-economic challenge rising out of advanced nation-states as each ruling regime struggled to satisfy its population's rising material expectations in a much more interdependent world system.

By defining the global politics of scarcity, Barnet saw, first, a worldwide employment crisis, for fewer and fewer jobs are leading to stable careers and material prosperity for many rank-and-file workers, and, second, a relative decline in the prominence of the United States in the world's economy. Unlike the analysts of the 1990s, however, Barnet saw blocs of truly multinational capital (or transnational businesses) building "global factories" for their own corporate benefit rather than serving any one nation's particular advantages. National capital formations (based exclusively in Japan, Germany, or North America) were not the culprit in these transformations.

Plainly, the geo-economic challenge for Barnet was how to develop a political economy of survival by reemphasizing the value of human life, enhancing local self-reliant economies, and extending democracy into economic governance to create an ethic of stewardship over the environment.[5] Otherwise, the fight over global resources would combine the principles of "Malthusian warfare against the surplus population" with a "reviewed technological assault on nature" that fuses "the drive for indiscriminate industrialization with the politics of austerity."[6] Ironically, the strategic designs of Reich, Thurow, and Luttwak paint their pictures of geo-economics for the 1990s in precisely these terms, whereas Barnet's vision of geo-economics in the 1970s is far less nationalistic. Barnet was extremely suspicious of transnational business, and not eager to politicize it for the pursuit of narrow national purposes.

His agenda, then, tends to be somewhat more cosmopolitan, seeking economic answers suitable for improving everyone's lot. By way of contrast, geo-economics in the 1990s often is highly chauvinistic, wanting to tout the merits of narrower strategies to enhance one nation's economic position vis-à-vis others.

One might argue that little has changed in geo-economic discourses over the past two decades; indeed, geo-economics has become more prominent in public and private debates over which ends and means can best provide for the collective welfare of each nation's population. Partly a response to global economic competition and partly a response to global ecological scarcities, a geo-economic reading of political economy now constructs the attainment of national economic growth, security, and prosperity as a zero-sum game. Having more material wealth or economic growth in one place, namely, any given nation-state, means not having it in other places, namely, rival foreign nations. It also assumes material scarcity is a continual constraint; hence, all resources, everywhere and at any time, must be subject to exploitation. Consequently, any effort to resist this agenda is tantamount to treason against the commonwealth of all.

Geo-economics accepts the prevailing megatechnics of mass- and niche-market consumerism as they presently exist, defines its rationalizing managerial benefits as the sole ends that advanced economies ought to seek, and then affirms militant programs of national productivism, now couched within rhetorics of politicized international competition, as the means for sustaining consumerist lifestyles in richer nations such as the United States. Creating economic growth, and producing more of it than other equally aggressive geo-economic countries, is the touchstone of "national security" in the 1990s. Mounting any resistance to this goal for ecological reasons is unpatriotic, unreasonable, and most important, unacceptable to advocates of geo-economic discipline. As Richard Darman, President Bush's chief of OMB, declared after Earth Day in 1990, "Americans did not fight and win the wars of the twentieth century to make the world safe for green vegetables."[7] Environmentalism in an age of geo-economics, in turn, can be tantamount to subversion of an entire way of life tied to using economic growth as an agency of the state power. During the 1990s, as the "wise use" movement indicates, many government bureaus and business interests have become much more aggressive in their reactions to both mainstream reformist environmental organizations and radical ecological activism. As former Reagan interior secretary James Watt argues, "If the troubles from environmentalists cannot be solved in the jury box or at the ballot box, perhaps the cartridge box should be used."[8]

Geo-Economic Theory: Reich, Thurow, Luttwak

In his book *The Work of Nations: Preparing Ourselves for Twenty-First Century Capitalism,* President Clinton's longtime friend, economic adviser, and secretary of labor in the first administration, Robert Reich, argues that the key economic issue of the 1990s and beyond is quite simple: what counts in calculations of national economic power is not which nation's citizens own what but how any nation's citizens learn how to do what, so that they are continuously becoming more capable of adding more value to the world economy. The primary economic assets of each nation-state are not tangible wealth but rather the intangible skills and insights of its citizens. Consequently, government's primary task becomes developing and upgrading those skills to increase the value-adding power of all citizens under its rule in networks of production run by truly transnational corporations. Reich's arguments are generally neutral about the nominal nationality of corporations. Who is "us," for him, is difficult to determine in an increasingly transnational economy. Therefore, he welcomes the trends toward increasing levels of foreign direct investment in the United States. "Nations," Reich argues, "can no longer substantially enhance the wealth of their citizens by subsidizing, protecting, or otherwise increasing the profitability of 'their' corporations; the connection between corporate profitability and the standard of living of a nation's people is growing ever more attenuated."[9] This skills-focused, transnationally disposed economic philosophy is an updated variant of the cold war era's hegemonic superpower orthodoxies, rearticulated and advanced by transnational liberalism.

In many ways *The Work of Nations* raises the most critical question in the geo-economic interpretations of the post–cold war era when Reich asks, "Who is us?" On one level, traditional discursive representations of "us" in terms of culture, kin, and country provide one vision of how the world works, a vision that Thurow and Luttwak tend to accept with less modification. As Reich shows, these categories are continually crosscut by globalizing tendencies in the world economy as capital, labor, technologies, and markets become more and more transnational. The discursive representations of "us" must recognize how thoroughly the members of allegedly different civilizations are enmeshed together on the same small planet by Boeing 747s, IBM PC clones, Coca-Cola, Toyotas, global warming trends, Sony Walkmen, Madonna videos, CNN cable feed, and Stephen Spielberg movies. Who owns and who controls what, under these circumstances, is more and more diffuse. So while neoconservatives such as Samuel Huntington see new civilizational barriers and conflicts growing in significance after the cold war, global mutual fund managers, transnational corporations, humanitarian organizations, and media networks keep jumping under, over, and around these allegedly inviolate civilizational divides.[10]

Other geo-economic intellectuals in the United States have less difficulty in answering the question "Who is us?" Management guru, media commentator, and sometime Democratic party adviser Lester Thurow articulates a much more traditional, if not almost mercantilist, vision of economic blocs in his *Head to Head: The Coming Economic Battle among Japan, Europe, and America.* Thurow's analysis of the post–cold war era both affirms and contradicts Huntington's clash of civilizations thesis. At the end of the cold war, Thurow sees "the economic leaders of the nineteenth and twentieth centuries, the United Kingdom and the United States," being forced "to alter their modes of playing the economic game" to cope with twenty-first century geopolitical realities.[11] The unipolar world of the Pax Americana has evolved into a tripolar world that will feature the United States going "head to head" with two new rivals. "In Europe an economic giant, the European Community, is in the process of being created. For the first time in modern history, an oriental tiger, Japan, has emerged as a competitor fully equal to any in Europe or North America. Because of their different histories and present circumstances, both of these new players are going to be infusing the capitalist economic game with strategies very different from those found in the Anglo-Saxon world."[12] Most important, with the quickened pace of change, lost national economic independence, and rising popular insecurity cited by Clinton and his advisers as threats to national prosperity, Thurow argues that the United States will be forced not only to change its economic and political arrangements fundamentally in order to deal with economic and technological equals for the first time but also to jettison outmoded institutions, procedures, and rules that it designed to manage the now vanished conflicts of the cold war era.

Arguing that the military competition of the cold war has ended, Thurow sees a new administrative, economic, and technical rivalry forming the strategic basis of twenty-first-century geopolitics. "Who can make the best products? Who has the best-educated and best-skilled work force in the world? Who is the world's leader in investment—plant and equipment, research and development, infrastructure? Who organizes best? Whose institutions—government, education, business—are world leaders in efficiency?"[13] Since he is an economist, of course, Thurow's analysis is decidedly ultraeconomic. Nonetheless, it does picture a particular set of conflicts and contradictions as the center of global power struggles, and this picture directly frames Japan and the European Union as the major threat to the United States.

Even though he sees no single force—Japan, the European Union, or the United States—dominating the twenty-first century, Thurow also asserts, "If one looks at the last twenty years, Japan would have to be considered the betting favorite to win the economic honors of the twenty-first century."[14] The United States is at a major disadvantage: its level of investment is not world class, its overall work force is poorly trained, its industrial productivity growth is slow, its Latin American trading partners are poor, and its political complacency is often paralyzing. Still, as the deep recession there during the 1990s suggests, Japan also faces major obstacles: it is an export-led economy, it has a weak domestic sector, its Asian trading partners are going their own ways, and its more insular culture often makes adaptation difficult. Hence, Thurow hedges his geo-economic bets by tagging the dark horse contender, the European Union, as the candidate most likely to dominate the next century, because in the final analysis, "strategic position is on the side of the Europeans."[15]

To respond to these dismal projections of geo-economic decline, the United States must adopt "an economic game plan." Thurow's version of this response basically maps elements of "Japanization," as Thurow reads Japan, into the political economy of the United States. Like Japan—or at least, like the images of Japan prior to the 1997 Asian economic meltdown in U.S. political discourses—the United States must begin saving and investing at higher levels, improving the skills of its work force, involving corporate business groups in collaborative enterprises, and innovating through coordinated nationwide industrial policies. Reaganism, as an experiment in old-time, laissez-faire, individualistic economics, has failed to make traditional Anglo-Saxon capitalism successful in the 1980s. Although individualism in the United States has failed, teamwork in Japan and Germany is working. Hence Thurow calls for some "bottom-line benchmarking" by the United States to emulate "their careful organization of teams—teams that involve workers and managers, teams that involve suppliers and customers, teams that involve government and business."[16] Despite what Huntington argues about conflicts between "the West and the rest," arguments like those advanced by Thurow indicate that real conflicts will center on who is "the best in the West." Aspects of these conflicts are perhaps "civilizational," but most of these struggles tie back to the ongoing modernization of megatechnical modes of production as noncultural criteria, such as technical proficiency, managerial acumen, labor efficiency, and social organization, separate rivals within the West rather than between civilizations.

Although we can distinguish between the "globalist" vision of Clinton's former labor secretary Robert Reich and the more nationally focused "Japanization" strategy of intellectuals such as Lester Thurow, it is unwise to see both of these geo-economic reinterpretations of the United States as incompatible. The Clinton administration, for example, resorts to either option as the occasion warrants. In his first inaugural address, Clinton echoed Reich's themes in declaring that "there is no longer a clear division between what is foreign and what is domestic."[17] Hence, his policies after 1997 have aimed at modernizing Japan's crisis-ridden financial sector.

Edward N. Luttwak's book *The Endangered American Dream* answers Reich's questions about "who is us" and responds to Thurow's observations on U.S. prospects in "head to head" economic competitions in the subtitle, *How to Stop the United States from Becoming a Third-World Country and How to Win the Geo-Economic Struggle for Industrial Supremacy.* This analysis casts the United States as already fighting a losing geo-economic war, even though it still is winning battles on some high-technology fronts. Like Reich, Luttwak sees the U.S. political economy splitting into two parts: in one segment, a successful one-fifth of the work force dedicates much of its energy to seceding from the other section, where 80 percent of all jobs are found in businesses that are stagnant or slipping backward. While the affluent segment of symbolic analysts in the prosperous 20 percent does well in Scarsdale, New York, or Scottsdale, Arizona, the rest of the country allegedly is beginning to become a Third World economy in appearance and reality.

The only way to reverse this slide into Third World mediocrity, Luttwak argues, is a conscious campaign by the nation-state to pursue a focused strategy of geo-economic maneuvering. Consciously targeting specific industries as the bedrock of *U.S.* industrial supremacy, Luttwak calls for the federal government to use any and all means necessary to win what is the technological, commercial, and managerial equivalent of war. "In traditional world politics," he observes, "the goals are to secure and extend the physical control of territory, and to gain diplomatic influence over foreign governments."[18] Geo-economic struggles instead are focused on the creation and domination of markets. In a world that blurs the nominal nationality and actual transnationality of business, Luttwak advocates that "nominally national" business professionals must act in the actual national interests of their home countries. Otherwise the nominally transnational guises of Japanese, German, or Taiwanese capital will actually peripheralize the United States, reducing it to a Third World nation. Geo-economics, then, becomes a noble calling to greatness "on the world scene of typically meritocratic and professional ambitions" shared by techno-economic corporate elites, who want to be "*in command* on the world scene, as markers of technology, not mere producers under license; as the developers of products, not mere assemblers; as industrialists, not mere importers."[19]

The project of geo-economics, however, is not likely to weaken statist intervention into everyday life. Under geo-economic orders, "The authority of state bureaucrats can be asserted anew, not in the name of strategy and security this time, but rather to protect 'vital economic interests' by geo-economic defenses, geo-economics offensives, geo-economic diplomacy, and geo-economic intelligence."[20] In addition, as a mobilization of national will and energies to counter the geo-economic strategies of other nations, state-managed designs for geo-economic industrial supremacy are spreading rapidly, "becoming the dominant phenomenon in the central arena of world affairs."[21]

Unlike Reich's quest to secure a high standard of living for as many workers as possible by upgrading the skills of all, Luttwak's agendas see a lessening of living standards as states such as the United States and Japan compete against all the other serious players in the world economy to sacrifice to the goals of capital accumulation and technological innovation. Geo-economics, then, does not necessarily aim to create the highest political standard of living for a nation's population. On the contrary, it seeks "the conquest or protection of desirable roles in the world economy."[22] The questions guiding political practices in geo-economic strategies are centered on technological leadership, product cycle domination, capital investment, and control over markets. Geo-economic strategists face a daunting set of challenges:

> Who will develop the next generation of jet airliners, computers, biotechnology products, advanced materials, financial services, and all other high-value output in industries large and small? Will the designers, technologists, managers, and financiers be Americans, Europeans, or East Asians? The winners will have those highly rewarding and controlling roles, while the losers will have only the assembly lines—if their home markets are large enough, or if fully assembled imports are kept out by trade barriers.[23]

States become players in the geo-economic game as their resource policies, industrial policies, tax policies, and fiscal policies all become "an *instrument of power*,"[24] especially after the Asian financial crises of 1997.

The Project of Ecodiscipline

Many individuals and groups who are focused on resisting the potential ill-effects of geo-economics stake their resistance on ecological principles, appealing to "the environment" to make their critiques. Certain that they must do everything possible to protect nature from geo-economic destruction, they often reduce environmental protection to a moral crusade. Unfortunately, as chapter 4 suggests, their struggles are often hobbled by a basic confusion over exactly what the environment might be. The specific meaning of "the environment" as a concept is frequently indistinct, but this vagueness becomes intriguing inasmuch as ecodisciplinary discourses spin alternative visions for economic growth, national stability, and political control by recasting the moral, psychological, and political significance of "environmental problems" for contemporary geo-economic states.

Such fundamentalist readings of the environment in terms of these individuals' own peculiar disciplinary "environmentality" ironically reveal much about the professional-technical intentions of many contemporary new class ecodisciplinarians. In and of itself, nature is meaningless. To find meaning, human beings must observe its significant patterns, choose to accentuate some over others, and then ignore what was not accentuated as insignificant. These preliminary interpretive acts construct realities that can then be read on various levels for their many manifest or latent meanings. As geo-economic agendas turn natural materials, sites, and energies into products, nature is already being transformed discursively into "natural resources." Once its complexity is reduced to these highly processed forms, nature can spark many forms of social resistance, including bureaucratic but green programs of ecodiscipline, which rise in defense against rampant geo-economic plundering of the planet in the name of national industrial supremacy.

Ecodiscipline as Anti-Industrialism

Andrew McLaughlin's ecological critique starts by retracing the familiar criticisms leveled against modern ways of life since the early days of the Industrial Revolution. In exchange for "ease and comfort" for a few in contemporary advanced industrial society, many must cope with greater levels of domination, exploitation, and competition. McLaughlin believes that basic material needs are easily satisfied in geo-economic industrialism, but everyone then struggles to overcome feelings of constant scarcity by seeking to accumulate or experience more. Traditional community, established status systems, and stable agrarian economies therefore all implode in the swirling markets of megatechnical polyarchies.

This happens, according to McLaughlin, because of a quest for identity and community in economic competition. Because "we are fundamentally insecure" within industrial societies, consumerism becomes an individual and collective quest "to relieve this insecurity and vulnerability by providing a feeling of strength through our possessions."[25] Geo-economic agendas for sustaining this kind of industrial dependency only aggravate human beings' reliance on the logic of planned obsolescence. Geo-economic struggles for technological supremacy guarantee that these possessions soon will create new insecurities and vulnerabilities with new feelings of inadequacy, insufficiency, and insubstantiality. Meanwhile, nature is plundered to provide the material wherewithal to drive this system of industrial order, causing a geo-economic society to become "a psychologically frustrating and ecologically lethal mode of forming personal identity."[26]

These linkages become the nub of geo-economic industrial society's most basic flaws. If the formation of personal identity lies at the heart of consumerism, and consumerism provides the most basic pretext for expanding industrialism, then any attempt to create an ecologically based social philosophy must address the processes of personal identity formation. Consequently, McLaughlin endorses social movements committed to the ideas of deep ecology. They have the "one perspective that beckons in the right direction."[27] Most important, deep ecology focuses on developing "life quality" instead of seeking, like geo-economics, "an increasingly higher standard of living." Contra Luttwak, such "sustainable communities" must feature much smaller human populations living outside "the mindless quest for growth,"[28] like those in many Third World countries.

Following Marshall Sahlin's anthropological observation about affluence—namely, that material wants can be easily satisfied by producing much or desiring little—McLaughlin valiantly asserts that consumers can renounce geo-economic mobilization programs and follow deep ecologists in choosing "poverty" over "affluence," bucking nearly two centuries of evidence to the contrary. The key question is "whether we can move forward toward a society that chooses a course of affluence by desiring less or whether we are compelled to continue the fruitless search for satisfaction through the relentless pursuit of industrial products."[29] Because the latter geo-economic choice is ecologically unsustainable, McLaughlin believes that the former ecodisciplinary option becomes politically necessary.

On one level, ecodisciplinarians, such as McLaughlin, do want to advance the "transformation of the masses into a new kind of society," but they have not developed many coherent political or organizational strategies for guiding this transformation.[30] Instead, ecodisciplinary tactics, like deep ecology, choose to operate on other fronts, primarily as "a spiritual-religious movement."[31] So the transformation of the masses envisioned by ecodiscipline either becomes a spiritual journey of inner personal change or it falls on state agencies to give a new identity to their clients by imposing on them the joy of owning fewer goods, doing less work, and having smaller families as improvements in their "quality of life."

McLaughlin's analysis of ecological ethics transforms correct ecodisciplinary thinking into a style of right reasoning that must avoid geo-economics' anthropocentrism. McLaughlin sees anthropocentric industrialism at the heart of megatechnical geo-economics; it is "the hub of a set of social practices that are destructive to the rest of nature."[32] In his vision of nature, "an ecologically based understanding of humanity that locates us *within* a community of communities composed of various centers of life . . . suggests that limiting concern to only human concerns is an undue, unjustified, and illegitimate bias, akin to the biases of racism and sexism."[33] At the same time, he is unwilling to quibble at length over the particular moral implications of taking this peculiar stand, because ethical theory is always "methodologically confined to developing and explicating currently dominant conceptions of what is moral and immoral."[34] Because all ethical theory is tangled within the rights and wrongs of industrial society, "any radical transformation of humanity's relations with the rest of nature requires going far beyond ordinary ethical discourse."[35] To transcend these species-centric limitations, then, McLaughlin tags deep ecology as the necessary transformative means for creating a new society that can midwife his new ethics. Most significantly, McLaughlin suggests that "an inclusive ecological ideology of nature would not legitimate the domination of nonhuman nature," but it apparently would legitimate radically decreasing the human population of the planet to protect "the right to life" of trees, frogs, and rivers.[36]

Critiques of contemporary polyarchies that simplistically tout alternative notions such as bioregionalism, ecocentrism, and sustainability, seeking thus to resist geo-economics with ill-defined rhetorical buzzwords rather than sharply specified policy programs, can play into the hands of administrative empowerment and communal disempowerment. On the one hand, ineffectual and divided groups, such as the American Green Party or the gaggle of North American bioregionalist fronts, talk at length about these ideas in warm, fuzzy terms, but these politicians have had little demonstrable political effect thus far in the United States' megatechnical polyarchies. McLaughlin might regard these factions as a genuine popular movement destined for greatness, but such forces mostly continue to be insignificant fringe elements that are incapable of organizing the few score in their own ranks as a coherent political agency, much less providing the organizational basis to reorder industrialist civilization. On the other hand, as Gore's book indicates, more establishment-based new class intellectuals in many nongovernmental organizations, environmentalist pressure groups, and international aid agencies are eagerly appropriating the rhetorics of bioregionalism, ecocentricity, and sustainability into their bureaucratic green practices, using them to rerationalize hyper-industrialist modes of agriculture, industry, and commerce in ways that can enhance the established workings of transnational capitalism and national state power.

McLaughlin does not effectively examine the fundamental ideologies within which "we moderns" allegedly are entrapped—anthropocentrism, capitalism, industrialism, scientism, and socialism. Instead he writes a shadow play, cast with characters bearing the most generic and simplistic attributes of capitalism and socialism (based on an impoverished cold war reading of both systems). Onstage in this theoretical theater, capitalism is Fordist corporate consumerism and socialism is Gosplannish bureaucratic collectivism. Scientism and industrialism are unstable assemblies of instrumental reason, reductionistic operationalism, materialistic ontology, and methodological falsificationism. At the bottom line, of course, science and its reductive images of nature are always fabricated in terms of creating technical control. And by using instrumentally rational science as its motive force, industrialism for McLaughlin becomes a sociological summation of a predatory mode of production resting on bureaucratically planned consumption, administratively managed production, and scientifically generated technics as it reposes with both capitalist and socialist economies.

As it is enmeshed with both capitalism and socialism, McLaughlin contends, industrialism reduces all nature to a reservoir of resources to fabricate more economic goods. Perhaps it is merely a question of his ecosophical attitudes, but this definition of industrialism sounds like a conflation of technology with the forms of contemporary industry. If this is true, then does industrialism not include most human actions since the earliest members of the human species first picked up stones from the reservoir of resources afforded by rockbeds to produce a variety of tools to work a variety of vegetable, mineral, and animal matter into goods for themselves? In throwing a rock (mineral nature) against a tree stump (vegetable nature) to extract grubs (animal nature) to put in their bellies (human nature), did not the first human beings regard nature—human and nonhuman—as a storehouse of resources, assume they could control nature, and expand their industrialistic facilities? Maybe it would be appropriate technology sustainably developed in their immediate bioregion, but such action essentially appears to be "industrialist" in McLaughlin's terms.

To resist anthropocentrism, McLaughlin hides its workings inside his new ecocentrism. This maneuver is not clever, but it is the honest option inasmuch as one can only wonder how humans could ever move beyond anthropocentrism. As long as humans are humans, they will be, and can only be, anthropocentric. The notion of ecocentrism tacitly acknowledges this inevitability, even though McLaughlin does not face this necessity. Ecocentrism simply says humans are nature, humans must coexist with all other life forms in the diversity of nature, and nonhuman life should be accepted as equally important as human beings. Although it is not clear that ecocentrism is really a radical break with most current practices, this rhetorical move merely broadens the notion of humanity to include nonhuman nature as a vital aspect of identity for human beings. So becoming radically ecocentric may mean only becoming softly anthropocentric, because humans could then correctly merge with nature to recenter their human being. Since the humanly defined ecology underpinning ecocentrism would then also be the center of human being, recentering social ontologies and axiologies on this humanly delimited ecology simply slips the *anthropos* into a stealth mode by embedding human beings more forthrightly into the being of nature. Unfortunately, in opposing geo-economics, McLaughlin does not explicitly face many concrete issues of fighting for wealth and power. At best he scribbles a morality play for a cast of straw men whose industrialistic foibles will be corrected by the deus ex machina of ecocentric bioregionalism. In the first act, the fictive science and oppressive technology of industrialism reduce nature to resources, but in the second act this conflict can be corrected by mobilizing "ecologically informed images of nature." So the morality play's lessons are totally in keeping with standard American operating procedures: concoct a techno-fix. Fortunately for us, McLaughlin concludes, the conceptual catalytic converters of ecology, if plugged into the industrialist engines of science by ecocentric deep ecology, will clean commerce's filthy combustion of all its noxious anthropocentric, capitalist, socialist, and scientistic pollutants, causing the rightly rebuilt vehicles of bioregionalism to run cleanly and freely.

Trapped by inaccurate notions of "industrialism" that cannot grasp the possibility of humanity's technological coevolution with nature in anthropogenic environments, McLaughlin wanders around the environmental ills of contemporary society as he avoids the geo-economic political economy of Reich, Thurow, and Luttwak. He assumes that everyone and everything in Western industrial civilization approaches nature as though humans lived totally separate from it rather than completely embedded within it. Human beings to McLaughlin are not "of nature"; instead, they stand over and against it. This is nothing new; at best, it is the old face-off of pastoralism and progressivism—the machine in the garden—that has dogged U.S. political thought since the Revolutionary War. Nature is outside, humanity is inside, and the artificial inside of "society" always works to dominate the natural outside of "environment" by reducing it to resources. Humanity, then, is the sole occupant of artificial spaces or nonnatural habitats, namely, cities or other essentially urbanized spaces in towns, suburbs, or tiny villages wherein people are industrially "liberated" from nature.

The realm of nature is identified as the green hills where small cabins are heated by wood stoves, the seasons are marked by complex changes in plants and the lack of indoor plumbing that still provides a chance to see the stars as one goes back and forth to the biffy. Unfortunately, this arcadian zone also is chockablock with the stuff of nonhuman nature that these unnatural humans regard as raw resources for their industrialist engines of economic growth. Modern society, on the other hand, is identified as cities where one lives in small apartments dependent on oil, electricity, subways, clocks, televisions, supermarkets, and flush toilets. The society is separate from nature, although its industrialism makes it depend on nature to survive. And the latter is conquered, dominated, and exploited by the former, causing all our environmental crises. Some of this is true, but not in the ways that McLaughlin thinks.

Nature and society may already be mutually embedded, wholly interpenetrated, and coincidentally codetermined. The little cabin and big apartment building, the green woods and concrete streets, pristine nature and corrupt society—all occupy shared coevolutionary spaces in the same modes of human production. *Homo sapiens* might be that animal species whose habitat *is* the city. What society is doing to the earth might be *natural* to and for humanity. And what is decried as industrialism could be, in fact, the natural human food chain operating in all the artificial ways that this highly efficient predator species—human beings—naturally uses as a hunting, gathering, cultivating, herding, digging, fishing animal. If humans are animals, and cities are being built in, on, and of this planet, then why are not society, humanity, and industrialism "natural"? Are we to believe that human beings are extraterrestrial, and therefore what people do is the work of space aliens? Or is McLaughlin merely drawing some indefensible distinctions that only substantiate his deep ecological biases, favoring some type of society whose members live in small cabins in the hills, burn wood, and use pit toilets, content that this lifestyle is deeply ecosophical? Even this move has dangers.

After all, given his own conceptual construction of industrialism, are not bioregionalists living in the woods "industrialistic"? Rustic cabins, outdoor plumbing, and wood-burning stoves rest on human assumptions that nature can be controlled by fabricating shelter systems, latrine technics, and heating mechanisms to evade the weather, eliminate body waste, and warm homes. All these acts take something from nature as a "resource reservoir" to produce each of these specific goods. Scale, numbers, and intensity surely modify the outcomes of this equation, but is it not merely a shift in magnitude rather than a qualitative change? These technics (like all technics) for bioregional society (like all forms of society) would simply reshape the human habitat out of coevolving ensembles of nature and humanity, environment and society, and industrialism and ecology.

This analysis of industrialism is naive. Without what is defined as "industrialism," humanity cannot exist at any material level of sophisticated civilization. As many anthropologists have recognized for decades, these industrialistic propensities are what has made humanity what it is. Humans arguably are tool users, tool using is instrumentalistic, and humanity always has been made and remade by its instrumentalistic tool using. Why should we attribute only negative qualities to industrialism as such when they may well be only contingent characteristics of industrial activity, rising from unchecked greed or plain laziness, capitalist traditions or corporate bureaucracy, and bad management or inefficient design? This sort of industrialism could work without the waste, inefficiency, despoiliation, and alienation that McLaughlin rightly condemns if it were designed and operated to avoid these failings. There is little intrinsic to all industrial techniques that is necessarily destructive beyond the inherent destructiveness of many "natural" processes. Indeed, McLaughlin's appeal to a successful utopian bioregional economy, which would have some sort of industrialistic economy to meet its human constituents' material needs, implicitly acknowledges this reality. However, this sort of utopian bioregionalism is not an effective antidote to geo-economics.

Ecodiscipline as Spiritual Environmentalism

The same antagonism that clicks in McLaughlin's endorsement of deep ecology also surfaces in Al Gore's environmental musings. On one level, Gore argues that "the task of restoring the natural balance of the earth's ecological system" could reaffirm the United States' longstanding "interest in social justice, democratic government, and free market economics."[37] As an identifying practice, ecology might even be seen as "a renewed dedication to what Jefferson believed were not merely American but universal inalienable rights: life, liberty, and the pursuit of happiness."[38] At another level, however, Gore takes the spiritual-religious fundamentalism of McLaughlin's opposition to geo-economics to new heights, arguing that the United States' new strategic goals after the cold war are to reestablish "a natural and healthy relationship between human beings and the earth," replacing the brutal exploitation of nature with an "environmentalism of the spirit."[39]

Gore confidently asserts that megatechnic industrial civilization, like all organized cultures, depends on "a web of stories" to explain what it is, where it is going, and why it exists. Industrialism's stories, however, are riddled with the themes of instrumental rationality, mindless growth, and possessive individualism. Such stories have led to the destruction of nature; hence, "new stories about the meaning and purpose of human civilization" must be devised.[40] To tell his new story, however, Gore labels advanced industrial societies as forms of "dysfunctional civilization." Its dysfunctionality has many origins: big science, instrumental rationality, capitalistic greed, industrial alienation, and growth mania are all cited in his diagnosis. Nonetheless, its most basic causes come from a worsening addiction to mass consumption. Because we (meaning everyone in advanced industrial society) allegedly have lost our direct, everyday connections to the natural world, we all are "addicted to the consumption of the earth itself."[41] Lonely, empty, and obsessive, Gore argues, everyone attempts to fill this void with the inauthentic surrogates of consumer goods. Thus we become biosphere abusers. Still, he does not call for us to face down the addiction by going cold turkey from the mall and reintegrating ourselves with the authenticity of nature's harmonies, as McLaughlin's deep ecology community does. Instead he argues that like all addicted individuals or any dysfunctional family, we are in denial; we must heal ourselves, however, and fortunately we can do so. Indeed, there is an easy way out of dysfunctionality.

Gore tells us that, as planetary perverts and consumption fetishists, we all must begin to feel the burning agony that our industrialized pleasures inflict on Mother Earth. When ordinary consumers return to "the original loss" while at the same time attempting to feel the pain that their dysfunctionality causes the Earth, Gore argues, these absolutions "can heal the wound and free the victim from further enslavement."[42] In paroxysms of healing self-condemnation, then, Gore finds the easy steps of civilizational therapy for redeeming nature and humanity from industrialism. By resorting to the faith-healing techniques of popular self-help books or late-afternoon television freak shows, Gore also shrewdly positions himself directly in the rhetorical mainstream of contemporary U.S. culture. In a dysfunctional civilization rationality is ineffectual. Instead, everyone expects a therapeutic script for escaping irrationality. Sensing the mass public's anxious need for such rough-and-ready redemption, he labels us all dysfunctional deviants, identifies the causes of our common neuroses, and provides the latest talking thought-cure needed to realize our collective salvation, namely, "the new story of what it means to be a steward of the earth."[43]

Gore's new story, in turn, rats out geo-economics by grounding it on the old stories of materialism, instrumentalism, and empiricism allegedly given to us by Bacon, Descartes, and Galileo. These old narratives wrongly divided fact and value, cause and effect, and faith and reason, causing our dysfunctionality. Something else is needed now. So Gore turns to new pantheistic or animistic tales for his curative ontology, eschewing old-fashioned scientific narrative in favor of New Age reenchantment. He says, "It is my own belief that the image of God can be seen in every corner of creation, even in us, but only faintly. By gathering in the mind's eye all of creation, one can perceive the image of the Creator vividly."[44] Yet Gore is no medieval mystic, seeking to glimpse God with the unaided eye of pure faith. On the contrary, this New Age epiphany is high-tech: God in his mind's eye can be seen very vividly as a hologram. "Due to the novel and unusual optic principles on which holography is based, when one looks not at a small portion but at the entire hologram," there are "thousands of tiny, faint images" that come together "in the eye of the beholder as a single large, vivid image"; something much the same happens with "the myriad slight strands from earth's web of life—woven so distinctively into our essence—that make up the 'resistance pattern' that reflects the image of God, faintly. By experiencing nature in its fullest—our own and that of all creation—with our senses and with our spiritual imagination, we can glimpse, 'bright shining as the sun,' the infinite image of God."[45]

Having gathered humanity, creation, and divinity into his mind's eye, Gore's spiritual imagination taps out an environmental hologram whose dots and dashes unfortunately only rehash a well-known story in their multistranded resistance pattern. The spirit of environmentalism that can restrike the balance of nature will need to assume a material manifestation to succeed. Here Gore's new story of Earth stewardship takes an amazing turn as he identifies contemporary dysfunctional industrial civilization with the fascist and communist threats of World War II and the cold war. "Then, as now, the real enemy was a dysfunctional way of thinking." Thus, good old-fashioned "totalitarianism" is made equivalent to today's new-fangled bad "consumptionism."

> In Nazi Germany, dysfunctional thinking was institutionalized in the totalitarian state, its dogma, and its war machine. Today, a different dysfunction takes the form

> of ravenous, insatiable consumption, its dogma, and the mechanisms by which ever more resources are obtained. Totalitarianism and consumptionism have led to crises peculiar to advanced industrial civilization: both are examples of alienation and technology run amok. Just as totalitarianism collapses individuals into "the state," the new ideology of consumption collapses individuals into the desire for what they consume, even as it fosters the assumption that we are separate from the earth. It is this strange and destructive way of thinking about our relationship to the physical world that is our real enemy. The struggle to save the global environment is in one way much more difficult than the struggle to vanquish Hitler, for this time the war is with ourselves. We are the enemy, just as we have only ourselves as allies. In a war such as this, then, what is victory and how will we recognize it?[46]

This effort to identify yesterday's dysfunctional Nazi stormtroopers with today's dysfunctional suburban Wal-Mart shoppers plainly is a tough reach, but Gore needs the linkage to continue the World War II theme in his story.

To win this new global war, Gore also claims there only is one workable model for guiding today's titanic struggle against "alienation and technology run amok" both here and abroad, namely, the Marshall Plan. In that historic program, Gore notes, several nations joined together "to reorganize an entire region of the world and change its way of life."[47] Like the Marshall Plan, Gore's Global Marshall Plan must (strangely, for a design dedicated to environmental spiritual renewal) "focus on strategic goals and emphasize actions and programs that are likely to remove the bottlenecks presently inhibiting the healthy functioning of the global economy . . . to serve human needs and promote sustained economic progress."[48] At this turn, Gore's new story of stewardship over the Earth gets to the punchline. Just as the Marshall Plan of the 1940s picked up and dusted off dysfunctional fascist totalitarians, putting them to work in U.S.-planned liberal democratic capitalism, so now must a new Global Marshall Plan round up and retrain dysfunctional suburban consumptionists, putting them to work in a new U.S.-planned spiritually refreshed green capitalism. Regrettably, "sustainable development" here apparently means finding ways of sustaining the economy on a global scale rather than sustaining the Earth's ecology at some more optimal natural balance.

Preserving Earth's natural ecology, however, may not be Gore's ultimate goal. The Global Marshall Plan instead provides megatechnical polyarchies with a global agenda for advancing a softer form of geo-economics as geo-environmentalization. Adopting this instrument as a central organizing principle, according to Gore, "means embarking on an all-out effort to use every policy and program, every law and institution, every treaty and alliance, every tactic and strategy, every plan and course of action—to use, in short, every means to halt the destruction of the environment and to preserve and nurture our ecological system."[49] Geo-economics is a predatory nationalistic attempt to monopolize material wealth for only a few in a handful of nation-states. Ecodiscipline recognizes that our "ecological system" is the global business environment as well as the world's natural environment. Both will be destroyed if we allow unchecked growth, mindless consumption, dysfunctional development, and obsessive accumulation to continue, but both can be saved if we plan on a global scale for environmentally appropriate growth, mindful consumption, sustainable development, and careful accumulation guided by an ethic of spiritual environmentalism.

Gore's ecodisciplinary designs outline a six-point course of action that necessitate the following actions: (1) stabilizing the world population, (2) deploying appropriate technologies, (3) devising techniques of ecological accounting to audit the production of all economic "goods" and ecological "evils," (4) imposing new regulatory frameworks to make the plan a success, (5) reeducating the global populace about environmental necessities, and (6) establishing models of sustainable development. McLaughlin's geo-environmental quest for personal identity and community in geo-economic societies pales beside this program, which can provide the new "central organizing principle" to replace the now lost sense of purpose and unity once provided by the cold war era's struggle against communism or the fight against fascism during World War II.[50]

Casting dysfunctional consumerists, who remain silent and supportive of unchecked development under geo-economics, as corrupt quislings and describing environmentalists of the spirit, who oppose mindless growth, as a green underground, Gore openly endorses U.S. intervention to aid any and all who "are standing in the path of destruction," recognizing only that "this time we are invading ourselves and attacking the ecological system of which we are a part."[51] And because there are no other institutional entities—the UN, OECD, or NATO—with the muscle to perform the heavy lifting needed to manage the global environment after this self-invasion is over, according to Gore, "The responsibility for taking the initiative, for innovating, catalyzing, and leading such an effort, falls disproportionately on the United States."[52] At the end of the cold war, we cannot simply show the interventionist central bureaucracies the door to retirement, nor can we allow them to remobilize society around geo-economic programs of mindless material development. On the contrary, we must bring the polyarchical state back in. Only now, the megatechnical bureaucrats will be green.

Ecodiscipline as Survivalism

David Oates begins, as do many government bureaucrats, with a simple insight: "Right thinking precedes right action."[53] The problem, of course, is specifying what *right* means. Still, Oates, like McLaughlin and Gore, is willing to ground a new ethics for green governance in the present crisis. For Oates, advanced industrial societies cling to flawed ideas—liberalism, progress, rationalism, growth, egoism, competitiveness, individualism—that can result only in wrong action. Consequently, one must find better ideological alternatives, which he believes can be discovered in "an ecological ethics." That is, a "healthy comprehension of the meaning of nature, of the inescapable network of natural interdependence—these ideas would result in a sane reaction to the problems of worldwide pollution, waste of resources, overpopulation, species extinction, and so forth. . . . The human and natural world can no longer afford the luxury of selfish and narrow ideas. For it turns out that ideas—values, beliefs, definitions of ourselves and nature—are part of the ecosystem."[54] "Right thinking" and "wrong thinking," then, are naturalized by embedding both sets of reasoning in the inner workings of the Earth's ecology. Humans engaged in rightly thought ecological action would resonate with nature's immanent harmonies, discovering "an inner guide, a secure sense of balance and timing, action and stillness," while humans enmeshed with wrongly thought ecological action unwisely diverge from nature's intrinsic order, clinging to "their crazy notion that they can destroy nature without destroying themselves."[55]

With these rhetorical moves Oates propounds an ecodisciplinary ethics that rests "on the notion that the human and the natural do fully coincide. And so the basis of value must be literal and sound, truthful to the facts of natural life as science relates them."[56] Having enlisted the deep structures of nature as definitive guides of right and wrong, and then having identified science as the most truthful means of decoding these rights and wrongs, Oates makes a simple, if dangerous, claim to ground his ethicopolitical project of ecological renewal. His reading of "ecological thinkers" reveals that they have found "an intrinsic value in biology to build a realistic ethic of life on earth. Their near-unanimous conclusion is that the sciences of life do indeed enable us to find—not invent—a basis for ethical value in the nature of life itself. That basic value is *survival.* Survival is the master concept of all life forms."[57] Realizing the harshness of this claim, Oates qualifies himself—unlike Luttwak, with his highly Darwinian geo-economics—by assuring the reader that his "survival ethic" is *not* a new Darwinian reading of nature. Instead, "it places the individual within his or her many contexts, and seeks well-being in the most comprehensive sense."[58]

A survivalist surveillance of nature by science and the state transforms it into ecodisciplinary "environments," elaborate natural systems of such complexity, diversity, instability, and connectivity that no one person, scientific discipline, society, or formal discourse can adequately comprehend or represent their workings. Discussions of nature in immediate terms through ordinary language as a localized cultural setting, a particular biophysical site, or a regionalized social ecology, then, disappear into much more arcane discussions of environmental complexities conducted in formalist technoscientific disciplinary discourses about the environment as an elaborate global system of systems. At the same time, this process of environmentalizing nature reduces its raw, unknown otherness to sets of purportedly rational, knowable relationships that can be defined, disciplined, and dealt with by administrative fiat guided by instrumental science.

This project of environmentalizing rationality articulates all the key assumptions needed for a new bureaucratic green state formation intent on Global Marshall Planning. Nature is reread not in the communal terms of immediate ecosocial settings or bioregional diversity but rather in accord with the findings presented by the life sciences. These scientific projects, according to Oates, find rather than invent a basis for ethical value in a new master concept: *survival.* Master concepts, however, are our rhetorical introduction to new groups of "master conceptualizers" in green bureaucracies who must be trusted to engage in right thinking and right acting as "environmental protection agents" in the administrative search for ecological well-being in its most comprehensive sense.

Oates is not pushing a gritty survivalist agenda for the "here and now" of every private individual viciously fighting to protect the "me and mine." Survival is much more. It boils down to defining a new time and space for an ecodisciplinary state's exercising social control beyond mere sovereignty over territory in the expanses of sustainability in the environment. Ecological governance, conducted in accord with a geo-environmentalizing regime's master concept of survival, accepts "the more genuine biological perspective on survival: the twin considerations of an organism's fitness and the environment's health. Both must be continually upheld for 'survival' to have any biological meaning . . . into future generations, and throughout the ecosphere, and for all those other organisms on whose lives our life depends. The ecological perspective is long and wide—it concerns all of us, here, forever."[59]

The "discovery" of such time frames, spatial realms, and population groups in Oates's technoscience-driven ecodisciplinary ethics also empowers green bureaucrats to police the fitness of organisms and the health of environments from within the state apparatus not only now but for all time. Guaranteeing the grasp of a master concept, such as survival or sustainability, empowers polyarchical green bureaucrats—as the scientifically legitimated master conceptualizers—to reinscribe the existing cultural, economic, and territorial order of the planet as an elaborate array of environments requiring constant supervision to be made safe for survival and sustainability. As Oates claims, the survival agenda of fitness and health "applies simultaneously to individuals, populations, communities, and ecosystems; and it applies simultaneously to the present and the future."[60]

This command to go anywhere at any time to defend the cause of survival also directs ecodisciplinarians to pursue other equally problematic values on a more global level with the full force of state power and positive science, namely, stability, diversity, and interdependence. A powerful nation-state is no longer empowered simply to defend its territory to protect its populations. It also must identify and police the surroundings of all its many environments to guarantee ecological stability, biological diversity, and environmental interdependence. Because some states are more sustainable than others, their survival imperatives can become guidelines for environmental colonialism. So to survive, the state may choose to impose the status of a green belt, forest preserve, nature reservation, or environmental refuge on other societies. Oates claims that the ecological ethic of stability as "a steady-state" would not result in stagnation. Such outcomes would, of course, offend the growth fixations of consumers and citizens living in liberal capitalist democracies. On the contrary, he believes that this ethic would mean "directing growth and change in nondestructive ways, generated within the standing pattern that supports life."[61] But who directs growth and change for whom? Is there a standing pattern that directs life? Does anyone really know enough about it to direct growth in accord with it? In practice, Global Marshall Planners in Washington or New York could use ecological criteria to impose sustainable development of economic growth at home as they also force ecological steady states on others abroad. If India's millions stay on foot or bicycles, then Germany's millions will stay in their cars. If Indonesia keeps growing trees, then Japan can keep consuming lumber. And if Brazil's ranchers keep turning rain forest into cattle ranges, then U.S. suburbanites will get their cheeseburgers.

Obviously, a "steadying state" designed and managed by green bureaucrats will be needed to enforce environmentalized stable states of dynamic ecological equilibrium, which Oates identifies as the sine qua non of stability. Ironically, then, green bureaucrats, who are directed to stabilize everyone's fitness and health, should restructure populations and growth by planning for sustainable patterns in timber harvesting, oil production, agricultural output, land use, and consumer marketing to contain but not end the growth fetishism of mass-consumption capitalism. Oates concurs with Gore and McLaughlin that all present geo-economic national economies run on a paradox: "Whatever is achieved instantly becomes inadequate when measured against the ethic of continual consumption. Satisfaction only creates dissatisfaction, in an accelerating cycle. 'More' is an unrealizable goal."[62] Since these consumerist values continually cause more and more damage, the environmentalizing strategies of ecodisciplinary regimes must enforce a new social commitment to their opposites, namely, the willing acceptance of "less" as the moral basis for new ecological values on a social and individual level. For survival's sake, "the ethical consciousness of earth's human population must therefore be as ecologically well regulated as the size of the earth's population."[63]

Protecting the whole, in the practice of environmentalizing green bureaucracies, also can become a strange administrative credo of *biophilia,* or love of life, in a framework of *biocentrism,* or placing earth-life-nature at the core of green thought and bureaucratic practice. If environments are to be protected, then all the life within them would, of course, anchor the practical forms of human engagement with the world. Yet this emotional commitment to "life," or life seen as the superorganism of Earth in ecology, might entail a condemnation of humanity in open misanthropy by containing, destroying, or limiting some traditional forms of human living in favor of the earth's ecological survival. It is not that geo-environmentalists love their lives less but that they might love other animal and plant life more—so green bureaucrats will reason as they prevent some human communities from developing to enhance environmental survivability. Such contradictions actually make sense, because they stand for placing limits on geo-economic excesses in those cases where the survivalist operatives of the green steady state see everyday social policies threatening nonhuman life's survival and stability. "Where survival of the whole seems threatened," Oates concludes, "as in issues of extinction and pollution, then the basic ethos of protecting the whole predominates."[64]

Beyond Geo-economics and Ecodiscipline

Ecodiscipline in many ways would counter the logic of the geo-economic by moving the polyarchy of existing liberal welfare states onto a new ecological footing, redeputizing their administrative personnel as bureaucratic greens. Because most consumers are willing participants in a dysfunctional geo-economic civilization not yet subject to full-blown green governance, they must be forced to be functional in accord with the regulatory goals of ecodisciplinarian bureaucracies. Entirely new identities built around ecological ends, such as survival or sustainability, can therefore be elaborated for megatechnics beyond the consumeristic personas that are the foundation of alleged dysfunctionality in national economic competitiveness. McLaughlin, Gore, and Oates urge state power to counter nationalistic geo-economic dysfunctionality with globalistic environmentality.

Inasmuch as economic and governmental techniques are a central focus of political struggle today, the complex interactions of populations with their surroundings in political economies and ecologies are forcing states to redefine what is within their competence. Ecodisciplinary discourses argue that to survive now, it is not enough for states merely to maintain legal jurisdiction over their allegedly sovereign territories. As new limits to growth are constantly discovered or redefined, states will be forced to guarantee their populations' productivity in all the environmental settings encompassed by the global political economy.[65] Rationally reforming the technosphere demands prudent administration of the biosphere to ensure sustainable development in the "marketsphere."

As Reich, Thurow, and Luttwak illustrate, governmental discourses must methodically mobilize particular assumptions, codes, and procedures to enforce specific understandings about the economy and society. Yet as McLaughlin, Gore, and Oates also show, other codes of ecological ethics about Earth in the balance could play the same roles. They can generate new administrative "truths" or managerial "knowledges" that will denominate codes of power with significant reserves of popular legitimacy. Inasmuch as they classify, organize, and legitimate larger understandings of ecological reality, such discourses can authorize or invalidate the options for constructing particular institutions, practices, or concepts in society at large. They frame the emergence of both new collective subjectivities (e.g., global ecologies as dynamic bioeconomic systems) and collections of subjects (e.g., individuals as bioeconomic units in such global systems) to protect the environment. Still, as both sides of these discursive streams in geo-economics and ecodiscipline show, one must remember how extensively the meanings of ecological subjectivity are still being contested among new class experts. Ecological subjectivity can be expressed in small-scale experiments by autonomous human beings following localistic political agendas in many bioregional communities, or it may be retooled in statist programs for postanthropocentric human organisms interacting within Global Marshall Plans, depending on which interpretations are empowered where.[66] International politics and global economics can be organized around either theoretical agenda. Whether geo-economists or ecodisciplinarians (or, indeed, some other rationalized system of ecological power and knowledge) will prevail is to be determined in political struggles of the near future. Both are likely to disserve the interests and agendas of local ecological movements or democratic populist networks.

The different understandings of environmentalism presented by McLaughlin, Gore, and Oates may simply be another guise for new class empowerment and communal disempowerment; in opposition to them, many ecological populists see how they must be resisted from below by other visions of localism, bioregionalism, and federalism. A bureaucratic green politics of conservation is centered on conserving state power as much as sustaining ecological balances in the ecosystem. Despite their pretensions of ecological omnicompetence, green bureaucracies are all too often too far away and too removed from almost every particular bioregional setting to be truly effective at safeguarding the environmental security of most local communities. What these communities need is not new justifications for environmentalizing state policies but rather the freedom and resources to embed their economies and societies in their particular ecological localities while guarding against negatively affecting other bioregional settings in doing so. This is the only way in which green governance from below, and nested within each particular ecological context, will be able to realize greater social justice, democratic government, or free exchange. Otherwise, as chapter 6 indicates, more attacks may come from the backwoods against the organization-dependent technologies of megatechnical polyarcharies.

Notes

1. See Robert Reich, *The Work of Nations: Preparing Ourselves for Twenty-first Century Capitalism* (New York: Knopf, 1991); Lester Thurow, *Head to Head: The Coming Economic Battle among Japan, Europe, and America* (New York: Morrow, 1992); and Edward N. Luttwak, *The Endangered American Dream: How to Stop the United States from Becoming a Third-World Country and How to Win the Geo-Economic Struggle for Industrial Supremacy* (New York: Simon and Schuster, 1993); as well as Andrew McLaughlin, *Regarding Nature: Industrialism and Deep Ecology* (Albany: State University of New York Press, 1993); Albert Gore, *Earth in the Balance: Ecology and the Human Spirit* (Boston: Houghton Mifflin, 1992); and David Oates, *Earth Rising: Ecological Belief in an Age of Science* (Corvalis: Oregon State University Press, 1989).

2. For a global overview of such reasoning, see Paul Kennedy, *Preparing for the Twenty-first Century* (New York: Random House, 1993).

3. Luttwak, *American Dream*, 34. James Fallows pursues a similar line of argument in *More Like Us: Making America Great Again* (Boston: Houghton Mifflin, 1989).

4. Richard J. Barnet, *The Lean Years: Politics in the Age of Scarcity* (New York: Simon and Schuster, 1980), 17.

5. Ibid., 310–16.

6. Ibid., 309.

7. Cited in Kirkpatrick Sale, *The Green Revolution: The American Environmental Movement, 1962–1992* (New York: Hill and Wang, 1993), 77.

8. Cited in ibid., 102.

9. Reich, *Work of Nations*, 153.

10. Samuel P. Huntington, "The Clash of Civilizations," *Foreign Affairs* 72 (Summer 1993): 22–49. Also see Samuel P. Huntington, *The Clash of Civilization and the Remaking of World* (New York: Simon and Schuster, 1996), 19–78.

11. Thurow, *Head to Head*, 15.

12. Ibid., 12.

13. Ibid., 23–24.

14. Ibid., 247.

15. Ibid., 257.

16. Ibid., 198.

17. Bill Clinton, "Inaugural Address," *U.S. Department of State Dispatches*, January 1993.

18. Luttwak, *American Dream*, 34.

19. Ibid., 310.

20. Ibid., 314.

21. Ibid., 310.

22. Ibid.

23. Ibid.

24. Ibid., 34.

25. McLaughlin, *Regarding Nature*, 78.

26. Ibid., 79.

27. Ibid., 172.

28. Ibid., 184.

29. Ibid., 80.

30. Bill Devall, *Simple in Means, Rich in Ends: Practicing Deep Ecology* (Salt Lake City: Peregrine Smith, 1988), 178.

31. Ibid., 160. For an extensive review of deep ecology's politics, see Timothy W. Luke, "The Dreams of Deep Ecology," *Telos* 76 (Summer 1988): 65–92.

32. McLaughlin, *Regarding Nature*, 172.

33. Ibid., 152.

34. Ibid., 169.

35. Ibid.
36. Ibid., 151.
37. Gore, *Earth in the Balance,* 270.
38. Ibid.
39. Ibid., 218, 238.
40. Ibid., 216.
41. Ibid., 220.
42. Ibid., 236–37.
43. Ibid., 237.
44. Ibid., 265.
45. Ibid.
46. Ibid., 274–75.
47. Ibid., 296.
48. Ibid., 297.
49. Ibid., 274. For a sense of where this all-out effort might lead policymaking, see Marian R. Chertow and Daniel C. Esty, eds., *Thinking Ecologically: The Next Generation of Environmental Policy* (New Haven, Conn.: Yale University Press, 1997).
50. Gore, *Earth in the Balance,* 274.
51. Ibid., 294.
52. Ibid., 304.
53. Oates, *Earth Rising,* 148.
54. Ibid., 146–47.
55. Ibid., 148, 146.
56. Ibid., 150.
57. Ibid.
58. Ibid., 151.
59. Ibid.
60. Ibid.
61. Ibid., 152.
62. Ibid., 155.
63. Ibid., 154.
64. Ibid., 163.
65. For more elaboration of the reasons state power must guarantee environmental security, see Norman Myers, *Ultimate Security: The Environmental Basis of Political Stability* (New York: Norton, 1993). Also see Tom Athanasiou, *Divided Planet: The Ecology of Rich and Poor* (Boston: Little, Brown, 1996).
66. See Kirkpatrick Sale, *Dwellers in the Land: The Bioregional Vision* (Philadelphia: New Society, 1991); Murray Bookchin, *Remaking Society: Pathways to a Green Future* (Boston: South End, 1990); and Brian Tokar, *Earth for Sale: Reclaiming Ecology in the Age of Corporate Greenwash* (Boston: South End, 1997).

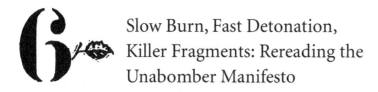

6 Slow Burn, Fast Detonation, Killer Fragments: Rereading the Unabomber Manifesto

One of the most extreme cases of personal resistance against the collectives built by new class expertise under contemporary corporate capitalism can be found in the thoughts and actions of the Unabomber. From 1978 to 1996 an unknown individual terrorist killed three and wounded twenty-three others in a string of sixteen bombings. These attacks seemed to be the work of one person, but the authorities believed for a while that a group might have been involved, because the Unabomber's communications also were signed in the name of a shadowy cell: "FC," the Freedom Club.[1] In part this terror campaign is intriguing because many of its victims were arguably members of the new class, comparatively obscure administrators, agents, or academicians who were actively working in the applied sciences, computer sciences, or mathematical sciences for small firms or universities. In addition, its conduct is a case study, first, in what new populist oppositional movements ought not to do—for both ethical and tactical reasons—as they test various strategies of resistance against the collectives organizing their everyday life and, second, in what too many ordinary, frustrated, angry men might do in reaction to the dead-end lives within which they have become trapped as the new class consolidates the 20:80 society around them.

The complicated story behind the arrest of Ted Kaczynski in April 1996 as the suspected Unabomber and the particularities of this eighteen-year-long strategic bombing campaign against "the System" nonetheless provide a broader backdrop against which to reexamine the details of this case, as well as an opportunity to scrutinize the finer points of the now infamous manifesto, "Industrial Society and Its Future" by "FC," which was published in both the *New York Times* and the *Washington Post* on September 19, 1995. The manifesto gave national audiences a glimpse of the same cultural, economic, and political issues over which radical ecologists and populists have tussled with new class experts during the last quarter century: modern leftist movements, big government, consumer capitalism, environmental destruction, and the loss of personal autonomy.

Slow Burn: The Life and Times of Ted Kaczynski

Until court proceedings proved otherwise during January 1998, Ted Kaczynski was regarded as only the "alleged Unabomber." David Kaczynski informed the authorities about his brother, Ted, after noting some disturbing parallels between Ted's personal letters, which espoused radical antiestablishment positions, and the Unabomber manifesto. Because he was not caught in the act of placing explosives in some academician's mailbox, the case against Kaczynski in 1997 rested exclusively on forensic and circumstantial evidence. Nonetheless, government press releases and mass media reports both indicated that Kaczynski's small cabin in the Montana woods yielded a considerable cache of potentially damaging discoveries, including typewritten initial drafts of the Unabomber manifesto, manual typewriters whose type matched that of copies sent out for publication, numerous bomb-making tools, explosive chemicals, pieces of a partially completed bomb, one fully operational bomb, and a detailed personal journal that accounted for his activities during the past three decades. The Justice Department found lists of actual and potential bombing victims, as well as a secret numerical code used by the Unabomber to verify his identity in communicating with the authorities. Kaczynski's DNA—as detected from saliva testing—apparently correlated positively with traces extracted from postage stamps affixed to the packaging from mail bombs dating back to 1978. Additionally, many witnesses at hotels, restaurants, and bus terminals put Kaczynski in or around Sacramento, California, a location frequently used to post the bomb packages, when mail bombs were either mailed or detonated.[2]

After many months of careful preparation, the government brought its case against Kaczynski to court in Sacramento, California, during January 1998. With all the evidence from Kaczynski's cabin, the FBI and the Department of Justice were intent on proving to other potential terrorists that they can always track down, convict, and if necessary, execute the most violent and intelligent criminals. Their confidence was so high that the Justice Department rejected Kaczynski's December 1997 offer to plead guilty in exchange for life without parole.[3] His lawyers then shifted strategies toward an insanity defense, but Kaczynski refused this option, maintaining throughout that he was not, in his words, "a sickie." He subsequently attempted suicide in his jail cell on January 14, 1998, and then moved the next day to fire his attorneys and to represent himself in court.[4] To affirm his competence, he reluctantly submitted to many hours of analysis by a state-appointed psychiatrist, Dr. Sally Johnson, who found Kaczynski to be competent—as well as a delusional paranoid schizophrenic.

With this information, Judge Garland Burrell Jr. rejected Kaczynski's request to serve as his own attorney, and left him back in the hands of his lawyers and their mental-defect defense strategy. Fearing jurors would be swayed by Kaczynski's antitechnology convictions or mental incompetence, the Justice Department then accepted the Unabomber's plea on January 22, 1998, a deal that gave him no possibilities for appeal or release.[5] On May 4, 1998, he was formally sentenced to four life terms in prison, and the next day he was flown to a maximum-security federal prison in Florence, Colorado, where Oklahoma City bomber Timothy McVeigh was also imprisoned. At his sentencing, Kaczynski maintained that he was a political prisoner who was being discredited by the government in an effort to undermine his ideas about technology. "By discrediting me personally," he claimed at the sentencing, "they hope to discredit my political ideas." This also prompted him to promise a more detailed rebuttal in the future: "At a later time I expect to respond at length to the sentencing memorandum. Meanwhile, I hope the public will reserve judgment against me and all the facts about the Unabomb case until another time."[6] Given the final disposition of his case, it is interesting to reconsider how Kaczynski was portrayed when he was at large as the Unabomber.

Newsweek's take on Kaczynski after his arrest in 1996 placed him in a long line of famous American oddballs who, beginning with Thoreau, had moved into shacks on the edges of civilization to pen jeremiads against society's oppression. On the one hand, *Newsweek* claimed that Kaczynski took up "a grubby, lonely existence in one of the most rugged regions of the North American outback," while on the other hand, it saw a pattern in Kaczynski's life that "bespeaks profound alienation—an estrangement so deep it makes Thoreau, with his two-year sabbatical at Walden Pond, look like a social butterfly."[7] Joe Klein, in a *Newsweek* column, asserted that his "essential left-wing orientation seems indisputable,"[8] which simply affirmed the spin taken by *Newsweek*'s editors the week before when they cast Kaczynski as "the diabolically elusive killer who, with his mail bombs, his manifesto and his taunts, hurled thunderbolts of prophetic judgement at the rest."[9] Other observers also have assayed the significance of Kaczynski's acts, ranging from Kirkpatrick Sale, writing in *The Nation*, who saw the Unabomber's activities as those of "a rational and serious man, deeply committed to his cause, who has given a great deal of thought to his work and a great deal of time to his expression of it,"[10] to Maggie Scharf, writing in *The New Republic*, who submitted that "the diagnosis of Narcissistic Personality Disorder seems to be the most illuminating explanation of the Unabomber's seemingly incomprehensible behavior."[11] Unfortunately these extreme, antithetical viewpoints provide the interpretative frameworks that much of the educated public has used to decipher the alleged Unabomber's behavior. In his eagerness to promote his then forthcoming book on the Luddites, Sale argued that "the Unabomber stands in a long line of anti-technology critics" who share a great many views with "a number of people today who might be called neo-Luddites—Jerry Mander, Chellis Glenndinning, Jeremy Rifkin, Bill McKibben, Wendell Berry, Dave Foreman, Langdon Winner, Stephanie Mills and John Zerzan among them."[12] For Scharf, the Unabomber is "deeply injured at the core and suffering from sorely depleted supplies to self-esteem . . . with a sense of inner emptiness and painful feelings of unworthiness, despair and desolation."[13] Neither of these pundits can be dismissed, nor can their views be confirmed. The final word on the Unabomber's mental state ultimately conforms to the personal sympathies, political persuasions, and ethical opinions of the journalists who have tackled the enigmatic story.

Whether Kaczynski is mad or reasonable, narcissistic or selfless, or evil or virtuous cannot be easily determined. Many rushed to make these judgments, but they often had little evidence to anchor their diagnoses. One must wonder how their accounts add up to little more than a disturbed body politic projecting its own fears and anxieties on this pathetic prisoner. More interesting perhaps are the more subtle elective affinities linking Kaczynski's life, the Unabomber manifesto, and the whole cultural context from which they emerged. Much of Kaczynski's *Newsweek/Time/U.S. News and World Report* persona shows so little of what might be regarded as "normal" that he could be considered a perfect case study in the (ab)normalization of individual subjectivity.[14] Here we might adopt, but also push beyond, the categories of individual subjectivity used by Foucault. Normalization is doubled back on itself as (ab)normalization inasmuch as the disciplinary structures of "the system" created a secretive agent who aspired to destroy what he considered wrong.[15] No vocabulary is fully adequate for reiterating what the Unabomber attacks in his manifesto or for explaining how someone could commit this sort of violent action. On one level, it is about power and knowledge turning an individual against technoscientific structures because of the frictions felt by all individuals living within industrial, bureaucratic society. On another level, it is a plea to recollectivize people and things on a smaller scale, at a slower pace, and in simpler ways. And on a third level, it is a shallow justification for mayhem and murder.

Fast Detonation: Rereading the Unabomber Manifesto

The Unabomber manifesto is a flawed document, one that crudely reduces the effects exerted by a complex, flexible transnational mode of production and consumption down to simple, rigid sets of national-level categories that are in turn seen as automata, functioning as "the system" in the ideal types of "industrial society." Nonetheless, there are interesting insights in this document, and it merits an extended reconsideration. This statement reveals a great deal in its own strange rhetorical registers about the collectivistic mechanisms needed for producing or reproducing the passive social individuality of contemporary corporate capitalist society.

There are no signs that the Unabomber pitched his arguments to catch the attention of today's many populist movements. A quick survey of the footnotes to the manifesto suggests that he did not have access to materials much more sophisticated than those anyone one might find in the second-hand bookshops or a public library in any small town. Not unlike Paul and Percival Goodman's analysis of the manner in which "the means of livelihood" structure "ways of life," the Unabomber's condemnation of those "man-made things" of "engineering and architecture" that are "the heaviest and biggest part of what we experience"[16] indicates that he recognizes how human liberation is continuously constrained by categorical imperatives embedded in the totalitarian design of ordinary technics.

Written as a disorganized series of short numbered paragraphs (the subsequent citations here are to paragraphs, not page numbers) and running some 35,000 words in length, the Unabomber's manifesto begins with radical sentiments that many have shared for nearly two hundred years: "The Industrial Revolution and its consequences have been a disaster for the human race," because the workings of "the industrial-technological system" have "destablized society, have made life unfulfilling, have subjected human beings to indignities, have led to widespread psychological suffering (in the Third World to physical suffering as well) and have inflicted severe damage on the natural world" (¶1). The Unabomber's critique, then, outlines a new vision of "what must be done" from the perspective of a burned-out one-time academician living in Montana's backwoods, on the rustic fringe of the United States' consumer society . Because of the author's reclusive existence outside all conventional networks of publication, the Unabomber's most recent bombings became a ploy to capture the attention of the nations' reading public. If the Unabomber had not committed any terroristic acts, he reasons, "and had submitted the writings to a publisher, they probably would not have been published." In order to get "our message before the public with some chance of making a lasting impression, we've had to kill people"(¶96). But how lasting was this impression? The Unabomber killed three people over thirteen years, and the message of his manifesto mostly was tossed away with the rest of the September 19, 1995, newspaper.

The Technification of Domination

The Unabomber admits the manifesto is neither a comprehensive nor a balanced account of modern life. Instead, it examines "only some of the negative developments that have grown out of the industrial-technological system," particularly those that "have received insufficient public attention or in which we have something new to say" (¶5). What the Unabomber believes has received inadequate consideration, or is "new," is to be found in his striking attempts to register how and why technology as "a means of livelihood" deprives people of their dignity and autonomy in modern "ways of life" while imposing a sense of inferiority and powerlessness as part of the processes of collectivization. Although some might dismiss the manifesto as another vacuous exercise in red-green confusion along the same lines as those articulated by most of Sale's "New Luddites,"[17] there is more to the Unabomber's writings than this superficial critique concedes.[18]

The Unabomber manifesto parallels Marcuse's reading of modern technology: complex technics simultaneously increase life expectancy and everyday ease as they decrease life enjoyment and ordinary freedom. Indeed, the daily operation of the industrial-technological system "provides the great rationalization of the unfreedom of man and demonstrates the 'technical' impossibility of being autonomous, of determining one's own life. This unfreedom appears neither irrational nor as political, but rather as submission to the technical apparatus which enlarges the comforts of life and increases the productivity of labor."[19] Although technology, industry, and business pose as vital mediations of cultural liberation and humanitarian progress, they also generate "the legitimacy of domination" that leads into "a rationally totalitarian society."[20]

This deadening combination of capital, research, and technics in collectives constituted by market-mediated choices is what has garnered too little attention. How can the allegedly emancipatory formations of technoscience, even with the countervailing legal institutions of capitalist liberal-democratic regimes, function as a regime of normalization so abject that it can be described only as a rational totalitarian order? The Unabomber approaches this question in several ways, but the concept of "oversocialization" captures much of his distaste for the regimen of normalization embedded within these collectives. Although he does not frame his analysis in terms of Foucault's capillary images of power,[21] the Unabomber sees human dignity and freedom bleeding away into preprocessed modes of subjectivity: "We are socialized to conform to many norms of behavior that do not fall under the headings of morality. Thus the oversocialized person is kept on a psychological leash and spends his life running on rails that society has laid down for him. In many oversocialized people this results in a sense of constraint and powerlessness that can be a severe hardship" (¶26). Even more ironically, Kaczynski sees this condition afflicting leftists even more acutely than it does most people, because the prevailing blocs of power and wealth in the United States have limited the modern left mostly to playacting its resistance as weakly focused mediations of artificial negativity that does not manifest itself as actual revolution (¶26–30).

As the Unabomber observes, the order of the industrial-technological system is rooted deeply in normalization, because "the system couldn't care less what kind of music a man listens to, what kind of clothes he wears or what religion he believes in as long as he studies in school, holds a respectable job, climbs the status ladder, is a 'responsible' parent, is nonviolent and so forth" (¶29). Conceding that this analysis is rough, he asserts that the highly rationalized totalitarianism articulated within oversocialization causes "low self-esteem, depressive tendencies, and defeatism," because this normalization regime "tries to socialize us to a greater extent than any previous society" (¶32). By stifling or distorting "the power process," the oversocializing routines of normalization defeat the average person's choice of goals, exertion of effort, and attainment of goals (¶33), which in turn eviscerates everyone's sense of autonomy.

To compensate for the real satisfactions of lost power processes, the normalization accords of oversocialization provide for, but also openly endorse, "surrogate activities" that all industrial-technological peoples "set up for themselves merely in order to have some goal to work toward . . . for the sake of the 'fulfillment' that they get from pursuing the goal" (¶39). Because "only minimal effort is necessary to satisfy one's physical needs" (¶39) in modern industrial society, most of what preoccupies anyone in everyday life is a surrogate: art, science, athletics, literature, as well as acquiring money, participating in office politics, engaging in social activism, and pursuing celebrity. These surrogates, however, are hollow substitutes that are "less satisfying than the pursuit of real goals . . . one indication of this is the fact that, in many or most cases, people who are deeply involved in surrogate activities are never satisfied, never at rest" (¶41). True satisfaction will never come, because everyone has acceded to personal irrelevance by embracing the empty surrogates of this rationalized system of totalitarian routinization. The Unabomber suggests that in our society "the effort needed to satisfy biological needs does not occur AUTONOMOUSLY, but by functioning as parts of an immense social machine" (¶41). When meeting real needs takes only trivial effort, and the search for surrogates is given such latitude, the stage is set for individual (ab)normalization on many interrelated levels.

The Unabomber's analysis again parallels Marcuse's understanding of technics as "instruments of social and political control," because every individual's sense of his or her current needs takes place through the scientific organization of labor and leisure, "which operate beyond and outside the work process and condition the individuals in accord with the dominant social interests."[22] Autonomy under these conditions is difficult to attain, or sustain, because each individual's power process is preempted by the highly rationalized regime of industrial-technological society, which in turn redefines the substantive qualities of rationality to suit profit targets set by its "merchants of desire."[23] As Marcuse notes: "The apparatus to which the individual is to adjust and adapt himself is so rational that individual protests and liberation appear not only hopeless but as utterly irrational. The system of life created by modern industry is defined in terms of expediency, convenience and efficiency. . . . Rational behavior becomes identical with a matter-of-factness which teaches reasonable submissiveness and thus guarantees getting along with the prevailing order."[24]

Even though this resistance was futile, and perhaps irrational, Kaczynski opposed the normalization routines of expediency, convenience, and efficiency (in a life that would seem sociopathic to many observers even before he was indicted for and convicted of serious crimes) by going against the prevailing social order of suburban normality. To live normally for him would have further interdicted his already tenuous grip on personal power processes. As the Unabomber maintains, this question of autonomy is decisive ground. It is where we stand or fall: "For most people it is through the power process—having a goal, making an AUTONOMOUS effort and attaining the goal—that self-esteem, self-confidence and a sense of power are acquired" (¶44). Industrial-technological society robs us of these conditions of autonomous powerful action by embedding us passively in collectives, which have required weak, unfree roles in reproducing every amorphous aspect of market-mediated social reproduction. Their sorry results are the reason this system is now in crisis and has become worthy of destruction in a vast popular revolution: "When one does not have adequate opportunity to go through the power process the consequences are (depending on the individual and on the way the power process is disrupted) boredom, demoralization, low self-esteem, inferiority feelings, defeatism, depression, anxiety, guilt, frustration, hostility, spouse or child abuse, insatiable hedonism, abnormal sexual behavior, sleep disorders, eating disorders, etc." (¶44).

An Abject Revolution

To crush the normalization regime of collectivized oversocialization and then revitalize the power process, the Unabomber touts the merits of violent revolt, which he somewhat naively believes certain to work as billed. An obviously poor sense of unintended consequences, however, pops up in his celebration of revolution, which the Unabomber claims must be "immediate" (¶166), "total" (¶179), "ecocentric" (¶183), "technoscientific" (¶193), "global" (¶195), and "communitarian" (¶199). The preservation of wild nature and individual autonomy depend on nothing less than dismantling "the system" through violent revolt.

With nearly complete naïveté, the Unabomber asserts that his revolutionary program is antithetical to the visions of the future espoused by those technophiles, leftists, or politicians who keep the present system running smoothly. Instead of outlining the democratic design for a populist transformation, he simply reinvents many devices for an elitist vanguard putsch. By positing that "the single overriding goal must be the elimination of modern technology, and that no other goal [social justice, material equality, popular participation] can be allowed to compete with this one" (¶205), he argues that everything else must be examined through an open-ended "empirical approach" (¶206). Not seeing how his revolutionary analysis mimics the elitist technoscientific managerialism of the industrial-technological system, the Unabomber merely reaffirms the credos of enlightened elitist self-empowerment co-opted by the captains of industry, inventors of tomorrow, or scions of commerce during the Second Industrial Revolution. In accord with the enlightenment schema of all vanguardism, he asserts that "history is made by active, determined minorities, not by the majority, which seldom has a clear and consistent idea of what it really wants" (¶189). Therefore, the coming revolution will follow an ideology packaged in two different versions: the "more sophisticated should address itself to people who are intelligent, thoughtful and rational" (¶187); the other "should be propagated in a simplified form that will enable the unthinking majority to see the conflict of technology vs. nature in unambiguous terms" (¶188).

The revolutionists of the Unabomber's Freedom Club would mistakenly follow the classic Bolshevik strategy of first energizing the committed radicals and then sensitizing the uninformed masses to ready themselves to coproduce their inevitable future under the leadership of the committed radicals' visionary vanguard: "Until the time comes for the final push toward revolution, the task of revolutionaries will be less to win the shallow support of the majority than to build a small core of deeply committed people. As for the majority, it will be enough to make them aware of the existence of the new ideology and remind them of it frequently; though of course it will be desirable to get majority support to the extent that this can be done without weakening the core of seriously committed people" (¶189). This peculiar vision of the transition is decisively negative: "We have no illusions about the feasibility of creating a new, ideal form of society. Our goal is only to destroy the existing form of society" (¶182). The possibility that such large majorities of disaffected people are there to mobilize only because the extraordinary productivity of this existing form of society works quite well is a point that eludes the Unabomber's otherwise thoughtful appraisal.

The Unabomber does not buy into the redistributive millenarianism of nineteenth-century socialism. He instead would guard against "leftists of the most power-hungry type" (¶217), because ultimately "leftism is a totalitarian force" (¶219) "characterized by arrogance or a dogmatic approach to ideology" (¶230). Social justice as a revolutionary goal also is forbidden, because it tends to attract too many leftist do-gooders with their own special power-hungry arrogance. Social justice agendas would compel the revolutionists to preserve large-scale, organization-dependent technology and would dilute the ecocentric focus of the revolution. In short, "It must not be allowed to interfere with the effort to get rid of the technological system" (¶201).

Despite all his efforts to anticipate the possible consequences of mounting a revolution whose "focus will be on technology and economics, not politics" (¶193), there are no guarantees that such a blow against the inevitabilities of technological progress would not self-destruct. In many ways the Unabomber seems committed only to replacing technocratic new class managerialists with small networks of green vanguardists who would rule by wise ecological fiat. There are no guarantees that his designs to empower antisystemic ecological technophobes, just like rule by the industrial-technological system's capitalist technophiles, would not also take us "all on an utterly reckless ride into the unknown" (¶180).

Technoculture: Domination and Resistance

The Unabomber embeds his critique of collectives in a fateful choice between two kinds of technology: "Small-scale technology and organization-dependent technology" (¶208). The former might lead to new collective associations of people and things that could be empowering, whereas the latter has culminated in the dehumanizing domination of the industrial-technological system. Pursuing a line of attack that concludes basically by celebrating the collapse of Rome and the rise of medieval feudalism, he observes that the Roman empire's organization-dependent technology (roads, aqueducts, urban sanitation, and large buildings) regressed as the empire collapsed, whereas its small-scale technology survived in many households and villages as feudalistic technics. Since "small-scale technology is technology that can be used by small-scale communities without outside assistance" (¶208), it must play the major role in any postrevolutionary scenario. Prior to the Industrial Revolution, "primitive INDIVIDUALS and SMALL GROUPS actually had considerable power over nature; or maybe it would be better to say power WITHIN nature" (¶198). Therefore, "one should argue that the power of the INDUSTRIAL SYSTEM should be broken, and that this will INCREASE the power and freedom of INDIVIDUALS and SMALL GROUPS" (¶199).

Following the Goodmans, Marcuse, or Mumford, the nub of the Unabomber's protest is here: how does complex technology, defined as large-scale or organization-dependent, dictate the nature of our lives and livelihoods, robbing us of real freedom by substituting empty surrogate activities for personal power in our everyday life? What must be done to escape the destructive consequences—on an individual, social, or global level—of this industrial-technological system? The demise of the industrial-technological system depends on effectively disrupting the system's propagation of empty surrogates as the false needs and choices of normalization. If the industrial systems behind such organizational dependence could be broken by violent revolution, terrorism, or popular disinterest, then the power/knowledge networks needed to operate them "would quickly be lost" (¶210). As the Unabomber explores this possibility, he welcomes the advent of a new "Dark Age," arguing:

> And once this technology had been lost for a generation or so it would take centuries to rebuild it, just as it took centuries to build it the first time around. Surviving technical books would be few and scattered. An industrial society, if built from scratch, without outside help, can only be built in a series of stages. You need tools to make tools. . . . A long process of economic development and progress in social organization is required. And, even in the absence of an ideology opposed to tech-

nology, there is no reason to believe that anyone would be interested in rebuilding industrial society. (¶210)

By embracing "a small is survivable" logic for a new Dark Age, the Unabomber shows how power ebbs and flows in organization rather than in technics per se, or the state as such, or any individual taken alone. According to the Unabomber, all people need power; it is what defines autonomous human beings. However, the Industrial Revolution was about the construction of new disciplinary networks in vast collectives that have concentrated individuals' power in abstract social machines. As a result, within these industrial-technological megamachines limited power for a few persists as nearly complete powerlessness for everyone else. "Modern man as a collective entity, that is—the industrial system—has immense power over nature" (¶197). But even more evil is the fact that "modern INDIVIDUALS AND SMALL GROUPS OF INDIVIDUALS have far less power than primitive man ever did," because "the vast power of 'modern man' over nature is exercised not by individuals or small groups but by large organizations" (¶197). Individuals can now wield the power of technology only "under the supervision and control of the system," for they "need a license for everything and with the license come rules and regulations," so the individual has *only* "the technological powers with which the system chooses to provide him" (¶198).

Here too the Unabomber identifies the source of operational survivability in organization-dependent technology. Its codes of authority, legitimacy, or use are embedded into the artifacts and structures needed for its application. Consequently, the Unabomber is unequivocal about his immediate revolutionary program: "Until the industrial system has been thoroughly wrecked, the destruction of that system must be the revolutionaries' ONLY goal. . . . if the revolutionaries permit themselves to have any other goal than the destruction of technology, they will be tempted to use technology as a tool for reaching that other goal. If they give in to that temptation, they will fall right back into the technological trap, because modern technology is a unified, tightly organized system, so that in order to retain SOME technology, one finds oneself obliged to retain MOST technology, here one ends up sacrificing only token amounts of technology. . . . never forget that the human race with technology is like an alcoholic with a barrel of wine" (¶200, 203). Fortunately for the Freedom Club, this tendency toward breakdown is already occurring on a global scale because of the intrinsic excesses and inherent flaws in the large-scale collectives of organization-dependent, industrial-technological systems. After all is said and done, "the industrial system will not break down purely as a result of revolutionary action," because its vulnerabilities are a product of the regime's own evolution: "It is already in enough trouble so that there would be a good chance of its eventually breaking down by itself anyway" (¶167).

The scale and complexity of these social machines forge a new order of things in their collectives that "has to regulate human behavior closely in order to function" (¶114) and "in ways that are increasingly remote from the natural pattern of human behavior" (¶115). So the collectives thrive with disciplinary expectations of technics as such and create all the "scientists, mathematicians and engineers" that the industrial-technological system needs to function (¶115). At the end of the day, "the system does not and cannot exist to satisfy human needs. Instead, it is human behavior that has to be modified to fit the needs of the system" (¶119).

The logic of analysis here confuses power with scale or mistakes complexity as organization, but the Unabomber hits on the decisive importance of organization-dependent technology as a new-class-making force. Any technology that is constructed on a vast, complex scale needs independent organizers of its technologies who in turn can use their power, knowledge, and position as a technological organization of dependence for all others. Small-scale technologies, on the other hand, produce independence by making individuals, or at most small groups, responsible for creating, using, and caring for their own tools. Such technified forms of freedom rest on an organic and humane power process in which people test their mettle against nature, whereas organization-dependent technology produces unfreedom out of organized dependence on large-scale complex technics. Their complicated operations require elite expertise and mass inexpertise to play out their oversocialized corruption through surrogate activities.

The Ecocentric Ideal

Beyond facing the obvious difficulties of constructing an antitechnological revolution from above out of a violent change in technology's scale and scope, the Unabomber employs a simplistic construction of nature as the fount of indisputable objective reason that the revolutionists should counterpose to the sullied irrationalities of technology. Again, his references suggest that he has not perused the works of Arne Naess, Bill Devall, or George Sessions, but his reading of nature parallels closely deep ecology. With no sense of irony at all, the Unabomber asserts, "The positive ideal that we propose is Nature" (¶183), and "it is not necessary for the sake of nature to set up some chimerical utopia or any new kind of social order" (¶184). This might be true, but could not nature itself, particularly when constructed along such deep ecological lines, become a kind of chimerical utopia for this new social order?

The Unabomber's categories of nature play ineffectually with Georg Lukács's two senses of nature.[25] "First nature," on one side, is a domain for "WILD nature; those aspects of the functioning of the Earth and its living things that are independent of human management and free of human interference and control" (¶183). It is set up, on the other side, against technology as "second nature," "an immense social machine" (¶41) composed of "technology that depends on large-scale social organization" (¶208). Human nature provides the central battleground between first and second nature, because "with wild nature we include human nature, by which we mean those aspects of the functioning of the human individual that are not subject to regulation by organized society but are products of chance, or free will, or God" (¶183). Destroy the disruptive collectives at the core of second nature, and first nature will be redeemed and reclaimed, allowing human nature to flourish amid personal tests of authentic power processes out in the wild and not to founder amid artificial surrogate activities. In addition to healing the scars left on nature by the Industrial Revolution, "getting rid of industrial society will accomplish a great deal. . . . it will remove the capacity of organized society to keep increasing its control over nature (including human nature). . . . it is certain most people will live close to nature, because in the absence of advanced technology there is no other way that people can live. To feed themselves they must be peasants or herdsmen or fishermen or hunters, etc. . . . local autonomy should tend to increase, because lack of advanced technology and rapid communications will limit the capacity of governments or other large organizations to control local communities" (¶184). Embracing wild nature, therefore, is the same thing as decollectivizing organization dependent technology and the mass populace.

These radical interpretations of nature, however, are no less artificial and no more certain than the positive ideologies of organization-dependent technology that the Unabomber opposes.[26] Instead, he simply conventionalizes a series of fashionable ecocentric assumptions about nature and transforms them into constant, timeless truths, like so many others who naively sign on to the good ship "deep ecology" without thinking about where its admirals might sail them. On this account, Joe Klein's dismissal of the Unabomber for his "essential left-wing orientation" is laughable.[27] The Unabomber's contempt for modern leftism seconds deep ecology's critique of modern socialism. Where Marx would trust in big science, complex technology, and vast organizations to create limitless material abundance for human beings, the Unabomber apparently would accompany Earth First! in its turn back to the Pleistocene. Even so, this commitment to "wild nature" does not lead all the way to a biocentric Gaia worship. Indeed, the Unabomber razzes such ecospiritualist devotions as frivolous playacting, even though he admits that nature does often inspire quasi-religious reverence among many of its devotees.

Rather than sing from Marxist hymnals, the Unabomber rehearses many problematic presuppositions cribbed from the primers of wild nature philosophies: nature is the opposite of technology, nature is beautiful, nature is popular, radical environmentalists must exalt nature and oppose technology, nature takes care of itself, nature is a spontaneous creation, humans once coexisted with nature without doing any damage to it, and only industrial societies really devastate nature (¶184). These assumptions follow from deep ecology's profound mistrust of the vast collectives propounded by industrial-technological society, but the voluntarily simplified technologies and small beautiful society of deep ecology would not necessarily ensure the realization of these ethical precepts in their systems of green collectivization. Most if not all these points of faith cannot be supported with evidence, because many of them are by-products of highly skewed misinterpretations. Nonetheless, from the horizon of this chimerical utopia, the Unabomber plots his course for a new social order constrained materially by this prime directive: nature's attributes make it necessary to destroy industrial technology so that small groups of autonomous humans can coexist with nature in ways that do not devastate it and thereby let it take care of itself. This image is clearly appealing, but it also coldly necessitates the destruction of a global web of contemporary capitalist collectives whose interrelated, organization-dependent, complex technologies provide a viable habitat for billions of people. Without such technologies, nature will take care of itself, killing off huge populations of human beings who cannot live autonomously like "primitive man," unable to "find and prepare edible roots . . . track game and take it with homemade weapons . . . protect himself from heat, cold, rain, dangerous animals, etc." (¶198).

Kaczynski maybe began to approach the Unabomber's ecological ideal in Montana, but unlike "primitive man," he also received a money allowance from his aged mother and perplexed brother. Many of his tools (a bicycle, his shack, the typewriters, various explosives, etc.) also were sophisticated machinic artifacts salvaged from industrial-technological society. Moreover, a protracted small-scale mail-bombing campaign against computer-store owners, timber industry lobbyists, or research university professors will not contribute much to the collapse of these vast social machines that sustain billions of human beings. Living autonomously in small groups might turn out well on the level of Rousseau's noble savages, but it also could turn sour on the scale of the Road Warrior's ceaseless quest for petrol that ends only in death. Bombing us back to the Stone Age, then, turns into an act of desperate eccentricity instead of becoming an ecocentric revolutionary program.

Killer Fragments: The Unabomber's Insights

The Unabomber's manifesto basically is an essay on the inescapable origins of inhumanity, inequality, and insensitivity as they arise from within the technoscientific collectives of the constructed environment made by megamachines. Second nature's artificial arcologies, the imbricated compounding of architecture, engineering, utility, transportation, and communication infrastructures with natural environments, are now such circumambient constraints on human beings that second nature is actively selecting autonomy, power processes, and small-group intimacy out of the human species.[28] The industrial-technological system is animated not by conventional political ideologies "but by technical necessity" (¶119). The survival of machinic networks of human and inhuman actors in these vast collective arcologies must rob once free individuals of their autonomy and power,[29] because the individual's fate now "MUST depend on decisions that he personally cannot influence to any great extent. . . . because production depends on the cooperation of very large numbers of people" (¶117). These biopowered populations accept all their daily disciplinary directives mostly within and merely out of the technics of their arcological habitats. The autonomy of local communities plainly disappears as these formations "become more enmeshed with and dependent on large-scale systems like public utilities, computer networks, highway systems, the mass communications media, [and] the modern health care system," for it becomes more obvious "that technology applied in one location often affects people at other locations far away" (¶118).

The Unabomber discloses the truths behind a key populist complaint: the colonization of our everyday lifeworld by the systemic effects of industrial-technological society's machinic metabolisms is becoming virtually irresistible and essentially irreversible as new class experts rob us all of our autonomous power potential so that we serve out their dictates in surrogate routines vended in state-corporate collectives.[30] Inasmuch as each new technical device appears to advance our lives in a desirable fashion, technological systems "as a WHOLE narrow our sphere of freedom" (¶128), and any real success in resisting it "can be hoped for only by fighting the technological system as a whole; but that is revolution, not reform" (¶130). The Unabomber attacks reform as the existing regime's most false promise: all reformist efforts to make any room for "a sense of purpose and for autonomy within the system are no better than a joke" (¶120). Reformers ask how personal freedom and small-group autonomy might be mixed with the benefits of high technology. The intrinsic operational requirements of the technical order, however, will eventually overrule any efforts to make true reforms as machinic demands must always reimpose inhumane consequences.[31] The existing order works much better without the policy uncertainties or lack of operational focus that humane values would introduce into its workings. As the Unabomber fears, "it is NOT in the interest of the system to preserve freedom or small-group autonomy. On the contrary, it is in the interest of the system to bring human behavior under control to the greatest possible extent" (¶139). Thus, the open-ended diversity of really autonomous human existence constantly faces the categorical instrumentalization of its continuance in serving the machinic requirements of immense industrial-technological collectives.

At one level, Kaczynski's close reading of technology and industrial society might be interpreted as a crude misinterpretation of Marcuse's "great refusal," one that has been carried on as a real revolution by a true "outsider" on a lonely long march outside the institutions. Indeed, his rehash of rhetorics used by Cal-Berkeley activists assailing "the system" in the 1960s at times sounds like the Zeitgeist of 1968 echoing back from the Montana Rockies. Fearing absorption by modern technological civilization, Kaczynski simply dropped out, refusing to cooperate within most of the high-technology systems that have transformed everyday life in United States since the 1880s. Living in a ten-by-twelve-foot shack with no indoor plumbing, electricity, telephone connection, gas, or municipal services, Kaczynski lived an intentionally frugal existence, his level of technological sophistication not exceeding that of 1896. With a woodstove for heat, a bicycle for transport, game animals for food, a manual typewriter for communication, and local library books for entertainment, the devoted Unabomber appears to have met his "single overriding goal . . . the elimination of modern technology" (¶7) in conducting his own daily existence. The delivery system for his mail bombs was a low-tech machinic montage of foot traffic, bike ride, bus trip, postal van delivery, and addressee detonation; nonetheless, it attacked the machinic collective's makers by using the collective's own goods and services. Unlike Kaczynski, few would forsake their surrogate activities in the contemporary industrial-technological system, and the unconsciously enjoyed conveniences of modern living, to accept planting, growing, and eating their own turnips outside a primitive shack in the backwoods as their liberatory version of an authentic power process.

One need not condone what Kaczynski has done to see the symmetries in his actions. As (ab)normalized as he was throughout his own life, much of what he did after leaving Berkeley in 1968 amounts to a one-man resistance movement against the industrial-technological collective and its market-mediated circuits of governmentality. For a regime run on the managerial models of consummativity's market demography and product design, the Unabomber greatly refused to act as expected by serving as another integer of collectivized biopower. He chose instead to remain (ab)normalized by the tacit knowledges of consumeristic acceptance in ordinary society.[32] He would be neither a market demograph nor a designer target who could be willingly guided by the behavioral expectations embedded in mass-consumption commodities.[33] Most significantly, in a marketing regime that fetishizes "family values" to hustle most of its goods and services, he spurned family, having very little to do either with his own small birth family or with any new nuclear family of his own making. Ironically, it was his own brother who tipped off the authorities on his activitites, and Kaczynski totally ignored his brother and mother throughout the trial. In a society of individualists that celebrates group conformity on the job and at home, he militantly chose a strictly feral existence.

Kaczynski, like Latour, questions the collectives in which we live. He too would have us reopen the black boxes built for us out of technoscience and corporate marketing to comprehend what it has cost us individually to spend our lives collectively around, for, or with these blackened boxes that have been constructed by the new class without our open consent to limit our power processes, oversocialize our families, and dominate our community habitats.[34] He does not claim that the end of industrial society is near; indeed, it can persist for many more decades simply by cranking out greater levels of ecological destruction and social anomie. Industrial-technological society has a future, albeit a bleak one that offers us more comfortable styles of solitary, nasty, brutish, and short lives. So Kaczynski attempted to capitalize on its bleakness to leverage a revolution out of mail bombs among those subjects who can still act and think on their own.

Whereas Latour pushes into the hyperecological terrains, pleading that political representation and real subjecthood should now be granted to objects in the all-powerful parliament of things governing "our modern constitution," the Unabomber lodges a more political question against this megamachinic assembly: who, whom? Latour recognizes that networks of association are creating collectives of quasi-subjective objects (technology) and quasi-objective subjects (human users), and their collective lives make the black boxes of modern industrial society work. The Unabomber, however, asks far more critical questions of Latour's associations, such as who associates with whom, whose collectives are powerful or powerless, who decides for whom what networks will operate where and at what known (and unknown) costs, and what human power processes are displaced by which inhuman power grids?

The conditions of association, or the mode of collectivization, that bring human beings into a coevolutionary coexistence with machines are rarely, if ever, discussed. In his manifesto the Unabomber focuses on this concern in his incomplete and unfulfilled critique of organization-dependent technologies, transnational corporate exchange, and coercive national states. Just as Gramsci asked how Fordism, a discrete social mechanism combining capital, technology, labor, markets, and culture in a determinate new assembly-line formation, creatively determined a formative new line of social assembly—"Americanism"—for the modern world,[35] so too does the Unabomber ask how this Americanized industrial-technological system has been reforging a new psychophysical nexus for technics, power, science, freedom, and organization of global scale that is dehumanizing, disempowering, and decommunalizing everyday life in today's unstable post-Fordist marketplace. The answer that he provides—technical necessity or organizational momentum—is neither completely convincing nor always all inclusive. Other forces also structure the conditions of association, but because the Unabomber is so averse to "modern leftism," he neglects to discuss in any real detail such added factors as market rationality, class bias, ideological expectation, bureaucratic stipulation, or disciplinary prejudice.

Populism and Freedom

Many radical populists have considered these questions in the past, and some continue parallel lines of critical investigation into the present.[36] In some ways populism in the United States has been the political movement that most directly focuses on questions of "who and whom" in the imposition of organization-dependent, large-scale technology on contemporary society. Believing that new associations of autonomous individuals working on levels more than local but less than national could invent new, viable alternatives to the surrogacies of industrial democracy, militarized nationalism, and personal consumption within the industrial-technological system of developed nation-states, some radical populists—old and new—advance their visions for finding alternative conditions of associating nonspecialist men and women with new arrangements of machines that would accentuate personal competencies, familial cohesion, and communal ecologies. These populist modes of forging technical collectives could also stand against the managerial elitism of industrial-technological society and for sane environmental practices, but they do not necessarily stand for colonizing the future with the past to revitalize personal power processes with Paleolithic hunting-and-gathering lifestyles.

In fact, even the Unabomber admits that the power processes in societies as developed as those found on the frontiers of nineteenth-century America were most likely quite satisfying (¶56–57). Hence, there may be no need to eradicate all forms of an industrial metabolism with nature to abolish the hypertrophied disorder of corporate consumerism and warfare-welfare statism as it has evolved in the United States since the 1880s. Likewise, myths of living in or for "wild nature" cannot save us from the domination embedded within of our existing arcological second nature; instead, its organization-dependent, large-scale systems with all their surrogate activities and technological controls need to be transformed from within to create workable populist communities that are less organization-dependent and smaller scale. What is amiss here is not technologies that create domination per se but rather inhumane systems of corporate control and statist domination that misinform and disorganize technologies as totalitarian systems of domination. Populist thinkers such as Christopher Lasch or Amory Lovins also attempt to disembed these insights from their current condition of inarticulation and then push people to answer these tough challenges using knowledge that they can find in their own communities, economies, and technologies.[37] Because of these face-to-face or small-group modes of economic interaction, even the Unabomber could envision U.S. frontier societies in the last century as ones in which the power process worked well: "the 19th century frontiersman had the sense (also largely justified) that he created change himself, by his own choice. Thus a pioneer settled on a piece of land of his own choosing and made it into a farm through his own effort . . . [He] participated as a member of a relatively small group in the creation of a new, ordered community . . . it satisfied the pioneer's need for the power process" (¶57). Bearing in mind the equally associated but wrongly unaddressed questions of Americans dispossessing Mexican and Native American communities in the process, the Unabomber feels "19th century American society had an optimistic and self-confident tone, quite unlike today's society" (¶56). These are the traces of humane living with smaller-scale technics that this nation's nineteenth-century populists struggled to keep in their battle with corporate managerialists and that contemporary populists now aspire to regain.

Real autonomy, for the Unabomber, would come from broadening the sphere of human freedom in the collectives of contemporary megamachines. By *freedom* he means "the opportunity to go through the power process, with real goals not the artificial goals of surrogate activities, and without interference, manipulation or supervision from anyone, especially from any large organization" (¶93). Reiterating one of the authentic goals of radical populism, he says that "freedom means being in control (either as an individual or as a member of a SMALL group) of the life-and-death issues of one's existence; food, clothing, shelter and defense against whatever threats there may be in one's environment" (¶93). This freedom is not the meaningless freedom of consumer choice—should I buy a Pontiac or an Oldsmobile? It means instead "having power; not the power to control other people but the power to control the circumstances of one's own life," because as most savvy populists observe with regard to big business and big government, "one does not have freedom if anyone else (especially a large organization) has power over one, no matter how benevolently, tolerantly and permissively that power may be exercised" (¶93). The "freedom to choose," as it is celebrated in soft drink, convenience market, sports sedan, or mutual fund ads, represents the false promise of industrial democracy that elitist managerial power imposed on much more populist democratic communities a century ago; such freedom is merely "an element of a social machine and has only a certain set of prescribed and delimited freedoms; freedoms that are designed to serve the needs of the social machine more than those of the individual" (¶97). Autonomy is more than political rights, buying discretion, or cultural liberation; it also should be an ecological condition in which people have the ability and latitude to determine the totality of their communities' and families' material interconnections in both nature and society.

Much of the Unabomber manifesto is a heated protest against a technics of normalization and its many interoperating tactics in the structures of schools, offices, factories, sciences, machineries, and states, which all work incessantly as normalizing devices. Kaczynski never led what many would consider a "normal life," and his personal experiences with the normalization regime appear to have done much to aid and abet his miserable slide into socially abnormal ways of behaving and thinking. The subtext of the mass media's reporting on these tendencies is that his own arrogance and intelligence got in the way of "fitting in," so he opted out and then finally decided to strike back violently. This is Kaczynski's key point: the human normalization routines of existing society are the heart of its inhumane reproduction. Strike at them successfully, and destabilization of everything in industrial society will be realized. Otherwise, they can remake you into something as awful as this.

Kaczynski is fascinating because he successfully eluded the authorities for nearly twenty years with hardly any material resources and no social support. Moreover, for a society that worships technology and all those university experts who have won the cold war, gone to the Moon, and created better living through big science, he is its most troublesome nightmare: "an insider" turned "outlaw," "the bright boy" gone "real bad," or a "smart guy" who read so many books that it made him antisocial, unsanitary, violent, and apparently insane. His life had been one of scholarly promise followed by consciously embraced internal exile and now imprisonment for murder. Yet the Unabomber's manifesto, which he did write, makes so many valid criticisms against industrial society that his twisted existence cannot be ignored. Unable to fit comfortably into the cold war university, he turned his back on the publish-or-perish grind at Berkeley to live as a recluse in the backwoods of Montana in accord with this idiosyncratic vision of self-reliance and voluntary simplicity. By bombing those whom he blamed for perpetuating a collective order embedded in large-scale technology and its ills, the Unabomber punctuated the theory of his manifesto with acts of serious violence.

More than a theorist, the Unabomber was a man of action who was ready, willing, and able to strike against those in the collectives whom he saw as contributing to the proliferation of their dehumanizing technology. Dismissing this statement, with all its flaws, as a demented screed from a wacko professor who turned to terrorism and a hermit's life to cope with his failures as a human being, which has been the media's evergreen take on Kaczynski since his arrest on April 3, 1996, dodges all the more important issues of this entire affair.[38] Even with everything that we know about the Unabomber, we should still heed his criticisms of megatechnics' inhumane arrangements for associating people and machines in the polyarchical collectives of our industrial-technological system. Chapter 7 continues this reconsideration by looking again at what alternative technologists and social ecologists have thought about the ways in which these unjust collectives operate.

Notes

1. *Washington Post,* June 22, 1996, p. A3. The moniker is a product of the FBI's investigation, which described the elusive bomber's attacks on universities (un) and air-

liners (a) as "Unabombs" from "the Unabomber." See the bound book version, *The Unabomber Manifesto: Industrial Society and Its Future* (Berkeley: Jolly Roger, 1995).

2. *New York Times,* June 16, 1996, p. A12.

3. William Claiborne, "Government Rejected Kaczinski Plea Offer: Unabomber Suspect Sought Life Sentence," *Washington Post,* December 30, 1997, p. A3.

4. Daniel Klaidman and Patricia King, "Suicide Mission," *Newsweek,* January 19, 1998, pp. 23–25.

5. Tamala S. Edwards, "Crazy Is as Crazy Does: Why the Unabomber Agreed to Trade a Guilty Plea for a Life Sentence," *Time,* February 2, 1998, p. 66.

6. William Booth, "Kaczinski Sentenced to Four Life Terms: Unabomber Is Unrepentant to the End," *Washington Post,* May 5, 1998, p. A2.

7. *Newsweek,* April 15, 1996, pp. 32–33.

8. Joe Klein, "The Unabomber and the Left," *Newsweek,* April 22, 1996, p. 39.

9. *Newsweek,* April 15, 1996, p. 33.

10. Kirkpatrick Sale, "Is There a Method in His Madness?" *The Nation,* September 25, 1995, p. 311.

11. Maggie Scharf, "The Mind of the Unabomber," *The New Republic,* June 10, 1996, p. 22.

12. Kirkpatrick Sale, "Method in His Madness," 301.

13. Maggie Scharf, "Mind of the Unabomber," 22. There is now more evidence to support claims of mental instability with regard to the Unabomber's activities. The court-appointed psychiatrist in Kaczynski's trial, Dr. Sally Johnson, reported on his first fantasies of murder developing allegedly after his inability to discuss a sex-change operation with a psychiatrist during his student days. Likewise, his personal journals reveal him gloating over a $25,000 reward being posted on him after one of his bombs killed a computer store worker in Sacramento, California, during 1985. See Sarah Van Boven and Patricia King, "A Killer's Self-Portrait: Charting the Mind and Motives of the Unabomber," *Newsweek,* May 11, 1998, p. 38. Nonetheless, it is still a stretch to allege, apart from these murders, that "a madman" is "someone who lived alone for 20 years in a shack in the semi-wilderness, in a cabin without running water or electricity" (Richard Cohen, "The Unabomber Case . . . ," *Washington Post,* December 30, 1997, p. A13).

14. *New York Times,* May 26, 1996, pp. 22–25.

15. Michel Foucault, *The History of Sexuality, vol. 1: An Introduction* (New York: Vintage, 1990), 135–59.

16. Paul Goodman and Percival Goodman, *Communitas: Means of Livelihood and Ways of Life* (New York: Vintage, 1960), 3.

17. Steven Marcus, "Rage against the Machine: The New Luddites, the Old Luddites, and Some Very Bad History," *The New Republic,* June 10, 1996, pp. 30–38.

18. See Kirkpatrick Sale, *Rebels against the Future: The Luddites and Their War on the Industrial Revolution* (New York: Addison-Wesley, 1996), 261–79.

19. Herbert Marcuse, *One-Dimensional Man: Studies in the Ideology of Advanced Industrial Society* (Boston: Beacon, 1964), xvi.

20. Ibid.

21. See Michel Foucault, *The Foucault Effect: Studies in Governmentality*, ed. Graham Burchell, Colin Gordon, and Peter Miller (Chicago: University of Chicago Press, 1991); idem, *The History of Sexuality;* idem, *Discipline and Punish: The Birth of the Prison* (New York: Vintage, 1979); and idem, *The Order of Things: An Archaeology of the Human Sciences* (New York: Vintage, 1970).

22. Herbert Marcuse, *Soviet Marxism: A Critical Analysis* (New York: Vintage, 1961), xii.

23. William Leach, *Land of Desire: Merchants, Power, and the Rise of a New American Culture* (New York: Pantheon, 1993), 3–38. One of the Unabomber's surviving victims, David Gelernter, a Yale professor of computer science, has written a personal account of his violent encounter with Ted Kaczynski, whom he in turn calls "the Hut Man." Ironically, Gelernter connects the Unabomber's mad bombing attack on him in his university office to a major change in the political fabric of the United States over the past generation, namely, the rise of the professional-technical intelligentsia, or the new class, to political hegemony during the 1960s and after. See David Gelernter, *Drawing Life: Surviving the Unabomber* (New York: Free Press, 1997), 61–74.

24. Herbert Marcuse, "Some Social Implications of Modern Technology," *Studies in Philosophy and Social Sciences* 9 (1941): 421.

25. Georg Lukács, *History and Class Consciousness: Studies in Marxist Dialectics* (Cambridge, Mass.: MIT Press, 1971), 83–110.

26. See Timothy W. Luke, "The Dreams of Deep Ecology," *Telos* 76 (Summer 1988): 65–92. The Unabomber's ultimate loyalties to peaceful ecological ends are actually quite dubious. On the one hand, Kaczynski posed as a dedicated antagonist of technology, conducting a protracted war for personal freedom against the dark designs of big science and big technology. On the other hand, his cabin yielded a cache of personal journals in which he records notes such as this: "I believe in nothing. I do not even believe in the cult of nature-worshippers or wilderness-worshippers. (I am perfectly ready to litter in parts of the woods that are no use to me. I throw cans in logged-over areas . . .) . . . My motive for doing what I am going to do is simply personal revenge" (*Washington Post,* May 4, 1998, pp. A6–7).

27. Klein, "The Unabomber and the Left," 39.

28. Timothy W. Luke, "The Politics of Arcological Utopia," *Telos* 101 (Fall 1994): 55–78.

29. See Lewis Mumford, *The Myth of the Machine* (New York: Harcourt Brace Jovanovich, 1970).

30. Bruno Latour, *We Have Never Been Modern* (London: Harvester Wheatsleaf, 1993), 1–12.

31. Christopher Lasch, *The Revolt of the Elites and the Betrayal of Democracy* (New York: Norton, 1995).

32. Foucault, *History of Sexuality,* 81–102.

33. Leach, *Land of Desire,* 153–90.

34. Latour, *We Have Never Been Modern*, 130–45.

35. Antonio Gramsci, *Selections from the Prison Notebooks*, ed. Quintin Hoare and Geoffrey Nowell Smith (New York: International, 1971), 272–318.

36. See the articles in *Telos* 103 (Spring 1995): Paul Piccone, "Postmodern Populism," 45–86; and Emory Roe, "Critical Theory, Sustainable Development, and Populism," 149–65.

37. See Christopher Lasch, *The True and Only Heaven: Progress and Its Critics* (New York: Norton, 1991).

38. For a more detailed study of Ted Kaczynski's life, although one captured and constrained by the conventional mass media frame on his unusual career, see Robert Graysmith, *Unabomber: A Desire to Kill* (Washington, D.C.: Regnery, 1997).

7 Social Ecology as Political Economy for Alternative Modernities

This chapter explores some popular but often ignored cultural alternatives promised by a political economy grounded on the principles of small-scale technology as they have been expressed by proponents of social ecology and voluntary simplicity. In one form or another, the spirit of this tradition can be traced back to Rousseau, Blake, Morris, or Kropotkin. Its most articulate contemporary exponents, such Bookchin, Commoner, Illich, or Schumacher, have become actively engaged in political debate only since the late 1950s, mainly in response to the changes being wrought by the newly emergent transnational corporate economy. Social ecology and voluntary simplicity outline some of the most thorough critiques of corporate capitalist production, because they articulate mostly populist strategies for social reconstruction. By reviewing the criticism of the prevailing polyarchical order made by Ivan Illich, Murray Bookchin, André Gorz, Karl Hess, Amory Lovins, E. F. Schumacher, and Hazel Henderson, one can closely examine the constant tension between economic necessities and moral imperatives. By placing moral preferences before economic necessity, these critics also identify some possible correctives for the excesses of megatechnics by revitalizing populist forms of both democratic citizenship and independent producership in everyday life. Their basic strategy attacks the passive, incompetent habitus of hyperecological lifestyles and shows how to remake the habitats of second nature by collectivizing people with different things on other scales that require new types of competent activity rooted in an alternative habitus.

Since 1945, as chapter 2 argued, an entirely new mode of megatechnical production based on the growth imperatives of transnational corporate capital has penetrated virtually every traditional economy, local community, and bioregional ecology on the planet. This energy-intensive, labor-displacing, capital-intensive, and market-generating system of exchange rapidly restructured everyday life in many diverse bioregions around the world to suit its operational imperatives. Social ecology and voluntary simplicity represent comprehensive critiques of megatechnics' operational imperatives—endless growth, unregulated waste, overspending of energy, overproduction of useless things, the valuation of technical expertise over users' needs, productive labor's displacement by underproductive leisure, and a consumer society's imposition of itself on a conserver society.

Although such outcomes have become increasingly characteristic of all advanced industrial societies—whether they are corporate capitalist, state socialist, or national corporatist in their predominant organizational and ownership patterns—the most extensive elaboration of the adverse ecological affects of megatechnics can be found in the polyarchical states and megatechnical economies of Western Europe, North America, and Japan. By the early 1960s the environmental corrosion intrinsic to the reproduction of this transnational corporate economy had stimulated a critical debate over the costs and benefits of "the affluent society" in the advanced industrial economies. The theoretical discourse of a populist resistance—expressed in diverse streams of social ecology as well as various social movements associated with the ideas of voluntary simplicity—represents one of the more sophisticated sides of these debates about the ends and means of living in the age of megatechnical abundance made possible by transnational corporate production.

Social Ecology and Voluntary Simplicity

After nearly a century of increasing environmental destruction under the factory system of the Second Industrial Revolution, the ecological costs inherent in advanced industrial production make necessary its immediate reorganization along ecologically sound lines.[1] Less and less of the corporate capitalist firms' productivity serves real human needs—feeding the hungry, employing the creative, sheltering the homeless, or clothing the cold. Advanced industrial society increasingly is a monoproduct economy specializing in the highly rationalized production of waste. This waste shows up today as short-run benefits in higher quarterly profits, greater corporate productivity, or larger administrative efficiencies. Its long-run costs, however, add up in acid rain, forest death, soil erosion, widespread desertification, aquifer exhaustion, dead lakes, and habitat pollution.

Under transnational corporate capitalism, the public goods of nature are increasingly despoiled for a historically limited group of individuals who are "fortunate" enough to be alive as relatively affluent consumers in the twentieth century, at the expense of all other human, animal, and plant communities. This consumerist social model, as packaged by capitalist megatechnics, thrives on the simultaneous denial and destruction of the ecological limits embedded in human habitats.[2] The project of social ecology and voluntary simplicity arises from the practical challenge of elaborating a new model for ecologically sound communities that could coexist in diverse habitats without qualitatively lowering many modern living standards.

"Ecology today," Donald Worster observes, "is not a single approach to nature; it embraces many approaches." Thus, "like the whole of science," ecology continues to be "a house with many doors, some leading to one view of nature, some to another."[3] In this chapter I will view ecology as another kind of critical social theory, carrying with it a new social understanding of human communities' interdependent interrelations with the biosphere. A social ecology rejects the "senseless, valueless, purposeless" worldpicture of positive science's "one-eyed reason, deficient in its vision of depth."[4] Instead, it seeks the logic for a "land ethic" or an "ecological ethic" for a new communal society grounded on a sophisticated sense of the community of living things.[5] This ethic in turn might guide a new political economy for every particular bioregion that would resist the univocal frameworks of corporate collective choice.

The issue behind social ecology is not simply disturbing the environment; "nature is not untouchable," as Gorz observes. Instead, the question behind a critical social ecology is knowing "whether the exchanges, which human activity imposes upon or extorts from nature, preserve or carefully manage the stock of nonrenewable resources; and, whether the destructive effects of production do not exceed the productive ones by depleting renewable resources more quickly than they can regenerate themselves."[6] The megatechnics of transnational corporate capital ignore these concerns. Megatechnics has been able to shift its corporate exploitation of resources from nation to nation, bioregion to bioregion, and hemisphere to hemisphere as resources became physically too scarce or marginally too expensive. A political economy of social ecology and voluntary simplicity, however, would seek to voice the interests of these communities of living things in each bioregion, serving their needs and fulfilling their ends along with those of independent human producers.

As a science that critically examines the totality of all relations between living organisms in their organic and inorganic environments, ecology continues to be a potentially powerful political force.[7] From the complex array of contemporary positive science, ecology—particularly the social and political modes of ecological investigation discussed here—is one of the few remaining approaches within corporate science and technology that retain a sophisticated subversive side. Through ecology's holistic interrelation of human economic production with the workings of its organic and inorganic environments, one can observe precisely how the production, circulation, consumption, and accumulation of commodities on a transnational scale progressively degrade the local ecologies of more and more bioregions around the globe. A social construction of ecology for populist resistances to polyarchy and megatechnics offers the conceptual map for taking the first steps to free nature from the anthropocentric culture of contemporary industrialism and to ground economic exchange on an ethic of voluntary simplicity.

Voluntary simplicity does not imply that people accept poverty as a way of life. As Duane Elgin argues, "The intention of this way of life is not to dogmatically live with less. It is a more demanding intention of living with balance. This is a middle way that moves between the extremes of poverty and indulgence. Simplicity, then, should not be equated with poverty."[8] In practice, a voluntarily simplified mode of living implies moving toward less consumption of consumer goods, more self-production of personal goods and services, greater use of energy-frugal appropriate technologies, less dependence on corporate and state services, and cultivation of new kinds of personal growth by devoting time to enlivening local institutions such as co-ops, extended families, collectives, churches, neighborhood organizations, and community schools. It is essentially an alternative vision of modernity waiting to be put into practice.

Against the backdrop of these developments, voluntary simplicity proposes a series of broad changes that Elgin sums up in these terms:

> a manner of living that is outwardly more simple and inwardly more rich; an integrative way of living that balances both inner and outer aspects of our lives; a deliberate choice to live with less in the belief that more of life will be returned to us in the process; a path toward consciously learning the skills that enable us to touch the world ever more lightly and gently; a way of being in which our most authentic and alive self is brought into direct and conscious contact with every aspect of living (working, relating, consuming, etc.); a way of living that accepts the responsibility for developing our human potentials, as well as for contributing to the well-being of the world of which we are an inseparable part; a paring back of the superficial aspects of our lives so as to allow more time and energy to develop the heartfelt aspects of our lives.[9]

Of course, these ideas are largely focused on the individual or personal level of change. Many social ecologists and voluntary simplicity practitioners agree with Schumacher that to answer the question "What can I actually *do*?" we must put our "own inner house in order."[10] Yet when these personal needs for individual or household-level transformation are linked to social ecology's critical analysis of the ways that households, firms, communities, regions, nations, and ecosystems interrelate in megatechnical exchange, the potential for reordering everyday life in a new political economy along morally sound lines could be quite considerable.

A New Economics for Social Ecology

To correct the ethical practices of conventional economics, the theorists of social ecology argue in favor of reintroducing moral ends and a substantive reasoning about morality into economic calculations. Schumacher, for example, argues that a new "metaeconomics" that reintroduces the moral dimension of ethical ends into economic reasoning must organize the workings of an ecological society. "The trouble about valuing means above ends—which, as confirmed by Keynes, is the attitude of modern economics—is that it destroys man's freedom and power to choose the ends he really favors; the development of means, as it were, dictates the choice of ends."[11] To correct this tendency, Schumacher claims that nonmaterialist values, which he sees exemplified by Buddhism, should be the new basis of determining the ends of economic and social activity.

The central ideal of Schumacher's social ecology, then, becomes attaining a "right livelihood," one centered on combining an ethical life of satisfying work, minimal wants, and careful consumption. Transnational corporate capital assumes that anyone who consumes more and works less has a higher "standard of living" than someone who consumes less and works more. An alternative economics, such as one guided by Buddhism, "would consider this approach excessively irrational: since consumption is merely a means to human well-being, the aim should be to obtain the maximum of well-being with the minimum of consumption."[12] Basically Schumacher advocates a revitalization of an ethical subjectivity devoted to the "living of standards" found in humility, simplicity, or sustainability to replace the materialistic "standard of living" vended in the corporate marketplace. Like Schumacher, Illich rejects the growing hegemony of exchange values, which are provided in the corporate market, over use values, which are created by every household or community. Instead of improving everyday living, the proliferation of useless things and excessive wants culminates in *modernized poverty.* That is, "when the intensity of market dependence reaches a certain threshold," many experience frustration, passivity, and domination in the face of "their overwhelming reliance on the riches of industrial productivity."[13] Similarly, Henderson observes that the excessive pursuit of superfluous needs in polyarchical societies actually aggravates the workings of modernized poverty. This system ultimately leads to the emergence of an "entropy state." The valuing of means over ends, artificial needs over real needs, and consumption over production slides into a general socioeconomic situation in which "complexity and interdependence have reached the point where the transaction costs that are generated equal or exceed the society's productive capabilities."[14] The result of not seeking a "right livelihood" evidences itself "in human maladjustment, community disruption, and environmental depletion."[15]

Schumacher, Henderson, Illich, and Elgin urge others to accept an economics based on concrete moral ends—simplicity, nonviolence, and frugality. "The ownership and the consumption of goods," from this perspective, "is a means to an end, and Buddhist economics is the systematic study of how to attain given ends with the minimum means."[16] Social ecologists such as Schumacher maintain that "a high degree of human satisfaction by means of a relatively low rate of consumption . . . allows people to live with the primary injunction of Buddhist teaching: cease to do evil; try to do good."[17] And Elgin agrees: "To simplify is to bring order, clarity, and purpose into our lives," which in turn implies a moral project of "new growth (growth that includes both a material and a spiritual, or interior, dimension)."[18] Voluntary simplicity, when practiced as an oppositional form of struggle against polyarchy with megatechnical regimes tied to transnational corporate capital, could undercut the "extravagant consumption, social passivity, and personal impotence" engendered in the everyday life of consumer society.[19] Living simply, as a rule for the conduct of everyday life in advanced industrial society, allows many others to simply live.

The key premise of social ecology's economics is the redefinition of human needs. As Schumacher asserts, "One of the most fateful errors of our age is the belief that 'the problem of production' has been solved."[20] Believing that corporate-generated science and technology have triumphed totally in the struggle against necessity, corporate marketing techniques continuously create new "needs" for new products, using more and more resources. Not only do these hyperecologies consume human time and energy at work, but, as Illich points out, they also consume "leisure" time and energy in unpaid "shadow work" to rationalize the work-time pursuit of artificial needs. As a result, corporate capitalist economies impose "a kind of forced labor or industrial serfdom in the service of commodity-intensive economies."[21]

"The modern economy," therefore, "is propelled by a frenzy of greed and indulges in an orgy of envy, and these are not accidental features but the very cause of its expansionist success."[22] Industrial production does not work to satisfy real human needs; instead, its output strains to meet the demands made by the institutionalized envy around which corporate consumer society organizes itself. Henderson labels this institutionalized greed "Jonesism," which represents "the cultural assumptions and economic arrangements associated with the game of 'keeping up with the Joneses.'"[23] This mode of generating economic growth is increasingly less effective and more unethical, however, "since such mass-consumption strategies in already affluent nations require an unfair portion of the world's diminishing resources and prevent needed economic growth in the less affluent countries."[24] Illich asserts that real equity demands a society directed toward simplicity, frugality, and fewer needs to ensure adequate consumption for the masses rather than excessive mass consumption for the elites.

Energy-intensive, resource-intensive, capital-intensive Jonesism must be replaced by ecological equity, because "only a ceiling on energy use can lead to social relations that are characterized by high levels of equity."[25] These illusions of solving the problems of production involved in meeting Jonesist marketing strategies are based on corporate capital's inability "to distinguish between income and capital where this distinction matters most."[26] Transnational corporate firms are not simply exploiting the limited income of natural resources that remain capable of being fully renewed periodically. On the contrary, they have begun to expend the natural capital of the biosphere, and as Schumacher claims, these nonrenewable reserves of ecological capital are now "being used up at an alarming rate, and that is why it is an absurd and suicidal error to believe, and act on the belief, that the problem of production has been solved."[27]

Schumacher challenges the existing definition of human needs in hyperecological technoregions on both materialist and nonmaterialist grounds. On the side of material constraints, the idea of unlimited needs being satisfied by endless growth must be challenged as an ideological falsehood. Basic resources are in fact less and less available, and the environment's capacity to sustain this excessive degree of human consumption is finite. On the nonmaterialist side, human needs that presume greed, envy, and senseless change are dangerous and destructive. Hence Schumacher favors an *economics of permanence* that can ensure the attainment of "a right livelihood" for all. Citing Gandhi, Schumacher affirms "that 'earth provides enough to satisfy every man's need, but not for every man's greed.'"[28] An economics of permanence, in this framework, should optimize "the organic, the gentle, the non-violent, the elegant and beautiful."[29]

To satisfy human needs in accord with the ideals of permanence, Schumacher states,

> we need methods and equipment which are
>
> —cheap enough so that they are accessible to virtually everyone
> —suitable for small-scale application; and
> —compatible with man's need for creativity
>
> Out of these three characteristics is born nonviolence and a relationship of man to nature which guarantees permanence.[30]

Accessibility, small-scale utilization, and creativity-compatible forms of productive capital are essential attributes of permanence in economic exchange. Using such tools, social ecologists maintain that "we can, each of us, work to put our own inner house in order. The guidance we need for this work cannot be found in science or technology, the value of which utterly depends on the ends they serve; but it can still be found in the traditional wisdom of mankind,"[31] which, of course, stresses the moral ends of prudence, frugality, simplicity, and balance. Even so, communities of ecological populists also should recognize that putting these values into practice as a basis for a new type of modernity requires new participatory approaches to political action in a populist economy and society.

The Politics of Social Ecology

Given the ethical and economic alternatives outlined by Illich, Elgin, Henderson, and Schumacher, the political options for ecological populists are spelled out provisionally in the works of Bookchin, Hess, and Gorz. All three propose many political changes to undo the coercive complexity inherent in corporate capitalist production. As Hess argues, complexity is "a familiar managerial defense against anything in which there is a suggestion that people generally can understand, operate, or change any process controlled by someone who wants to keep the controls firmly in hand."[32] Here, then, a critique grounded on social ecology asks *the* central political questions: Who dominates whom? And in so doing, who decides who gets what, when, and how? As Bookchin claims, social ecology is the most political framework available for contemporary critical analysis inasmuch as "ecology raises the issue that the very notion of man's domination of nature stems from man's domination of man."[33] Social ecology, to a very real extent, looks for the political pivot in all aspects of everyday life. The polyarchical politics of corporate capitalist society, like its ethics, economics, science, and technology, is under the control of professional public administrators, corporate managers, and party or parliamentary politicians. Citizens are at best reduced to consumers. Merely being a consumer impels citizens "always to accept and take what is and never to share what could be."[34]

The politics of social ecology rejects the economic and social roles of polyarchies and megatechnics that inform everyone "you are a consumer[;] somebody *else* is a producer. Production is not a community matter; it is an 'expert' matter, best left to managers and politicians."[35] It rejects this direction because "the material base for local liberty exists. The decision to have or not have local liberty is just that, a decision, a decision derived from human will."[36] Bookchin maintains that these choices, like all collective decisions, can be made democratically, effectively, and communally to reclaim personal producership, self-identity, and complete citizenship. Social ecology implicitly asserts that to "replace social domination by self-management, a new type of civic self—the free, self-governing citizen—must be restored and gathered into new institutional forms such as popular assemblies to challenge the all-pervasive state apparatus."[37]

The modern welfare state became all-pervasive under liberal democratic capitalism because of the concomitant decline of a civil society under the polyarchical regime of megatechnical corporate capitalist production. "The rift," Gorz observes, "between production and consumption, between work and 'leisure,' is the result of the destruction of autonomous human capabilities in favor of the capitalist division of labor."[38] As the dense fabric of social relations between individuals within social groups and local communities unraveled, the state and its bureaus interposed themselves directly in the macromanagement of production and consumption. Therefore,

> the destruction of autonomous capabilities is thus to be understood as part of a process, in part deliberately planned, tending to strengthen the domination of capital—or of the state which assumes it functions—over the worker not only as a worker but also as a consumer. By making it impossible for individuals to produce, within the extended family or the community, any of the things which they consume or aspire to, capitalism (and the state) forces them to satisfy the totality of the needs by commodity consumption (i.e., by the purchase of institutionally produced goods and services); at the same time, *capitalism reinforces its control over this consumption.*[39]

As Illich, Henderson, and Schumacher hold, this fetishization of commodity consumption as the main mediation for realizing personal identity, cultural purpose, and social meaning becomes the primary political problem of polyarchically governed corporate society. This psychosocial order values having over being and then destroys the environment to provide the materialistic means of controlling who will have what, as well as when and how they will have it.

To oppose this polyarchical regime, Bookchin turns to a more populistic politics of direct action in which individuals "function outside it and *directly* enter into social life, pushing aside the prevailing institutions, its bureaucrats, 'experts,' and leaders, and thereby pave the way for *extra-legal, moral,* and *personal* action."[40] In particular, Bookchin favors the creation of new communities and technologies in exercises of direct action. Most important, direct action becomes the practical means for local communities to recover individual control from bureaucratic agencies of the nation-state and corporate firm. In acting directly, Bookchin maintains,

> we not only gain a sense that we can control the course of social events again; we recover a new sense of selfhood and personality without which a truly free society, based on self-activity and self-management, is utterly impossible. We often speak of self-management and self-activity as our ideals for a future society without recognizing often enough that it is not only the "management" and "activity" that has to be democratized; it is also the "self" of each individual—as a unique, creative, and competent being—that has to be fully developed. . . . A truly free society does not deny selfhood but rather supports it, liberates it, and actualizes it in the belief that everyone is competent to manage society, not merely an "elect" of experts and self-styled men of genius. Direct action is merely the free town meeting writ large. It is the means whereby each individual awakens to the hidden powers within herself and himself, to a new sense of self-confidence and self-competence. . . . It is the means whereby individuals take control of society directly, without "representatives" who tend to usurp not only the power but the very personality of a passive, spectatorial "electorate" who live in the shadows of an "elect."[41]

In the populistic critiques of social ecology, direct action constitutes an entirely new political ideal, suffusing all aspects of individual attitudes and behavior with a theme of self-reliance. Through direct action, individuals can immediately begin to restructure their own communities and technologies to suit their purposes without professional-technical new class intervention.

The moral necessity of protecting the organic biosphere from advanced industrial societies' tendency to render it inorganic in their technosphere moves Bookchin and other social ecologists to call for the creation of these "ecocommunities" grounded on new kinds of "ecotechnologies." Both ecocommunities and ecotechnologies can be characterized by their ecological populism, in which the optimization of personal control, communal participation, and individual choice are stressed in opposition to corporate managers' instrumental rationality. In addition to standing for totally new spatial arrangements in the built environment, an ecocommunity could become the core of a balanced, humane ecosystem of humans within more carefully guarded organic and inorganic environments. That is, in Bookchin's view,

> if the word "ecocommunity" is to have more than a strictly logistical and technical meaning, it must describe a decentralized community that allows for direct popular administration, the efficient return of wastes to the countryside, the maximum use of local resources—and yet it must be large enough to foster cultural diversity and psychological uniqueness. The community, like its technology, is itself the ensemble of its libertarian institutions, humanly-scaled structures, the diverse productive tasks that expose the individual to industrial, craft, and horticultural work, in short, the rounded community that the Hellenic polis was meant to be in the eyes of its great democratic statesmen. It is within such a decentralized community, sensitively tailored to its natural ecosystem, that we could hope to develop a new sensibility toward the world of life and a new level of self-consciousness, rational action, and foresight.[42]

The intention of ecological populists in building ecocommunities is to overcome the antinomies of theory and practice at the core of corporate capitalist economies: mind and body, town and country, factory and farm, mental and manual work, consumption and production.

These transformations would also require popular initiatives for reinventing of technology in new and more ecological forms

> composed of flexible, versatile machinery whose productive applications would emphasize durability and quality, not built-in obsolescence, and insensate quantitative output of shoddy goods, and a rapid circulation of expendable commodities. . . . Such an ecotechnology would use the inexhaustible energy capacities of nature—the sun and wind, the tides and waterways, the temperature differentials of the earth and the abundance of hydrogen around us as fuels—to provide the ecocommunity with non-polluting materials or wastes that could be easily recycled.[43]

As I will discuss in more detail later, an ecotechnology is a central goal of social ecologists' reformation of contemporary economies, because it implies a nondestructive approach toward nature as well as the active exercise of individual initiative, self-reliance, and judgment. Again, ecological technology should broaden, not constrict, the choices and freedoms of individual households and communities in their experience of local citizenship and individual producership.

The direct action of social ecology could overturn, bit by bit, the administrative regime of centralized welfare states and transnational firms used in megatechnics. "Ecocommunities and ecotechnologies, scaled to human relationships," Bookchin maintains, "would open a new era in face-to-face relationships and direct democracy, providing the free time that would make it possible in Hellenic fashion for people to manage the affairs of society without the mediation of bureaucracies and professional political functionaries."[44] As a result, and in accord with the ethical vision propounded by Illich, Henderson, and Schumacher, the politics of ecological populism would ideally reintroduce the moral ends of simpler, more frugal living into the economic struggle against necessity. In a somewhat utopian vein, Bookchin concludes that

> the antagonistic division between sexes and age-groups, town and country, administration and community, mind and body would be reconciled and harmonized in a more humanistic and ecological synthesis. Out of this transcendence would emerge a new relationship between humanity and the natural world in which society itself would be conceived as an ecosystem based on unity in diversity, spontaneity, and non-hierarchical relationships. Once again we would seek to achieve in our own minds the respiritization of the natural world.[45]

By generating a new substantive rationality from the ecological needs of communities of living things coexisting in the biosphere, a more balanced, equitable, and democratic exercise of instrumental rationality could emerge from the many diverse local ecocommunities and their bioregionally appropriate ecotechnologies. The political economy of social ecology would redefine, balance, and reintegrate economic needs with moral necessities. In the project of social ecology, citizenship would extend into the organization of collectives, and it would ask everyone to rethink their uses of technology, tools, and organization of production. As the following section indicates, technical institutions also could be treated more as accessible communal utilities rather than as private properties or corporate resources.

Technology As Social Ecology

To ground the ethical ideals of an economy of permanence and a politics of direct action on a solid material foundation, the proponents of social ecology and voluntary simplicity pay special attention to the technical base and organizational infrastructure required for ecocommunity. Their program seeks to reorder the collectives associating people and things with new forms of technics for new modes of community. The shift to such a base would be quite difficult. Nonetheless, the problems and prospects of developing an ecotechnology are addressed by Bookchin, Hess, Lovins, and Schumacher. Despite their diverse approaches to the issues of energy and technology, all concur that ecological populism could work well: "Ordinary people are qualified and responsible to make these and other energy choices through the democratic process, and on the social and ethical issues central to such choices the opinion of any technical expert is entitled to no special weight."[46] Likewise, they all would agree that the alternative, appropriate ecologies or low technologies needed for an ecocommunity are neither fantastic, anachronistic, nor inadequate systems for rational action.

In many respects, as Commoner claims, World War II was the decisive turning point in this corporate application of primary scientific knowledge to new megatechnic technologies of industrial and agricultural production. Although coal smoke and many industrial wastes had been well known for over a century prior to the 1940s, "most pollution problems made their first appearance, or became very much worse, in the years following World War II."[47] In fact, "many pollutants were totally absent before World War II, having made their environmental debut in the war years: smog (first noticed in Los Angeles in 1943), manmade radioactive elements (first produced in the wartime atomic bomb project), DDT (widely used for the first time in 1944), detergents (which began to displace soap in 1946), synthetic plastics (which became a contributor to the rubbish problem only after the war)."[48] Ecological populism affirms that economic growth per se is not to blame for the ecological crisis. Instead, a particular kind of energy-intensive, pollutant-intensive, and capital-intensive growth promoted by polyarchical megatechnics is at fault. It has accelerated ecological degradation exponentially, while it has improved the general standard of living only arithmetically.

These unintended social costs of growth, complexity, scale, and productivity, then, are the real root of the social ecology critique of megatechnics. By the early 1970s, Commoner suggests, the evidence was quite clear:

> The chief reason for the environmental crisis that has engulfed the United States in recent years is the sweeping transformation of productive technology since World War II. The economy has grown enough to give the United States population about the same amount of basic goods, per capita, as it did in 1946. However, productive technologies with intense impacts on the environment have displaced less destructive ones. The environmental crisis is the inevitable result of this counterecological pattern of growth.[49]

By optimizing large-scale economies of energy intensivity, planned efficiency, capital intensivity, and global marketing, transnational capital rebuilt the world economy after 1945 along these ecologically destructive megatechnical lines. Social ecology as a critical social project seeks to find the technological and organizational means to restructure this global corporate order along more small-scale, energy-sensible, locally managed, labor-intensive, bioregionally structured lines of economic growth.

Social ecologists also agree that alternative technologies do more than just protect the many organic exchanges of the biosphere and regenerate local networks of social cooperation; in addition, they provide very practicable options for rebuilding our technosphere. During and after a transition to an ecocommunal living standard, ecotechnology "simultaneously offers jobs for the unemployed, capital for business people, environmental protection for conservationists, enhanced national security for the military, opportunities for small business to innovate and for big business to recycle itself, existing technologies for the secular, a rebirth of spiritual values for the religious, traditional virtues for the old, radical reforms for the young, world order and equity for globalists, energy independence for isolationists, civil rights for liberals, states' rights for conservatives."[50] The questions connected with the entropy state of transnational corporate capital, then, "far from being too complex and technical for ordinary people to understand, are on the contrary too simple and political for experts to understand."[51]

The technology and organizational forms most suitable for an ecocommunity are "a technology with a human face, which instead of making human hands and brains redundant, helps them to become far more productive than they have ever been before."[52] "This technology, Bookchin notes, is "the basic structural support of a society; it is literally the framework of an economy and of many social institutions."[53] Over the last four decades transnational corporate production has constructed a peculiar technology that explicitly and implicitly organizes liberal polyarchies around the unecological, antihumane, and amoral social institutions of consumer society. A "liberatory ecotechnology" might provide new structural supports for communities that could be more ecologically sound, humanly scaled, and morally grounded. As Bookchin suggests, this decentralization of technological power should promote democratization. Under an ecotechnology not all societies' economic activities "can be completely decentralized, but the majority can surely be scaled to human communitarian dimensions. This much is certain: we can shift the center of economic power from national to local scale and from centralized bureaucratic forms to local, popular assemblies. This shift would be a revolutionary change of vast proportions, for it would create powerful economic foundations for the sovereignty and autonomy of the local community."[54]

Ecotechnology, then, would be closely integrated into the local environment and the larger biosphere instead of into the nation-state and its economics. Social ecologists suggest that an ecotechnology is morally worthwhile, ecologically necessary, and already present in undeveloped forms within corporate science and technology. Megatechnical corporate technologies are concrete examples of the transnational economies' present ecological failures. Pieces from this technical complex can be given new functions in an ecotechnological community, but there are no guarantees.

First, the recent development of miniaturized, automated, microelectronically controlled production units by transnational flexible production makes a decentralized communalization of manufacture technically possible. Such new technology obviously would lend "itself to a system of small-scale production, based on a regional economy and structured physically on a human scale."[55] The technologies will not create these social changes on their own. However, they do create the technical possibilities for such a thoroughgoing social transformation when combined with new forms of popular organization and control.[56] Moreover, the entrepreneurial revolution attending the post-1973 "hollowing out" of vast corporate capital formations is another indication that independent producership and personal enterprise do work under advanced technological conditions. Small is beautiful for contemporary high-tech *kanban* capitalism, where more and more work is outsourced to smaller independent operators. The questions of equity, fairness, and ecological responsibility are often not now addressed by such enterprises. Nonetheless, they could be.

Second, the technical potentialities in present-day corporate science and technology also constitute ecologically necessary changes. The "present-value" accounting of transnational corporate production, which casts the unending growth in world resource exploitation as megatechnical growth, mystifies the fact that, in an environmental sense, we are burning our house, clothes, furniture and food in midwinter to keep warm for the next few hours. Forest death, acid rain, and widespread desertification are signs that the carrying capacities of many bioregions have broken down under the destructive growth of consumer society. Ecotechnologies, based on less use of fewer resources in more efficient ways, have become ecologically necessary. An ecotechnology must be seen as this complex social ensemble of techniques, bioregion, and communal productivity. "This ensemble," Bookchin claims, "has the distinct goal of not only meeting human needs in an ecologically sound manner—one which favours diversity within an ecosystem—but of consciously promoting the integrity of the biosphere. The Promethean quest of using technology to 'dominate nature' is replaced by the ecological ethic of using technology to harmonize humanity's relationship with nature."[57]

Finally, accepting a partnership with nature instead of dominating nature reframes the moral importance behind living frugally in accord with an ecotechnology. Living more simply in unison with the biosphere's cycles of generation and regeneration would make possible a new moral-political order for ecocommunities. The reduction of nature's domination could also reduce human domination of other humans. New forms of self-management, community empowerment, and household production in keeping with the ecological constraints of every bioregion could liberate both nature and humanity. Protecting nature would make all human minds and hands useful in a new system of "production for the masses" based more fully on nonmaterial ends. As Schumacher outlines, an ecological system of production using more appropriate technology mobilizes

> resources which are possessed by all human beings, their clever brains and skillful hands, *and supports them with first-class tools.* The technology of mass production is inherently violent, ecologically damaging, self-defeating in terms of non-renewable resources, and stultifying for the human person. The technology of *production by the masses,* making use of the best of modern knowledge and experience, is conducive to decentralisation, compatible with the laws of ecology, gentle in its use of scarce resources, and designed to serve the human person instead of making him the servant of machines. I have named it *intermediate technology* to signify that it is vastly superior to the primitive technology of bygone ages but at the same time much simpler, cheaper, and freer than the supertechnology of the rich. One can also call it self-help technology, or democratic or people's technology—a technology to which everybody can gain admittance and which is not reserved to those already rich and powerful.[58]

Using these technical means, social ecologists argue, ecocommunities would more easily realize the nonmaterial ends—justice, balance, frugality, enjoyment—that most persons seek to attain.

These tools also would enable human societies to realize "convivial" values—self-empowerment, individual choice, household autonomy, and independent subsistence.[59] Soft energy and technology paths, particularly in contrast to the moral vacuum of the corporate marketplace, could revitalize many vital values, such as "thrift, simplicity, diversity, neighborliness, humility, and craftsmanship."[60] Every modern tool contains many self-subversive dimensions that ecotechnologies might tap to meet the purposes of ecological populist development. Much of the inaccessible science of corporate and state specialists also can be reconstituted as accessible knowledge useful to nonspecialists. It now is possible to design instruments that are simple, durable, useful, and manageable in individual, household, or community use. These tools, once disengaged from corporate control, could produce the energy and productive power necessary for a humane standard of living. Many ecotechnologies, then, might grow out of the communal projects of dismantling megatechnical systems for corporate capitalist production.

Revolutionizing Everyday Life

With the globalization of megatechnical production and its consumerist model of commodity consumption, a transnational political economy has stripped individuals and communities of their rights to self-direction, self-determination, and self-definition with a mix of corporate economics and polyarchical politics. These games of "rationalization without representation" have imposed destructive new forms of ecological domination upon the order of everyday life. The presumed authority of technical experts and their specialized knowledge exerts itself through the material artifacts, market processes, and organizational infrastructure of corporate culture. While many costs pile up in the biosphere, a few benefits mainly flow to the anonymous controllers, managers, and designers in the technologically competent classes of transnational enterprises. This is precisely the organization-dependent technology that the Unabomber attacked. Ecologically inspired populist political action represents a new emancipatory form of opposition within the transnational corporate order, organizing individuals and families communally to rebuild everyday life globally by recollectivizing themselves and things in their immediate localities. The activism of many such new populist movements also defines the class conflicts of advanced industrial societies.

In the last analysis, ecological populism far surpasses leftist resistances. Social ecology and voluntary simplicity are the sharpest critical responses to the contemporary post-Fordist mode of advanced megatechnical development. Fordism, as Gramsci argues, represents "the organization of a planned economy," concentrating on the large-scale production of consumer durables with Taylorized productivity schemes, such that the workers as a mass undergo "the entire process of psycho-physical transformation so that the average type of Ford worker becomes the average type of worker in general."[61] Speculating that the techniques of Henry Ford's Highland Park automobile plant, featuring the first continuous assembly line, would become generalized, Gramsci saw this energy-, capital-, and technology-intensive system as the core of a new corporate economy. Today it is "a shorthand term for the organizational and technological principles characteristic of the modern large-scale factory,"[62] signifying the organizational model that big business, big government, and big labor push on contemporary society through polyarchical rule.

Post-Fordism implodes the social contract of fair wages and social security for nationally defined working classes by truly globalizing the megatechnical production process. Segmenting the production process transnationally into different value-adding steps located in various national labor markets also permits transnational business to reduce costs by paying less overhead costs for such concessions as social security and high wages. Instead of reproducing this global system of wage and benefit reduction within high-tech industrial capitalist firms, a populist social ecology would push for greater independent producership both inside and outside the commodity chains of transnational corporate capitalism. Rather than promote higher wages and better benefits, this strategy would push for communities to reassert their economic autonomy, technical choice, and political freedom. To revitalize opportunities for local commonwealths, alternative technologies and ownership arrangements in social ecologies could offer an avenue for ordinary people in their own communities to secede from the systems of coercive complexity sold by corporate firms in polyarchical systems as "free markets."

Voluntary simplicity stands for the repudiation of a modernity oriented toward the production and consumption of consumer durables within the impoverished lifeworld fabricated by big business.[63] The experts' Taylorization of labor into mindless subroutines of semiskilled and unskilled work represents a mode of coercive complexity that is no longer worth its psychic or social costs. Similarly, the destruction of the biosphere in the process of feeding the global post-Fordist factory system's needs for energy, resource, and land in hyperecological technoregions disrupts the community of living things in many of the planet's bioregions. Post-Fordism, with its system of globalized flexible specialization, is the direct antithesis of social ecology's "right livelihood," and the political economy of social ecology aptly criticizes the many moral flaws and cultural failings in megatechnical post-Fordism by pushing for new alternatives rooted in fresh collectives tied to local commonwealths, ecotechnologies, and simpler values. Chapter 8 explores more closely how these resistances might begin to change the existing economy and society by finding within them alternative collectives in other modernities, which are or can be more social and ecological.

Notes

1. For further discussion in this vein, see Barry Commoner, *The Closing Circle: Man, Nature, and Technology* (New York: Bantam, 1971); Ivan Illich, *Toward a History of Needs* (New York: Bantam, 1978); and Jeremy Rifkin, *Entropy: Into the Greenhouse World* (New York: Bantam, 1989).

2. For a critique of consumerism, see Jean Baudrillard, *For a Critique of the Political Economy of the Sign* (St. Louis: Telos, 1981); Ivan Illich, *Energy and Equity* (New York: Harper, 1974); William Leiss, *The Limits of Satisfaction* (Toronto: University of Toronto Press, 1976); and Timothy W. Luke, "Regulating the Haven in a Heartless World: The State and Family under Advanced Capitalism," *New Political Science* 2, no. 3 (Fall 1981): 51–74.

3. Donald Worster, *Nature's Economy: The Roots of Ecology* (Garden City, N.Y.: Anchor Doubleday, 1979), 347, 349.

4. Alfred North Whitehead, *Science and the Modern World* (New York: Macmillan, 1925), 58–59.

5. See Joseph Wood Krutch, *The Great Chain of Life* (Boston: Houghton Mifflin, 1957); and Aldo Leopold, *Sand County Almanac* (Oxford: Oxford University Press, 1949).

6. Andre Gorz, *Ecology as Politics* (Boston: South End, 1980), 21.

7. For the first discussion of "ecology" as a science, see Ernst Haeckel, *Generelle Morphologie der Organismen* (Berlin: Reimer, 1866).

8. Duane Elgin, *Voluntary Simplicity: Toward a Way of Life That Is Outwardly Simple, Inwardly Rich* (New York: William Morrow, 1981), 33–34.

9. Ibid., 33.

10. E. F. Schumacher, *Small Is Beautiful: Economics As If People Mattered* (New York: Harper and Row, 1973), 297.

11. Ibid., 51.

12. Ibid., 57.

13. Illich, *History of Needs*, vii.

14. Hazel Henderson, *Creating Alternative Futures: The End of Economics* (New York: Berkley Windhover, 1978), 83–84.

15. Ibid., 84.

16. Schumacher, *Small Is Beautiful*, 58.

17. Ibid.

18. Elgin, *Voluntary Simplicity*, 37.

19. Ibid., 199.

20. Schumacher, *Small Is Beautiful*, 13.

21. Ivan Illich, *Shadow Work* (Boston: Marion Boyars, 1981), 13.

22. Schumacher, *Small Is Beautiful*, 31.

23. Henderson, *Creating Alternative Futures*, 339.

24. Ibid.

25. Illich, *History of Needs*, 134.
26. Schumacher, *Small Is Beautiful*, 14.
27. Ibid., 15.
28. Ibid., 33.
29. Ibid., 34.
30. Ibid.
31. Ibid., 297.
32. Karl Hess, *Community Technology* (New York: Harper and Row, 1979), 14.
33. Murray Bookchin, *Toward an Ecological Society* (Montreal: Black Rose, 1980), 15.
34. Hess, *Community Technology*, 10.
35. Ibid., 21.
36. Ibid., 37.
37. Bookchin, *Ecological Society*, 13.
38. Gorz, *Ecology as Politics*, 34.
39. Ibid., 35–36.
40. Bookchin, *Ecological Society*, 47.
41. Ibid., 47–48.
42. Ibid., 110.
43. Ibid., 69.
44. Ibid.
45. Ibid., 69–70.
46. Amory B. Lovins, *Soft Energy Paths: Toward a Durable Peace* (Cambridge, Mass.: Ballinger, 1977), 14.
47. Commoner, *The Closing Circle*, 124.
48. Ibid., 125.
49. Ibid., 175.
50. Lovins, *Soft Energy Paths*, 23.
51. Ibid., 24.
52. Schumacher, *Small Is Beautiful*, 153.
53. Murray Bookchin, *Post-Scarcity Anarchism* (Berkeley, Calif.: Ramparts, 1971), 87.
54. Ibid., 112.
55. Bookchin, *Post-Scarcity Anarchism*, 106.
56. Hess, *Community Technology*, 38–107.
57. Bookchin, *Ecological Society*, 109. For more discussion of Bookchin's project, see Andrew Light, ed., *Social Ecology after Bookchin* (New York: Guilford, 1998).
58. Schumacher, *Small Is Beautiful*, 154.
59. See Ivan Illich, *Tools for Conviviality* (New York: Harper and Row, 1973), for further discussion of "convivial technologies" and their influences on community life.
60. Lovins, *Soft Energy Paths*, 57.
61. Antonio Gramsci, "Americanism and Fordism," *Selections from the Prison Notebooks*, ed. Quintin Hoare and Geoffrey Nowell Smith (New York: International, 1971), 279, 312.

62. Charles F. Sabel, *Work and Politics: The Division of Labor in Industry* (Cambridge: Cambridge University Press, 1982), 33. See also Alain Lipietz, *Miracles and Mirages: The Guises of Global Fordism* (London: Verso:, 1987); Dani Rodrik, *Has Globalization Gone Too Far?* (Washington, D.C.: Institute for International Economics, 1997); and Michael Storper and Richard Walker, *The Capitalist Imperative: Territory, Technology, and Industrial Growth* (Oxford: Blackwell, 1989).

63. Populist resistance against the new class is essential. Illich's questioning of expertise is where a new social ecology rooted in populism might begin: "The credibility of the professional expert, be he scientist, therapist or executive, is the Achilles heel of the industrial system. Therefore, only those citizen initiatives and radical technologies that directly challenge the insinuating dominance of disabling professions open the way to freedom for nonhierarchical, community based competence. . . . The first step . . . is skeptical and nondeferential posture of the citizen toward the professional expert. Social reconstruction begins with a doubt raised among citizens" (Illich, *History of Needs,* 17).

8 Searching for Alternative Modernities: Populism and Ecology

This concluding chapter tackles directly several difficult issues raised in the preceding sections. It argues in favor of a communal democratic populism and against control by the new class, whose members are seen as the key privileged social bloc benefiting under the current arrangements of state and corporate power. It calls for a revitalization of radical popular imagination and rebukes tendencies toward unthinking popular inaction. It speaks in favor of choosing a habitat requiring individual property, self-reliance, and local community power against a habitus based on collective propertylessness, personal dependence, and bureaucratic administration. It advocates taking some new risks and forgetting old fears, suggestions that are never welcome in many quarters. At the very least, it might initiate some fresh discussions about several critical but too often ignored questions raised by populist forms of politics.

This chapter continues arguments from chapters 6 and 7 by reconsidering linkages between the economics of everyday modern life and populist communitarian resistance in terms of how these ecologies have been organized for over a hundred years as urban-industrial hyperecologies. In addition, retracing ideas raised in chapter 6, it also looks at the populist revolt of the 1890s as one of the last serious oppositions to the organization-dependent technologies of megatechnics in the process of assuming their current cultural forms as "industrial democracy" or "suburban consumerism."[1]

By asking why the populist revolts were eclipsed, however, it also investigates how recent shifts in the world economy are undercutting the existing hyperecological macroenvironments still populated by industrial democrats and suburban consumers and raising the prospects for new populist resistances to rethink the institutions of U.S. federalism and practices of corporate capitalism. As corporate downsizing and government cutbacks renege on social contracts hammered out over the past century in the form of industrial democracy, a new and unstable entrepreneurial economy of independent subcontracting, temp workers, and structural underemployment emerging from post-Fordist informationalism is forcing many to revisit old communitarian ideas, which were last considered seriously by the populists.[2] This chapter, then, surveys all these developments and considers how populist ways of living might lead into new ecologies of everyday life.

Informationalism, Populism, and Ecology

In the transformations being wrought today by post-Fordist informationalization, radical changes arguably "can be translated or transcoded into a narrative account in which agents of all sizes and dimensions are at work."[3] The choice between various alternative interpretations of their workings as the specific operations of political agency and social structure often "is a practical rather than a theoretical one."[4] This observation is important. Now political spaces are being generated by some determinate set of contemporary material forces, and they are being inhabited by new agents of all sizes and dimensions that are neither statist nor corporate.

This postmodern condition also may signal the rise of "a new social system beyond classical capitalism" emerging from "the world space of multinational capital" on both a local and a global level.[5] More specifically, as David Harvey argues, this new social system of multinational capital is developing its own world spaces by disintegrating the Fordist regime of industrial production, capital accumulation, and state intervention formed during the 1930s through the 1970s in national welfare states.[6] Since then it has been replaced by a new regime of flexible accumulation, productive specialization, and state deregulation in loosely coupled transnational alliances of market centers, factory concentrations, technology generators, capital suppliers, and public administrators.

From this mix transnational firms, on the one hand, produce world cars, global hamburgers, planetary pants, or "Earth Shoes" from nowhere and anywhere to sell everywhere, making a travesty of nationalist campaigns to "Buy American" and xenophobic reactions to resist "Americanization." Like Chernobyl, "America," as an economic formation, a mass culture, or an ecological system, is everywhere. It is no longer simply the substance of a nation-state or one ethnonational population; its hyperecologies become the signs of both a new consciousness and a mode of production at the nucleus of a global chain reaction. In addition, as it melts down to its most critical mass, the fallout is changing all life forms everywhere. Spatial barriers and time zones collapse in the compression of multinational capital's acceleration of global production. As Harvey observes, "flexible accumulation typically exploits a wide range of seemingly contingent geographical circumstances, and reconstitutes them as structured internal elements of its own encompassing logic. . . . the result has been the production of fragmentation, insecurity, and ephemeral uneven development within a highly unified global space economy of capital flows."[7]

Under this horizon of flexible accumulation, Lyotard's vision of performativity comes to anchor the disorganized regime following classical economic liberalism. Today, "the State and/or company must abandon the idealist and humanist narratives of legitimation in order to justify the new goal: in the discourse of today's financial backers of research, the only credible goal is power. Scientists, technicians, and instruments are purchased not to find truth, but to augment power."[8] New class meritocracies and professional-technical elitists hiding behind these codes of performativity are global, not regional, local, or maybe now even national in their interests and loyalties.[9] On the other hand, new resistances from beneath the nation-state and outside big business now stress the viability of the local community, immediate environment, and regional commerce against the designs of large national bureaucracies and firms. Post-Fordist informationalism's rise to existential and cultural dominance marks one of the most basic forces at work within the current world system, which is marked also by "the moment of the multinational network, or what Mandel calls 'late capitalism,' a moment in which not merely the older city but even the nation-state itself has ceased to play a central functional and formal role in the process that has in a new quantum leap of capital prodigiously expanded beyond them, leaving them behind as ruined and archaic remains of earlier stages in the development of this mode of production."[10] Scanning these ruins for clues of life is essential. What are now "traditional structures" of industrial cities and nation-states, the accustomed seats of sovereign power and typical sites of economic exchange, play less central roles in either forming the economy or fixing the functions of the society.[11]

After the consolidation of the Second Industrial Revolution, the necessities of everyday life were no longer the product of individual artisans or cultivators.[12] Instead, new formations of finance capital, professional organizations, interventionist bureaucracy, and applied sciences crystallized into an elaborate organization of high-tech production that linked together the workings of many complex machines—namely, all those new devices, routines, and institutions that arose from many resistant but constrained parts to form larger entities intended to transmit motion and modify force in performing many different desired forms of work so as to provide for the needs of urban industrial workers and consumers.[13] Small-holding agriculture gave way to corporate farming, little shops were displaced by big factories, local economies imploded under global trade, and skilled trades were restructured as professional technical science or unskilled wage labor. The ecology of human communities was totally transformed as these megamachines infiltrated the structures of everyday life in the name of efficiency, progress, or development to fabricate urban-industrial hyperecologies.[14] What once was homemade now could be store bought. Items that once came from local fields, streams, forests, and soils arrived from faraway. Corporate marketing needs, professional scientific opinions, and uniform government requirements all set the measure of ordinary existence, not local communities based locally among neighbors and friends.

The Populist Movement: Conflict in the 1890s

American populism in the 1890s was, to a significant extent, a widespread popular revolt against the new systems of human ecology fabricated by hyperecological machines. If all were to serve the new agendas of major corporations, big banks, national bureaucracies, academic professions, and applied sciences, the more sustainable communities of small local producers, who already were following appropriate technologies, frugal lifestyles, and democratic philosophies, had to be crushed.[15] The remaining fragments were integrated, not on terms of their own choosing or in ways fitting their material interests, into new networks of social reproduction suited to the megamachines rising out of the Second Industrial Revolution.[16] If ecologies are the totality of all relationships between organisms and their environments, then the relation between human organisms and their environments completely shifted when Americans allowed major corporations, pretending to be the sole legitimate incarnations of science and technology, to bring good things to life for them or permitted better living to come through chemistry, physics, or biology instead of hard work, self-reliance, or individual effort. For all their other faults, the populists sensed these dangers in the emergent state-corporate alliances of a century ago and strongly resisted them.

Populism has been a negative figure of political speech in the United States largely because of the meanings it acquired in the now outmoded cold war political lexicon, meanings that were defined by new-class-oriented social sciences created for bureaucrats and managers of industrial democracy. Anxious to contain mass resistance from below in apparently right-wing forms, the prevailing political opinion in the 1950s, for example, largely bought into S. M. Lipset's characterization (or caricature) of populism as a rancid strain of working-class authoritarianism.[17] Ignoring enlightened establishment elites in big business or big government offices, such populists allegedly would give sway to their authoritarian tendencies by throwing in with either fascist or communist movements to upend the status quo. Set within this negative frame, other populistic initiatives in the 1960s and 1970s among the civil rights movement, environmental groups, or religious revivals were often dismissed as being promulgated by mobs of dangerous deviants threatening the basically progressive harmony of liberal welfare states. President Reagan's anti-statist and anti-elitist rhetoric in the 1980s, however, unleashed populism from many of its negative associations, henceforth allowing many new initiatives to lay claim to "populism" as their watchword.[18] New Leftish versions from Jesse Jackson, George McGovern, or Bill Clinton clash with New Rightish visions from Jack Kemp, Newt Gingrich, and Dan Quayle as all post–Reagan era politicos try to outmatch one another in their attacks on the liberal welfare state of the New Deal, Great Society, or cold war era. So far, this talk mostly has been only talk. Meanwhile, for many middle-class groups, the economic, political, and social unrest of the past decade remains, as Harry Boyte argues, "emblematic of deep and traumatic disruptions in values and ways of living themselves. . . . in such an environment, the call for a return of power to ordinary people—the defining project of populism—gains tremendous force. If experts, distant problem-solvers, and the rich and powerful seem perplexed, impotent and avaricious, the appropriate solution is to devolve authority to those closer to home and to institutions grounded in communities."[19] But how, where, when, and why?

Populism in the 1890s as well as now during the 1990s represents a struggle over the best way to organize the economy and society in modern industrial systems. It contests the prevailing corporate or statist rules of "who and whom," arguing in favor of supporting small freeholding against corporate collectivism, local economies over global diseconomy, face-to-face community against in-your-face commercial culture, and self-rule over bureaucratic clientage.[20] American populism, as it rose and fell in the Midwest, West, and South from the 1890s through the 1930s, was many things for many people. In some respects, however, it constituted a antisystemic resistance against a new industrial ecology that emerged in the 1880s as the Second Industrial Revolution remade much of America around a political economy rooted in corporate capitalism, national statism, and technocratic professionalism.

During the generation leading up to the 1890s, the social and economic environment of the United States was transformed radically. In 1860 the United States trailed England, France, and Germany in the total value of its manufactured output, yet by 1894 its manufactures almost equaled all those from England, France, and Germany together.[21] Before the Civil War, the working class was outnumbered by slaves. By the mid-1890s, the American working class was the largest in the world. At the end of the 1860s, half the nation's manufacturing establishments still were powered by water. By the mid-1890s, electricity and steam drove much of America's manufacturing enterprise.[22] Before Taylorism and Fordism colonized American workplaces and working-class communities, hard work was experienced by many exploited workers, but a four-day work week and a three-day weekend characterized many other places of business and manufacturing, for artisanal work habits and skills still gave many workers tremendous control over both "work rules" and "company time." Families and friends, good drink and good discussion, frequent breaks and fine naps—all were not uncommon features of those workplaces, workdays, and worklives grounded in economies of independent producership.[23]

Instead of capital enforcing its monopolies over access to capital, technology, and markets, independent producers in agriculture, commerce, and industry worked separately and together to produce goods, circulate commodities, and accumulate property in local networks keyed to notions of commonwealth. Populists wanted to avoid narrow national concentrations of owning class-monopolized wealth. Plainly the artisanal economy was not perfect, but in many ways it was far more humane, democratic, and accessible as a project for developing commonwealth than was the corporate order for maximizing choice and demanding productivity in terms of industrial democracy. Although post-Fordist informationalism brings many new uncertainties with it, some of its practices might also eliminate much of the standardized mechanization and centralist disempowerment that undercut the producership of artisanal labor a century ago. Within the hollowed-out, downsized, and disorganized old Fordist industrial system, new artisan-based forms of labor, independent entrepreneurialism, and communal production might be tested again. And with such autonomous economic activities, individuals and communities could begin uniting in an effective opposition to big firms and bureaucracies that impede their progress or disrupt their enterprise.[24]

As Lasch observes, the loose alliance of corporate capital and national bureaucracy forged in the 1870s and 1880s sought to replace independent producership and classical citizenship with a narrow array of feeble surrogates tossed out of a mix of consumerism and clientage. That is, "attempts to achieve a redistribution of income, to equalize opportunity in various ways, to incorporate the working classes into a society of consumers, or to foster economic growth and overseas expansion as a substitute for social reform can all be considered as twentieth-century substitutes for property ownership; but none of these policies created the kind of active, enterprising citizenry envisioned by nineteenth-century democrats."[25] The freedom and equality believed to be necessary for a truly popular form of democratic commonwealth early in the 1800s were never realized, because the Fordist wage system, Taylorist corporate organization, Keynesian financial regime, and Sloanist commercial culture became established as the vendors of a new "industrial democracy" with its own peculiar forms of economic freedom and legal equality.

One can, however, connect American populism to a producerist ideology shared by small farmers, skilled artisans, and small-town tradespeople all working to resist the innovations of a new national industrial economy and state from the 1880s through the 1930s, although the heyday of populism clearly comes from 1894 through 1914. Although independent agrarianism was a bedrock foundation of the movement, as Lasch notes, its ranks included far more than just America's small-holding farmers:

> Artisans and even many shopkeepers shared with farmers the fear that the new order threatened their working conditions, their communities, and their ability to pass on both their technical skills and their moral economy to their offspring. In the nineteenth century, "agrarianism" served as a generic term for popular radicalism, and their usage reminds us that opposition to monopolists, middlemen, public creditors, mechanization, and the erosion of craftsmanship by the division of labor was by no means confined to those who worked the soil.[26]

Populism at that time represented a wide range of people still directly tied to the land, trading on their craft, touched with real artisanal abilities, and turning over goods immediately between local producers and consumers. In such settings individual producership tied families and communities to their immediate environment in ways quite unlike those in the corporate capitalist and welfare state economies of the present.

Because of deep shifts in the organization of labor for information-based commercial enterprises, however, as well as changes in the property relations most suited to flexible modes of production, new possibilities are emerging now that strangely parallel or continue much of what was once attacked as populism. As Lasch suggests, these attributes would include now as they did then such attitudes as "producerism; a defense of endangered crafts (including the craft of farming); opposition to the new class of public creditors and to the whole machinery of modern finance; [and] opposition to wage labor. Populists inherited from earlier political traditions, liberal as well as republican, the principle that property ownership and the personal independence it confers are absolutely essential preconditions of citizenship."[27]

The myths of complete and total abundance on which consumer capitalism and the new class continue to base their legitimacy as a form of industrial democracy in the light of environmental constraints are proving to be nothing more than myths. If everyone in China, or perhaps even just in the United States, lived at the consumption levels of upper-middle-class LA suburbanites, the world would soon choke to death on its own smog, CFCs, styrofoam, and CO_2. Luxury for all tomorrow will never happen; such promises survive only to mask and measure luxury for the few today. The populists' awareness of limits pushed them toward notions of widespread competence, shared governance, and ordinary ownership—ideas that progressive new class managers contained with their utopias of consumption and clientage from big business and big government. "Populists, on the other hand," as Lasch argues, "regarded a competence, as they would have called it—a piece of earth, a small shop, a useful calling—as a more reasonable as well as a more worthy ambition. 'Competence' had rich moral overtones; it referred to the livelihood conferred by property but also the skills required to maintain it. The ideal of universal proprietorship embodied a humbler set of expectations than the ideal of universal consumption, universal access to a proliferating supply of goods. At the same time, it embodied a more strenuous and morally demanding definition of the good life."[28]

The living standards of the affluent cannot be extended to the poor on either a global or a national scale. Endless economic expansion will collapse the planet's biotic sustainability long before universal material abundance on the scale of U.S. suburban consumption is realized, because a higher material standard of living never has been much more than a high living of material standards imposed by corporate design and state regulation. Not surprisingly, then, corporate ecological authoritarianism, which has forced many forms of new-class-organized cultural, social, and technical rationalization on society without popular representation, is under fire today for the anti-ecological arrogance it displays in impoverishing culture and abusing technology. Even more ironically, what worked imperfectly in the United States from the 1880s through the 1960s has worked even more imperfectly on a global scale since the 1970s as corporate commerce has unsustainably misdeveloped the world economy and its many ecologies.

The acceptance of consumer capitalism on a national scale has proven to be highly destructive as well. State regulation of everyday life has created dependencies, insecurities, and incapacities in almost every class that begin to undermine the general reproduction of society. President Clinton's ratcheting down on "big government," like President Reagan's moves before him, are not likely to reverse these trends. Greater and greater state intervention into the routines of families, individuals, cities, and firms has only made them less survivable while creating major inefficiencies and massive deficits. Complete and total abundance, as the progressive utopias of industrialism and statism foretold, is illusory. Just as state communism collapsed of its own weight, so too is corporate consumerism proving to be an impossible dream. *Perestroika* in the United States may first appear as Reaganism, but what will follow these moves after that kind of restructuring's failures remains to be seen. As Lasch observes, American populism possibly had some answers:

> The need for a more equitable distribution of wealth ought to be obvious, both on moral and on economic grounds, and it ought to be equally obvious that economic equality cannot be achieved under an advanced system of capitalist production. What is not so obvious is that equality now implies a more modest standard of living for all, not an extension of the lavish standards enjoyed by the favored classes in the industrial nations to the rest of the world. In the twenty-first century, equality implies a recognition of limits, both moral and material, that finds little support in the progressive tradition.[29]

When populist resistances lost their preeminence as practical guides for living, new ideologies and institutions arose in the commercial sphere to define individual values, organize urban society, and foment cultural revolution in the name of "industrial democracy," which was made possible by corporate capitalist entities charged with the operational tasks of administering this new hyperecological mode of production and consumption.

As William Leach suggests, "from the 1890s on, American corporate business, in league with key institutions, began the transformation of American society into a society preoccupied with consumption, with comfort and bodily well-being, with luxury, spending, and acquisition, with more goods this year than last, more next year than this. American consumer capitalism produced a culture almost violently hostile to the past and to tradition, a future-oriented culture of desire that confused the good life with goods."[30] During the 1990s, in the lands of desire carved from commercial artifacts, new populist resistances are also asking whether "commodity production and consumerism alter perception not just of the self but of the world outside of the self. They create a world of mirrors, insubstantial images, illusions increasingly indistinguishable from reality . . . The consumer lives surrounded not so much by things as by fantasies."[31] Such fantasies can be, and have been, normalizing for polyarchies. From the mass media, market pressures, and peer practices, these corporate goods acquired tremendous force, allowing anyone to see him- or herself in them and everyone to see them as self-constituting agents of this unstable industrial democracy.

Hyperecologies in Industrial Democracy

Once such hyperecological webs were woven, as chapter 2 suggested, uncontaminated ecologies in pristine nature became problematic. Indeed, after the Second Industrial Revolution, one might ask whether nature exists anymore. Where is it; can we go there and live self-reliantly? On the other hand, is nature gone for good now that the corporate modernization project has expanded over the entire planet as a hyperecological macroenvironment? All organisms are products of their environments. They may, of course, shape their environments by their actions, but they too always are shaped by their environmental settings. Human beings are no exception to the rule, even though there has been little consideration of the way that the rule might work for people. Why? Because the human environment is no longer nature, despite environmentalists' frantic railings about humanity's domination of nature. Bill McKibben and Carolyn Merchant are absolutely right, even though they are often not taken seriously.[32] We may now live *after* "the end of nature." Nature *is* perhaps dead. To take these insights to heart, as chapters 3 and 4 argued, we should admit that our real ecosystem, our environment, is composed largely of commercialized artifacts, mediating the metabolism of immense megamachines of production and consumption thriving in their habitats of elaborate, artificially built environments.[33]

Mumford describes these elaborate environment-forming apparatuses as megamachines, "mass organizations able to perform tasks that lie outside the range of small work collectives and loose tribal or territorial groups," which have "progressively multiplied the use of the more reliable mechanical components while not merely reducing the labor force needed for a colossal operation but, through electronics, facilitating instantaneous remote control."[34] Through bureaucratic surveillance and commercial normalization, the agendas of these machines are to exert "control over the entire community at every point of human existence," because the global human ecology generated by such machines "escapes spatial and temporal limitations; it can operate as a single, largely invisible unit over a wide area, its functioning parts operating as a unit through instant communication."[35] The daily existence of millions of individuals and thousands of urban settlements turns on the workings of hundreds of these machines, which interlock labor and capital, matter and energy, technology and technician, and producers and consumers in megatechnical exchanges that sustain the life of these human beings in their artificial environments. In other words, human beings are mainly products of the products that constitute the environment: supermarket foods, mall fashions, suburban housing, automotive transport, electronic telecommunication, petrochemical energy, and corporate entertainment. We exist only there.

Maybe this is the by-product of natural fission, creating a "first nature" of the green outside and a "second nature" of the manufactured inside. Either way, the key ecosystems of the human environment are centered in a hyperecological second nature and its megamachineries. The acts and artifacts of this global system are charged with significant conventional understandings about accepting or employing as well as resisting or disrupting this totalitarian monoculture, namely, its megamachines and the inscripted commodities or packaged form that they produce to reproduce their order. Everyone who lives mostly in a money economy now depends on the artifacts produced by these megamachines—commodified forms of shelter, food supplies, dress, climate control, work, social control, entertainment. When easy access to this environment is interrupted by war, natural disasters, crime, or international sanctions, survival itself is imperiled. Without the megamachines, life turns into the solitary, nasty, brutish, and short kinds of existence endured in Sarajevo, Haiti, Beirut, Rwanda, or Grozny.

This is the generic ideology of commodities under industrial democracy: the primacy of the totality. Everything must work this way, because everything does work this way. There is an ironic concordance with Commoner's first law of ecology here: "everything is connected to everything else," and the whole depends on each part doing its part to sustain these complex habitats.[36] Ecologies of megamachinic artifacts shape their inhabitants even as the inhabitants shape these artifacts. Without linking into its transnational commodity chains as value-adding and value-appropriating co-operators, few humans now can live any kind of satisfying life. The independent producership of dignified labor within autonomous communities that American populists dreamed of during the 1890s is almost impossible unless, of course, one sees poor peasants combing the hills for firewood and food in these terms. Nature becomes a utopia, existing at best as the glossy imagery of Sierra Club photos or in the slick packaging of ecotourism trips, because many of its old secrets are now completely commodified products—nuclear fission, calendar art, genetically engineered vegetables, and prepackaged wilderness experiences.

Ironically, Commoner's second law of ecology is met as well: "everything has to go somewhere," and strangely enough it does, as both city and country are architecturally integrated, technologically linked, and institutionally managed to function in corporately administered shelter, diet, energy, dress, and labor megamachines.[37] These business-based apparatuses obtain their inputs globally and deliver their outputs locally—albeit in extremely inequalitarian levels of concentration and rates of production—to promote the daily survival of six billion human beings. Most of these habitats are to be found in cities, which are not nature's metropolis but rather Nature's necropolis.[38] High-performance machineries of speed, light, power, comfort, security, choice, and fun realize their ideological ends in each individual's use of their commodities in the everyday lifeworld. Separate and apart from this environment, few humans today live any kind of satisfying existence as "satisfaction" is specified now. Without access to their ordinary habitats in the mall or familiar ranges in the supermarket, modern hunter-gatherer cultures created by the suburban consumerism of industrial democracy will wither and die.

Maybe the abolition of nature with the formation of such hyperecologies can be seen as a by-product of shifting collective megamachines in which individual men and women get caught along or inside the boundaries of two technologies, such as those provisionally discussed by Foucault. These technologies rarely operate autonomously or discretely, but the circuits of commodity-production-consumption perhaps permit a closer examination of the constant interaction of "(1) technologies of production, which permit us to produce, transform, or manipulate things," and, "(2) technologies of the self, which permit individuals to effect by their own means or with the help of others a certain number of operations on their own bodies and souls, thought, conduct, and way of being, so as to transform themselves in order to attain a certain state of happiness, purity, wisdom, perfection, or immortality."[39] Do these coaligned technologies of production and the self cogenerate new amalgams of objective systemic productivity and subjective idiosyncratic consumption in consummativity? The end users of corporate commodities are reassigned through commodities to the role of capital asset, causing "the ultimate realization of the private individual as a productive force. The system of needs must wring liberty and pleasure from him as so many functional elements of the reproduction of the system of production and the relations of power that sanction it."[40]

For the megamachines, the liberation of technically imagineered fictions, such as the "wants" or "needs" allegedly felt by men and women, the young and the old, minorities and majorities, the East Bloc and the West Bloc, or straights and gays, is often centered on commodities hitherto inaccessible to these groups. Liberating these needs, as chapter 2 has shown, will be matched by mobilizations of need fulfillments in commodities. Consumer goods can be supplied once new subjects are recognized as having the will demanded of good consumers. Subjectivity becomes refined into material needs, and then subjection can be defined in the absolution of commodities designed to satisfy these needs materially. The habitus serves as habitat when each and every commodity co-modifies its makers and users, buyers and sellers, and haves and have-nots. Disciplinary objectivities define disciplined subjectivity, because, as Baudrillard observes:

> The *consumption* of individuals mediates the *productivity* of corporate capital; it becomes a productive force required by the functioning of the system itself, by its process of reproduction and survival. In other words, there are these kinds of needs because the system of corporate production needs them. And the needs invested by the individual consumer today are just as essential to the order of production as the capital invested by the capitalist entrepreneur and the labor power invested in the wage laborer. It is *all* capital.[41]

One here sees elective affinities drawing technologies of the self (consumer decisions to exercise purchasing power) together with technologies of production (producer choices to organize adding value) in megamechanical ecologies. Ideologies of competitive progress are inscribed by industrial democracy on each commodity delivered to consumers as tokens of their collective liberation, and bizarre ideologies of individual empowerment arise from each act of product appropriation as signs of that consumer's social development.

Consummativity is, as chapter 2 suggested, the operational summation of industrial democracy under megatechnical conditions of transnational corporate capitalist exchange. It represents the first principle of the megamachines sustaining the development of a global human ecology:

> Everything has to be sacrificed to the principle that things must have an operational genesis. So far as production is concerned, it is no longer the Earth that produces, or labor that creates wealth . . . rather, it is Capital that *makes* the Earth and Labor *produce*. Work is no longer an action, it is an operation. Consumption no longer means the simple enjoyment of goods, it means having (someone) enjoy something—an operation modelled on, and keyed to, the differential range of sign-objects. Communication is a matter not of speaking but of making people speak. Information involves not knowledge but making people know.[42]

In this setting the megamachinery of second nature's energy production, resource extraction, materials processing, service delivery, and built environments becomes "the environment," the action setting and surrounding influences determining human existence.

Commoner's third law of ecology is "nature knows best," and the logic of consummativity also ironically affirms that second nature knows best.[43] Or at least, the professional-technical new class experts in charge of making and managing this logic know best. Maybe, to paraphrase McLuhan, who saw all technologies as media providing psychical and physical "extensions of man," men and women become psychic and physical media in second nature, impersonating extensions of these technologies.[44] Is it not true that consummativity, as a mechanism of power, depends on the cultivation of the body and what it does, allowing capital to extract time, energy, and labor from what the body does in production and consumption? As the American populists feared, the material coercion of consummativity is to be found within its authoritarian confinement of local choice and totalitarian denial of global alternatives. Consummativity is liberating, but only in the peculiar fashions that it will determine within its macroenvironments. Through commodified freedoms, it can "increase subjected forces" and "improve force and efficacy of that which subjects them" in the circulation of its commodified artifacts.[45]

The "values and ways of living" embedded in contemporary transnational capitalism and national welfare states are predicated on this ecology of complex megamachines designed and managed by new class experts to create clientalistic dependencies on the corporate firm and nation-state among the mass population. When General Electric exclaims in its ads, "We bring good things to life," it captures the essence of these vast global ecologies that center themselves on bringing huge bureaucratic machines of production and consumption into life by dropping their goods and services into the lives of consumers and clients to whom "the good life" is "good things." The cycle is complete: goods and services are produced, packaged, and purchased on a global scale to bring to life for corporate capital the power of those good things under corporate control.

The transition to intensive modes of economic production over the past century also transforms the logic of governmentality, coordinating the administrative interactions of populations, political economy, and government. Increasingly, "the instruments of government, instead of being laws, now come to be a range of multiform tactics."[46] Unlike sovereignty, which expresses directly the privileges or prohibitions determined by some powerful sovereign in acts of violence, law, or favor, governmentality works through things and people's interactions with them in the materialized force fields of "public" and "business" administration. "To govern," Foucault asserts, "means to govern things," in accordance with the claim that "government is the right disposition of things, arranged so as to lead to a convenient end."[47] Both state services and corporate commodities provide a wide range of multiform tactics for corporations, state bureaucracies, banks, and professional experts to rightly dispose of things and thereby also people, arranging them to lead to useful ends that both advance their interests and enhance the existence of their many end users.

In Simon Patten's vision of the system of mass production and individual consumption in the 1890s, "the standard of life is determined, not so much by what man has to enjoy, as by the rapidly with which he tires of the pleasure. To have a high standard means to enjoy a pleasure intensely and to tire of it quickly."[48] What the American populists once touted, deeper, more organic relations to others, communities, or the land—as the old nature myths once dictated to society—must be devalued. Such commitments imply husbanding resources, preserving nature on its own merits, or respecting networks of mutual aid in close-knit communities. Rapid destruction of resources in permanent programs of quickly grazing over intense satisfactions of highly imagineered commodities only to push on relentlessly to new experiences with others is the mark of "the highest standard of living." Frugality, stability, and durability, by definition, become tawdry signs of inferior "lower forms of life."

Federalism and Populism

While reflecting about their own lives in the 1900s, many long-lived Victorians realized that when they were born in the 1820s or 1830s, the mass of humanity mostly still lived in first nature, much as it had for centuries. Rural life in A.D. 1830 was not tremendously unlike life in A.D. 1030 or A.D. 30. Urban life was not like rural living, mostly because of the rise of urban capitalism in the late Middle Ages. Even so, in many ways, city living in most towns during 1830 had not changed much since 1780 or even 1330. By the time the last Victorians passed away in the 1920s, however, almost everything had become very different. Entirely new ideologies of existence emerged along with immense new technologies for producing and consuming the hyperecologies of second nature, which remade almost everything in their everyday lifeworld. In generating this vision of the good life, then, we must admit that "in its sheer quest to produce and sell goods cheaply in constantly growing volume and at higher profit levels, American business, after 1890, acquired such power and, despite a few wrenching crises along the way, has kept it every since."[49] As the American populists anticipated in the 1890s, this shift has been the most revolutionary movement of this era, bringing new values and alternative institutions that obliterated many of the old beliefs and fixed ways of the past.

New populist movements today confront tremendous obstacles as they cope with the aftermath of this revolution. The built environment, global webs of trade, and basic ecologies of existence, as they are now structured, embody the agendas and prerogatives of state bureaucracies or corporate enterprises that have worked for over a century to bolster the centralizing federal government and Fortune 500 companies by minimizing individual autonomy and communal freedom. At the same time, the old established ways are failing. In the meantime, states and firms are shedding responsibilities and services in waves of restructuring that create new opportunities for populist communitarian innovation. With industrial democracy, corporate capitalism decisively defeated both American populism and European socialism with the countermeasures of polyarchy and megatechnics. Yet these victories were won only to the degree that new hyperecologies with special ideologies of power, subjectivity, and value could articulate their ends and expectations in the realm of artificial commodities. Advanced standards of living mean more than the enjoyment of affluence; they also imply the ongoing advancement of living in accord with normalizing standards that are continuously enforced by industrial democratic citizenship—that is, most individuals' acceptance of the imperatives at work behind megatechnical firms' designing, operating, and possessing consumer goods. Acquiring these material possessions repositions individuals and communities to become possessed, if only in part or merely for a while, by the megamachineries devoted to such systems of material acquisition. At each nexus of consumer and commodity in consumption, complex alliances of many powers elicit all those normalized subjectivities, ideological expectations, and authoritative subjugations perpetuating the megamechanical ecologies of industrial democracy.

Federalism in the United States after 1861 has plainly operated in much more centralizing bureaucratic terms, shifting power and authority away from localities, counties, and states and toward Washington.[50] These developments occurred rapidly: first, the acquisition of all or most of the territory on the North American continent in what became the trans-Mississippi West; second, the control of the development of free wage and unfree slave labor in the entire federation, leading ultimately to the Civil War, for the extractive agrarian economies of the southern states practiced a more state-based Jeffersonian vision of federalism against Washington both before and after their secession; third, the reconstruction of the South after the Civil War to impose the victorious federal reading of law and order as well as northern terms of trade on the defeated Confederacy; fourth, the pacification of the indigenous peoples through warfare and resettlement as well as the determination of the economic development of the territories in the trans-Mississippi West in accord with nation-based federal policies set in Washington by Congress and the president; and finally, support for the sustained industrialization of the entire nation through new policies for railroad construction, easy immigration, colonization, naval expansion, inflation, and military conquest. Federalism in the 1890s was something far different from what Hamilton, Jefferson, Madison, Washington, Jay, and Adams had envisioned, as federal state power moved with and against corporate capitalism to construct an urban industrial democracy capable of Americanizing millions of immigrants, normalizing millions of consumers, and disciplining millions of workers to accept strange forms of commercial reacculturation, political disempowerment, and economic dependency as a progressive modern way of life. What little sense of U.S. federalism's original approach to separation of powers, division of powers, or balance of powers remained after the crushing of most populist resistance by World War I typically boiled down to intraregime squabbles among different factions of new class experts over the way to divide the goodies in pork-barrel federalism from 1933 to 1975 or to allocate the evils in shift-and-shaft federalism from 1975 to 1998.

The key problem in American federalism since the early to mid-1970s has been how to deal with the impact of the global economy on all the communities and citizens of the United States. Caught within the territorial domain of Washington's rule are small economies tied to competitive capital capable of besting everyone or anything in the global marketplace.[51] Yet there are also smaller economies bound up with much less flexible monopoly capital or military support systems that cannot compete nationally, much less globally. Of course, the able wish to secede from the federation, and in many ways they already have, for able members of the new class build private telecommunication systems, patronize private schools, trade globally, live in gated communities, employ private security guards, and tax themselves in various systems of protective covenants. At the same time, the less able are left seeking new entitlements from a weakened federal regime still coasting on the momentum of its cold war authority; the power to tax, borrow, and spend; and the prerogatives of territorial sovereignty. Those who cannot find a place are joining the patriot movement or the narcocapitalist economy or finding some other escape from the ravages of neoliberal globalization.

In the 1990s statist instruments of power have been less efficacious, as the "new world disorder," a four trillion dollar deficit, and post-Fordist informationalism increasingly make a mockery out of Washington's once strongly centered ability to control world events, regulate its currency or steer the economy, and police its own ideological frontiers, geographical boundaries, or technological domains. A revitalized federalism centered on the people and not the state, the locality and not nationality, the national state and not the federal government, or the sharing of powers and not the concentration of powers might well be what is needed to adapt to the realities of post-Fordist informationalism for both the able and the less able segments of our society. It is clear that Washington does not have the answers after nearly three decades of ineffective Democratic and Republican administrations. In struggling to solve the problems involved, it has nearly bankrupted the treasury, mostly corrupted many local communities, and mainly disrupted regional economies by maintaining the hyperecologies of industrial democracy long after native civil society lost its ongoing ability to pay out of current cash flow. The benefits of suburban consumerism have been retained only by robbing the future and ransacking the biosphere to keep the myth of industrial democracy alive, the new class in power, and corporate America strong. Many populists believe that Americans can do better, but economic and environmental justice cannot be attained in the polyarchical traces to which they have been harnessed over the past century.

New class managerialism, bureaucratic state interventionism, and transnational corporate capitalism have all coaligned in a corruption of American federalism, creating a peculiar ecology that binds atomized societies of individual consumers to complex chains of commodity production on a global scale. Every product increasingly depends on matter, energy, and information outsourced from everywhere to operate anywhere. Consequently, almost no one can act truly autonomously as an authentically independent producer, and no place is capable of sustaining its economy or society without considerable dependencies on outside sources of supply. As chapters 2 and 3 assert, new class experts generate a host of social theories to justify these ecological insecurities as economic efficiency or instrumental rationality. Large state bureaucracies create demand for their services by coordinating these exchanges through legal, fiscal, institutional, and regulatory mechanisms. In addition, big corporate concerns continue to control markets, technologies, and resources by embedding more and more buyers in their megatechnical networks of demand creation and supply satisfaction. Unless and until these ecologies break down or redirect themselves, more populist forms of communitarian federalism cannot fully develop. Just as federalism assumes that the forms of rule will work at the level and on the scale to which they are most suited, so too must a new sense of ecological settlement begin to pervade the political economies of the present. The complex forces of new class expertise, bureaucratic statism, and transnational corporate capitalism tend to be centralizing, disempowering, and atomizing influences that can further erode communal autonomy, bioregional complexity, and local decision making unless populist movements can protect the prerogatives of their subsidarity against their overweening authority.

Ecology and Populism

Of all the fragmentary positive sciences, ecology still retains a fairly potent subversive dimension inasmuch as it can comprehensively and critically examine the totality of all relations between human beings and all other nonhuman organisms in their inorganic and organic environments. The megamachines of transnational corporate capitalism, aided and abetted by the liberal welfare state, have entirely reordered both the urban-industrial and rural-agricultural ecologies underpinning ordinary everyday life. In turn, a populist reconstitution of these economies and societies must disrupt the existing ecologies of such state-corporate macroenvironments even as they search for new ordering logics for human settlements tied to new kinds of independent producership in local microecologies.

Huge corporate bureaucracies have been constructed since the 1880s on a regional, national, and global scale to produce the goods and services huge populations need to survive. Consequently, a few score of vast monoculture, monoproduct, monoservice networks now supply most of the matter, energy, and information needs of millions of people in the United States at virtually unsustainable and ungeneralizable levels of output. Without the work of these megamachines, there can be no life as most people know it in its urban-industrial or suburban consumer forms. Yet as the cold war has ended, welfare-state liberalism and consumer capitalism, which emerged hand-in-hand with these megamachines during the Second Industrial Revolution, are clearly suffering crises in their ongoing reproduction. In new populist circles ranging from NIMBY site-defense groups to multicultural environmental justice fronts, many citizens are now asking the same questions raised by the populists a century ago. Like the militia movement, they are challenging the benefits of interventionist welfare states and transnational corporate capitalism given that the social contract of industrial-era Fordism is being rolled back, broken, or ignored in the 1990s.

Boris Frankel's essentially dogmatic antipopulism is trapped in the shallow antinomies of industrial-era politics, in which the easy divisions of labor versus capital are seen as somehow providing all the answers.[52] Given these simple abstractions of proletarian struggle, everything on the contemporary political scene allegedly can be explained and then solved. Yet this sort of "with us or against us" vision of current environmental politics, as Wendell Berry suggests, is "a sad little pair of options," and many populists hold out for the possibility that one "can live decently *without* knowing all the answers, or believing that he does—can live decently even in the understanding that life is unspeakably complex and unspeakably subtle in its complexity."[53] Like many orthodox leftists, Frankel still does not comprehend how labor is not simply the poor but pure proletarian facing capital in the form of the rich and corrupt bourgeoisie. Ordinary people recognize that they work and consume and that the new class also works and consumes; hence, effective populist environmental politics admits that everyone contributes to the problem. No one is innocent in the cycles of production and consumption that drive contemporary polyarchies and megatechnics. Again, Berry's observations on this new reality are quite astute, inasmuch as he admits that

> the environmental crisis rises closer to home. Every time we draw a breath, every time we drink a glass of water, every time we eat a bit of food we are suffering from it. And more important, every time we indulge in, or depend on, the wastefulness of our economy—and our economy's first principle is waste—we are causing the crisis. Nearly every one of us, nearly every day of his life, is contributing *directing* to the ruin of this planet. A protest meeting on the issue of environmental abuse is not a convocation of accusers, it is a convocation of the guilty.[54]

Too much of everything that is amiss today is rooted in the lives of all people. This system of authoritative efficiency thrives in part by the design of the new class in search for new efficiency and greater authority and in part from the complicity of those clients, consumers, and consumers who are "the people." The necessary changes amount to a radical reorganization in the ways that we all live, both ecologically and economically.

Few, however, are considering what will replace the megamachineries embedded in the hyperecologies of everyday life. If the welfare state is dismantled, will its regulationist apparatus, which has underpinned the collective cultivation of monocultures and monoproducts during several generations of modern hyperecology, also be closed down? Will the national state apparatus accept alternative forms of rule to end deficits, reduce regulation, and control costs? If corporate capital downsizes its presences or realizes its power in these megamachines, will its organization of production, which has set product design, service delivery, quality control, access rules, and behavior norms in modern ecologies, be eliminated? Will it tolerate alternative webs of production and consumption to reduce payrolls, rationalize product lines, and revitalize profitability?

There is no definitive program for populists that articulates what to do. Populism does not provide a failsafe recipe for the future or a surefire method for realizing successful commonwealths. Rather, this unorthodox reading of contemporary populism simply outlines strategies for the present by elaborating clearly what to undo. The notion of an industrial democracy was commandeered largely by small groups of new class professionals working to serve bureaucratic and technical interests in the welfare state or transnational firm. Its political concerns, then, usually focused on policies of damage control or codes for technical legitimation within advanced industrial society. By taking the ideas of federalism away from these narrow interests and integrating their untapped potentials into a political critique of domination under corporate capitalism, popular social forces could reconstitute contemporary consumerist ecologies, removing them from their present scientific functions and economic purposes, as an initial step toward reconstructing advanced industrialism's destructive exchanges with the environment.

Populists may be caught within the system, but they should refuse to submit to their entrapment. Populist resistances arise from advanced industrialism, but they do not have to be for it. In the 1990s as they were in the 1890s, populist resistances are about recollectivizing people and things by finding alternative modernities in modernity to serve more people more fairly more locally. As chapter 7 indicated, even the most system-affirming corporate technologies contain self-subversive moments within their makeup. Populists must work to exhume and exploit that subversive potential by revealing the unseen flexibility, unknown possibilities, and untested alternatives that contemporary technologies contain for developing an ecologically sound economy. The society of bureaucratically controlled consumption as a whole can be totally undone. Yet its revolutionary "undoing" will be attained only by destructively reconstituting pieces and parts of its institutions, technologies, and values in a new ecological "doing"—reorganized on a small-scale, nonhierarchical, noncentralized basis in new forms of real community building in specific localities outside the megamachines. Frankel's glib dismissal of populist strategies as "the panacea to the contemporary malaise" unjustly ignores Lasch's ready admission that "the populist tradition offers no panacea for all the ills that affect the modern world. It asks the right questions, but it does not provide a ready-made set of answers."[55]

Any effort to embed ecological constraints in a more populist form of society must enhance the accessibility of tools and economies to ordinary individuals, whom artificial skill monopolies and corporate-driven regimes of capital accumulation have for nearly a century excluded from individual autonomy as producers.[56] What is in fact an extremely simple and fairly brittle transnational commerce in food, fuel, and fiber tied to a few monoproduct output networks or monocrop extraction systems must become much more diversified in many more complex regional and flexible local economies.[57] Forgetting how to provision most parts of a basic everyday life from their own microecologies in favor of producing a few things for cash to buy everything else produced elsewhere and sold everywhere for immense profits in the urban-industrial macroenvironments has only disempowered the many by empowering the few who control the megamachines forming this highly environmentalized industrial ecology.

Systems of cultural normalization, which now underpin a transnational trade in identical hamburgers, automobiles, movies, and shoes, could well succumb to new zones of particularity where populist communities define and satisfy their own material wants at home. Biodiversity should mean more than protecting insects and fungi in the Brazilian rainforest canopy; it could also imply safeguarding diverse forms of human life in different economies, cultures, and societies tied to artificial microecologies held mostly apart from the transnational circulation of suburban consumer goods. Independent producership also suggests a production of independent relationships with sufficient complexity, diversity, and density to generate alternative kinds of civilization.[58] This ecological outcome, however, is to be expected and even applauded as people define their own communities in their own bioregions to sustain their own cultures of contentment free from the colonizing governmentalities that have defined global Fordism. A federal system of populist commonwealths, then, should not involve, as did new class managerialism from the past century, a forcible reorganization of industrial capitalism to make it better serve the collective choicelessness of the powerless populace. Rather, these complex federalist transformations can begin only when ecologically informed independent producers undo consumerist dependencies in everyday life with another style of collectivization resting on a new technics and democratic communities.

Reconstructing the Subpolis

Since the onset of the Second Industrial Revolution, as the American populists so intensely argued, technical advances have progressively robbed individuals and communities of their rights to self-definition, self-determination, and self-direction. This process of rationalization without representation has engendered new modes of personal and community domination in the ecologies of everyday life, yet these dynamics are ironically treated as the progressive side of modernity. The authority of technical experts and specialized knowledge exerts itself through the material artifacts and organization processes of corporate culture, benefiting its anonymous controllers and designers in the technologically competent ranks of the new class. Populism takes root whenever and wherever people recognize the merit of Wendell Berry's worries about the neglect of agriculture and land in the United States. That is, populism requires a revitalization of private life:

> We are going to have to gather up the fragments of knowledge and responsibility that we have parceled out to the bureaus and the corporations and the specialists, and we are going to have to put those fragments back together again in our own minds and in our families and households and neighborhoods. We need better government, no doubt about it. But we also need better minds, better friendships, better marriages, better communities. We need persons and households that do not have to wait upon organizations, but can make necessary changes in themselves, on their own.[59]

It is this anonymous authoritarianism that populist communitarians need to attacked. Being grounded in a modern welfare state that tends toward total administration, any meaningful ecological critique also must recognize that transnational capital inescapably works to moderate, limit, and define its revolutionary thrusts.

The environmental crisis typifies much of the old paradigm for new class power. Concerned mostly with their own technical success, administrative authority, and scientific power, scientific and technical experts constantly served the operational performativity of capital by externalizing noxious industrial by-products in the appropriation of profitable industrial products. The occupants of externalization zones—ordinary people—have rarely shared equally in the economic profits or working benefits of these arrangements. Instead they suffer; they are poisoned; they pay. Hence, populist resistances problematize the disposition of toxic wastes produced by the modernized subpolis in the subcivics of environmentalism. Left to its own devices, the new class chooses to kill a few to service the many, because the risks of any one person's death are sold to all as acceptable tradeoffs for everyone's allegedly joint benefits. This tradition of arrogant expertise, however, is now being questioned and pushed toward more the fault-resistant, damage-avoiding, or risk-averse practices of negotiated collective decision making and management. In this respect, populists are remaking the rules by contesting as well as collaborating on "the rationalization of rationalization," in which their efforts are "the assertion of political civil rights within the world of work, a synthesis of democracy and economics yet to be invented."[60]

Continuing success for the populist resistance, however, also depends on turning many individuals in the new class against the technocratic powers, privileges, and positions misused by too many others in the ranks of professional-technical experts. The cross-pressures of abusing one's post as a rational guardian must be pitted against the moral imperative of acting otherwise as a guardian of rationality. Thus, an essential role "is played here by the *issue of how deeply alternative activity affects and splits even the ranks of expert rationality.*"[61] Even then, of course, the populist challenge to new class authority is a strange amalgam of symbolic and material politics, and "action within the operation becomes dependent on publicity, legitimation and also on consent."[62]

With all their practical engagements in megatechnic management or polyarchical policymaking, new class workers now see the economic imperatives behind their technological innovation "being eclipsed by questions of the political and economic 'management' of the risks of actually or potentially unlisted technologies—discovering, administering, acknowledging, avoiding or concealing such hazards with respect to specially defined horizons of relevance."[63] With a new populist resistance, the industrial ecologies of megatechnics—with their entire man-made populations of industrial by-products, agricultural chemicals, construction materials, artificial foodstuffs, nuclear waste, automotive fuels, food packaging, and synthetic pharmaceuticals, to name only a few problem areas—become contested ground, brimming with actual or potential questions of rational or irrational modernization that must be subjected to further interpretation.[64] Populism essentially "presumes a turning away from mere criticism and a transition to *a siege of the status quo by alternatives.*"[65] Within the built environments, which constantly experience further revolutionization with megatechnics, industrial production and by-production now construct a transnational subpolis of technoscience acts and artifacts set beneath, within, and above each territorial polis still being composed from political acts and ideological artifacts.

This technified mode of permanent revolution by the new class contributes to the poor environmental and economic quality of life in the modernized subpolis. More specifically, narratives of continuous ecological and economic revolution simply underscore how thoroughly

> the potential for structuring society migrates from the political system into the sub-political system of scientific, technological and economic modernization. A precarious reversal occurs. *The political becomes non-political and the non-political political.* . . . The promotion and protection of "scientific progress" and of "the freedom of science" become the greasy pole on which the primary responsibility for political arrangements slips from the democratic system into the context of economic and techno-scientific non-politics, which is not democratically legitimated. A *revolution under the cloak of normality* occurs, which escapes from possibilities of intervention, but must all the same be justified and enforced against a public that is becoming critical.[66]

Polyarchical institutions in the territorial polis ordinarily accept these changes without much contest, because such technoscientific revolutions are believed to bring progress, modernity, or the good life, albeit at times with a few risks or those unwanted but allegedly quite controllable noxious by-products of technological action. In fact, however, the subpolis of technoscientific artifacts deeply undercuts the workings of conventional political life: new class empowerment and popular apathy are the main characteristic of the subpolitics created by the revolutionization of advanced industrial technics. The political system, on the one hand,

> is being threatened with disempowerment while its democratic constitution remains alive. The political institutions become the administrators of a development they neither have planned for nor are able to structure, but must nonetheless justify. On the other hand, decisions in science and business are charged with an effectively political content for which the agents possess no legitimation. Lacking any place to appear, the decisions that change society become tongue-tied and anonymous. . . . What we *do not* see and *do not* want is changing the world more and more obviously and threateningly.[67]

Populist challenges to the new world order make the same point about the way in which megatechnical modernization takes place under the cover of normality within global markets: what we do not see and do not want is obviously changing the world quite thoroughly and threateningly.

In this subpolis, however, these ordinary processes of polyarchical legitimation fail. Modern megatechnics, with all their toxic by-products and economic disruptions, are still producing highly technified but still mostly performative polyarchical goods. Each "remains shielded from the demands of democratic legitimation by its own character" inasmuch as "it is *neither politics nor non-politics*, but a third entity: economically guided action in pursuit of interests."[68] With populist countermovements against new class authority, however, the inhabitants of the subpolis admit how "the structuring of the future takes place indirectly and unrecognizably in research laboratories and executive suites, not in parliament or in political parties. Everyone else—even the most responsible and best informed people in politics and science—more or less lives off the crumbs of information that fall from the tables of technological sub-politics."[69]

Populist movements to politicize technology are "the reflection of human actions and omissions, the expression of highly developed productive forces," which underscores how "the sources of danger are no longer ignorance but *knowledge;* not a deficient but a perfected mastery over nature; not that which eludes the human grasp but the system of norms and objective constraints established with the industrial epoch."[70] Against Foucault's visions of governmentality, populist oppositions to new class expertise indicate how the right disposition of some people and things in one set of intended assemblies, such as interstate highway driving or ordinary household gardening, simultaneously creates a wrong indisposition between other people and other things in many different unintended collectives, such as urban lung cancer cases or pesticide-poisoned bays.[71] Because these improper relations escape or are ignored by the rational means-ends calculations of new class experts, the irrational events of mismeant or badly ending technological operations will inevitably occur. These events are systemic, not sporadic; widespread, not isolated; chronic, not episodic. Nonetheless, such instrumental irrationality is rarely recognized as an endemic product of modernity. Instead such events are mislabeled as accidental by-products and then called inaccurate names, such as "pollution," "toxins," "contamination," or "hazards."

What is irrational in one register often is confused with being free in another, and liberal philosophies of agency and society have purposely intertwined themselves with new class power prerogatives in a most unproductive fashion in the name of more choice and less regulation. This wrong indisposition of all other things and people, which often attends the right disposition of a few things and people, is now an intrinsic by-product of every product launched by new class experts into world marketplaces as megatechnical production. Much of this by-production reappears as the toxic wastes, industrial pollutions, artificial biohazards, and chemical contaminants that cause tremendous environmental destruction. Yet most of this comes from planning, knowledge, and affluence, not carelessness, ignorance, and scarcity. Moreover, this process of unchecked or undivided power is in turn what many populists now oppose.

Populist resistances are necessary pointers toward alternatives—untested and tested, good and bad, useful and frivolous. Without constant questioning, the new class continually evades important questions in its members' standard operating procedures. Yet the technocratic usurpation of popular will can end when and where

> alternatives open up in the techno-economic process and polarize it. These alternatives become fundamental and detailed, professional and profitable, found careers and open markets, perhaps even global markets. They divide up the power bloc of business in this way and thereby enable and enforce new conflicts and constellations between and inside the institutions, parties, interest groups and public spheres of all types, and to the extent all this occurs, the image of the self-referentiality of social systems shatters.[72]

Here the covert collaboration of expertise and capital can be exposed by political pressures, and in the light of deep doubt, informed analysis, and shared resolve, new alternatives freely chosen and openly decided can be provisionally mobilized and continuously revised to do the most good and the least bad by some public's leave rather than by that of a handful of elite experts.

Politics, Ecology, and Populism

This book has reviewed the workings of the various microecologies and macroenvironments in the subpolis constructed and controlled by the new class that now in turn sustain human beings in contemporary advanced capitalist societies. In another register, it has probed the links between habitus and habitat in the global economy. To a significant extent, the last authentic alternative challenge posed to this peculiar organization of production and consumption in the United States came around one hundred years ago from the short-lived and much misunderstood populist revolt. At that juncture many microecologies in most human settlements were still bioregionally based, sustainably developed, and appropriately tooled, letting communities of independent producers live more or less autonomously in their own bioregions as locally governed commonwealths. However, the technoregions built from megatechnics were fabricating new macroenvironments of nationalized administered space, industrially standardized time, and corporately colonized lifeworlds. As they advanced further and further into everyday life, they smashed apart the many microecologies that had maintained a form of human existence that presumed independent producership and free markets.

For nearly a century large state bureaucracies and major corporate enterprises have organized and operated the economic, political, and social environments of advanced industrial society by shifting human life away from independent producership and toward dependent consumerism, out of free markets and into administered systems of commerce, and beyond individual self-reliance and into statist regimes of clientalistic entitlement. What the populist resistance opposed did come to pass, in the forms of Fordist industrialism and welfare state liberalism; in succeeding, however, the loose operational alliances of polyarchy in liberal welfare states and megatechnics in large corporate enterprises have so abused the natural environment, most institutions of civil society, many sites of urban settlement, and the culture of American society that their authority is no longer respected. On the one hand, self-styled patriots are trying to launch revolutions by blowing up federal administration buildings, and on the other hand, self-absorbed hermits are mail-bombing new class experts in their office suites, computer labs, and university offices. However, other more promising developments are unfolding in the aftermath of the welfare state's collapse and the modern corporation's fragmentation. New populist movements are mobilizing people and resources to cope with a declining quality of life in the interlinked microecologies and macroenvironments being patched together under post-Fordist informationalism. They aim at environmental justice.

Flexible modes of production, disorganized regimes of accumulation, and post-Fordist systems of regulation are fostering a new entrepreneurialism in the economy and society, because big government and big business either have failed to make advanced industrial society work rationally or have chosen to spin off their social control functions in numerous deficit reduction, personnel cuts, organizational downsizing, or company restructuring campaigns during the past fifteen years. The writing has been on the wall for the new industrial state and affluent society since 1973, but the instructions began to be read only after 1989. With the end of the cold war, the raison d'être of modern bureaucratic society in the public and private sectors now faces many new questions. In addition, as did American populism in the 1890s, a new populist communitarianism is testing new answers by probing the notions of social solidarity, community commonwealth, and personal producership in which individual ownership and enterprise might provide effective solutions.

The downsizing of public- and private-sector bureaucracies threatens to take with it the hyperecologies of modern life as well as the massive megamachines of production and consumption that sustain everyday life for millions in the United States. The exhaustion of welfare-state interventionism over the past ten to fifteen years, as well as the bureaucratic immobility engendered in corporate behemoths such as GM, IBM, and Exxon, is plainly behind many experiments with both independent producership and populist politics. Government downsizing will reduce the level and number of statist redistribution programs. Often what is being done now is clearly inefficient and frequently ineffective, and other populist institutions will need to supplant some of the welfare state's current responsibilities. Moreover, corporate cutbacks are forcing many workers back into independent producer status as consultants, small businesspersons, or temp workers. A very high, perhaps even higher, standard of living can be realized from the local microecologies that populist reformers want to reclaim from the dependent consumership and clientage of today's existing global macroenvironments organized around the policies of polyarchical megatechnics: industrial Fordism, fiscal Keynesianism, and cultural Sloanism. For many populists, seeing these dilemmas is what they need to change, and it works well because it requires greater self-reliance. Resisting the collectives constructed by the new class can begin at home when a person becomes "answerable to at least some of his own needs, by acquiring skills and tools, by learning what his real needs are, by refusing the merely glamorous and frivolous. When a person learn to act on his best hopes he enfranchises and validates them as no government or public policy ever will."[73]

Nothing, or at least very little, necessarily remains settled forever in the economic, governmental, and social institutions of advanced capitalist economies. Advanced urban industrial life is never necessarily the way that we find it simply because it grows in accord with invariant laws of modernization and development. Rather, what is taken to be modern and developed represents the latest winning political coalition or ascendent market logic prevailing over all the others that have lost these battles, if only temporarily. The collectives behind modernity are full of alternative formations, untested possibilities, and potential innovations simply not yet implemented as lived activities. There are few inevitabilities or necessities beyond the constant struggle over who will dominate whom, with those in power then pretending afterward that political contingency was in fact structural inevitability.

Populism today is a complex, variegated, multidimensional phenomenon that no one analysis can fully articulate—much of it stands on the right, some of it veers to the left, a bit of it is a step back, a piece of it strikes out ahead. This book has touched on only a few of its ecological implications, examining how American populism in the 1890s stood for one sort of social ecology against a new alternative, as well as how the deteriorating macroenvironments of the 1990s suggest that another mode of collectivization, or a whole new social ecology, might now emerge to restructure the megatechnical polyarchies that have operated for over a century. One might aver that ecology is insignificant in the current scheme of things. In fact, nothing could be further from the truth.

One kind of human relationship with the environment presumes collectives rooted in microecologies of independent producership, regionalistic communitarian exchange, and personal citizenship. Another entails collectives chained to a hyperecology of dependent consumerism, globalistic corporate exchange, and personal clientage. Habitat is shaped by habitus. For ecologically minded populists to reorder the economy and society, another set of collectives in this new social ecology, which is basically another alternative modernity potentially quite different from the one that has prevailed for over a century, must be developed as forms of individual competence from within the universal incompetence engendered by this failing modernity. Even this is no surefire recipe for realizing the future. Following Marx and his warnings about the future vis-à-vis stock recipes for communism, each populist ecological community must ultimately craft its own cuisine in its own kitchen, although some ingredients for the best mix—as this book concludes—should be taken from the shelves of Marxian critical theory, localist democratic populism, and ecotechnical social ecology.

Notes

1. For a more extensive discussion of industrial democracy and suburban consumerism as forms of life, see Stuart Ewen, *Captains of Consciousness: Advertising and the Roots of Consumer Culture* (New York: McGraw-Hill, 1976); Thomas Hine, *Populuxe* (New York: Knopf, 1986); and Stuart Ewen, *PR! A Social History of Spin* (New York: Basic, 1996).

2. See, for example, Jeremy Rifkin, *The End of Work* (New York: Viking, 1995); and Daniel A. Coleman, *Ecopolitics: Building a Green Society* (New Brunswick, N.J.: Rutgers University Press, 1994).

3. Fredric Jameson, *Postmodernism, or the Cultural Logic of Late Capitalism* (Durham, N.C.: Duke University Press, 1991), 408.

4. Ibid.

5. Ibid., 59, 54.

6. David Harvey, *The Condition of Postmodernity* (Oxford: Blackwell, 1989).

7. Ibid., 294, 296.

8. Jean-François Lyotard, *The Postmodern Condition* (Minneapolis: University of Minnesota Press, 1984), 46.

9. Christopher Lasch, *The Revolt of the Elites and the Betrayal of Democracy* (New York: Norton, 1995), 25–49.

10. Jameson, *Postmodernism,* 412.

11. Lasch, *Revolt of the Elites,* 80–92.

12. David Noble, *America by Design: Science, Technology, and the Rise of Corporate Capitalism* (New York: Knopf, 1977).

13. Lewis Mumford, *The Lewis Mumford Reader,* ed. Donald Miller (New York: Pantheon, 1986), 345.

14. William Cronon, *Nature's Metropolis: Chicago and the Great West* (New York: Norton, 1991).

15. See Carleton Beals, *The Great Revolt and Its Leaders: The History of Popular American Uprisings in the 1890s* (New York: Abelard-Schuman, 1970).

16. David A. Hounsell, *From the American System to Mass Production, 1800–1932* (Baltimore: Johns Hopkins University Press, 1984).

17. S. M. Lipset, *Political Man* (Garden City, N.Y.: Anchor Doubleday, 1960).

18. For additional discussion of this point, see Kevin P. Phillips, *Post-Conservative America: People, Politics, and Ideology in a Time of Crisis* (New York: Random House, 1982) and *The Politics of Rich and Poor: Wealth and the American Electorate in the Reagan Aftermath* (New York: Random House, 1990).

19. Harry C. Boyte, *Community Is Possible: Repairing America's Roots* (New York: Harper, 1984), 213.

20. For a similar view, see Christopher Lasch, *The Agony of the American Left* (New York: Knopf, 1969), 3–31.

21. Herbert G. Gutman, *Work, Culture, and Society in Industrializing America* (New York: Vintage, 1977), 33.

22. Ibid.

23. See Daniel T. Rodgers, *The Work Ethic in Industrial America, 1850–1920* (Chicago: University of Chicago Press, 1978), 1–29, 94–124.

24. See Margaret Canovan, *Populism* (New York: Harcourt Brace Jovanovich, 1981).

25. Christopher Lasch, *The True and Only Heaven: Progress and Its Critics* (New York: Norton, 1991), 224–25.

26. Ibid., 217.

27. Ibid., 224.

28. Ibid., 531.

29. Ibid., 532.

30. William Leach, *Land of Desire: Merchants, Power, and the Rise of the New American Culture* (New York: Pantheon, 1993), xiii.

31. Christopher Lasch, *The Minimal Self: Psychic Survival in Troubled Times* (New York: Norton, 1984), 30.

32. See Bill McKibben, *The End of Nature* (New York: Doubleday, 1989); and Carolyn Merchant, *The Death of Nature: Women, Ecology, and the Scientific Revolution* (San Francisco: Harper and Row, 1990).

33. For a parallel discussion, see Bruno Latour, *We Never Have Been Modern* (London: Harvester Wheatsleaf, 1993), 142–45.

34. Mumford, *Mumford Reader,* 345.

35. Ibid.

36. Barry Commoner, *Making Peace with the Planet* (New York: Pantheon, 1990), 8.

37. Ibid., 9.

38. Cronon, *Nature's Metropolis,* 207–59.

39. Michel Foucault, *Technologies of the Self* (Amherst: University of Massachusetts Press, 1988), 18.

40. Jean Baudrillard, *For a Critique of the Political Economy of the Sign* (St. Louis: Telos, 1981), 85.

41. Ibid., 82.

42. Jean Baudrillard, *The Transparency of Evil: Essays on Extreme Phenomena* (London: Verso, 1993), 45–46.

43. Commoner, *Making Peace,* 11.

44. Marshall McLuhan, *Understanding Media: The Extensions of Man* (New York: Signet, 1964), 19–67.

45. Michel Foucault, *The History of Sexuality, vol. 1: An Introduction* (New York: Vintage, 1980), 104.

46. Michel Foucault, "Governmentality," in *The Foucault Effect: Studies in Governmentality,* ed. Graham Burchell, Colin Gordon, and Peter Miller (Chicago: University of Chicago Press, 1991), 95.

47. Ibid., 94, 93.

48. Simon Patten, *The Consumption of Wealth* (New York: Lippincott, 1892), 51.

49. Leach, *Land of Desire,* xiii.

50. For more analysis of the growing power of the U.S. state and the retreat from its early federalistic ideals, see Stephen Skowronek, *Building a New American State: The Expansion of National Administrative Capacities, 1877–1920* (Cambridge: Cambridge University Press, 1982); as well as Jackson Lears, *No Place of Grace: Antimodernism and the Transformation of American Culture, 1880–1920* (New York: Pantheon, 1981).

51. See Kevin P. Phillips, *Staying on Top: The Business Case for National Industrial Policy* (New York: Random House, 1984); James Fallows, *More Like Us: Making America Great Again* (Boston: Houghton Mifflin, 1989); Robert B. Reich, *The Work of Nations: Preparing Ourselves for Twenty-first Century Capitalism* (New York: Knopf, 1991); or Michael Storper and Robert Salais, *Worlds of Production: The Action Frameworks of the Economy* (Cambridge, Mass.: Harvard University Press, 1998).

52. Boris Frankel, "Confronting Neoliberal Regimes: The Post-Marxist Embrace of Populism and Realpolitik," *New Left Review* 226 (Nov.–Dec. 1997): 68.

53. Wendell Berry, *A Continuous Harmony: Essays Cultural and Agricultural* (San Diego: Harcourt Brace, 1972), 51.

54. Ibid., 74.

55. Frankel, "Confronting Neoliberal Regimes," 68; Lasch, *True and Only Heaven,* 532.

56. See David Dickson, *Alternative Technology and the Politics of Technical Change*

(Glasgow: Fontana, 1974); and Ivan Illich, *Energy and Equity* (New York: Harper and Row, 1974).

57. As Wendell Berry notes, some localities will never be sustainable ("New York City cannot be made sustainable, nor can Phoenix" [63]), but many others can be and should be; see "Out of Your Car, Off Your Horse," *Atlantic Monthly*, February 1991, pp. 61–63. Also see David Morris, *Self-Reliant Cities: Energy and the Transformation of Urban America* (San Francisco: Sierra Club Books, 1982); and Richard Register, *Ecocity Berkeley: Building Cities for a Healthy Future* (Berkeley, Calif.: North Atlantic, 1987).

58. For more discussion, see Paul Goodman and Percival Goodman, *Communitas: Means of Livelihood and Ways of Life* (New York: Random House, 1960).

59. Berry, *A Continuous Harmony*, 79–80.

60. Ulrich Beck, *The Reinvention of Politics* (Cambridge: Polity, 1997), 49.

61. Ibid., 157.

62. Ibid., 49.

63. Ulrich Beck, *The Risk Society: Towards a New Modernity* (London: Sage, 1992), 19–20.

64. See, for example, Sandra Steingraber, *Living Downstream: An Ecologist Looks at Cancer and the Environment* (Reading, Mass.: Addison-Wesley, 1997).

65. Beck, *The Reinvention of Politics*, 160.

66. Beck, *The Risk Society*, 186.

67. Ibid., 187.

68. Ibid., 222.

69. Ibid., 223.

70. Ibid., 183.

71. See Ted Bernard and Jora Young, *The Ecology of Hope: Communities Collaborate for Sustainability* (East Haven, Conn.: New Society Publishers, 1997), 182–209, for one vision of ecological populism. See also Christopher H. Foreman Jr., *The Promise and the Peril of Environmental Justice* (Washington, D.C.: Brookings Institution Press, 1998), 112–36.

72. Beck, *The Reinvention of Politics*, 157.

73. Berry, *A Continuous Harmony*, 123.

Index

Timothy W. Luke is a professor of political science at Virginia Polytechnic Institute and State University. He is the author of *Ideology and Soviet Industrialization* (1985), *Screens of Power: Ideology, Domination, and Resistance in Informational Society* (1989), *Social Theory and Modernity: Critique, Dissent, and Revolution* (1990), *Shows of Force: Politics, Power, and Ideology in Art Exhibitions* (1992), and *Ecocritique: Contesting the Politics of Nature, Economy, and Culture* (1997).

Typeset in 10.5/13 Minion
with Flightcase display
Designed by Dennis Roberts
Composed by Celia Shapland
for the University of Illinois Press.